Forbes®
To the Limits

Forbes®

To the Limits

Pushing Yourself to the Edge— in Adventure and in Business

James M. Clash

WILEY

John Wiley & Sons, Inc.

Published by John Wiley & Sons, Inc., Hoboken, New Jersey.
Published simultaneously in Canada.

For general information on our other products and services please contact our Customer Care Department within the United States at (800) 762-2974, outside the United States at (317) 572-3993 or fax (317) 572-4002.

Wiley also publishes its books in a variety of electronic formats. Some content that appears in print may not be available in electronic books. For more information about Wiley products, visit our web site at www.wiley.com.

ISBN: 0-471-21093-5

Printed in the United States of America
10 9 8 7 6 5 4 3 2 1

This book is dedicated to two people very dear to me who passed away in the summer of 2001: my mother, Winifred, who lost her battle with colon cancer on July 4; and Laury Minard, founding editor of *Forbes Global,* who died climbing Mount Rainier on August 2. Without their support and mentoring, this would not have been possible.

Contents

Foreword by Tim Forbes   xi

Introduction   xv

1   Commercial Adventure Today   1

2   Because They're There   7

    Grand Teton: America's Matterhorn   8

    Mount Aconcagua: Shiver and Pray   12

    The Matterhorn: Crowds in the Clouds   23

    Mont Blanc: Monarch of the Alps   28

    Mount Kilimanjaro: Wide as All the World   32

    Mount Kosciusko: The Seventh Summit   40

3   Everest, According To . . .   43

    Sir Edmund Hillary: Dean of Everest   45

    Dick Bass: Father of Mountaineering
       Adventure Travel   56

    Conrad Anker: The Mallory Question   62

    Jamling Norgay: Like Father, Like Son   65

    Ed Viesturs: 8,000 Meters or Bust!   71

    Lawrence Huntington: When to Say When   76

    Robert Anderson: The Art of Guiding   81

Contents

4 The Business of Adventure   95

   Geoffrey Kent: Mr. Abercrombie, I Presume?   96

   Robert Lutz: High on Speed   100

   Farhad Vladi: Islands for Sale   103

   Greg MacGillivray: IMAX Man   107

5 Tops and Bottoms of the World   111

   Svalbard: The Long Arctic Night   113

   The North Pole: A Different Kind of Cold War   117

   Antarctica: Climbing with Penguins   122

   The North Pole: Swimming with Santa   126

   A *Titanic* Trip: Voyage to the Bottom of the Sea   130

   Dead Sea: How Low Can You Go?   135

6 Racing with the Wind   139

   Rick Mears: Four-Time Indy 500 Champ   140

   Nazareth: Testing My Own Mettle   145

   Skip Barber: Grand Prix Racing at Daytona   147

   Fontana: 200 Miles per Hour or Bust!   151

   Racing for Kids: Second Chance to Speed   156

   Italy: Lamborghini at 200   162

   Vintage Cars: Let Them Eat Dust   166

   George Hall: Cigarette Boats and Hedge Funds   171

7 Adventures in Physics and Metaphysics   177

   New Mexico: Ground Zero   178

   Edward Teller: Father of the Hydrogen Bomb   180

   Ham Radio: Vicarious Travels   194

   Roger Bannister: Four Minutes to Fame   197

Contents

Tommy Moe: Olympic Gold   202

Baker and Bruce: Cream of the Musical Crop   205

Survivor: Escape from the World Trade Center   211

8 Space: The Final Frontier   215

The Right Stuff: Tourists in Space   216

Buzz Aldrin: The View from Number 2   219

Dennis Tito: Executive in Space   225

Kathryn Sullivan: Spacewalker Turned CEO   230

Mach 2.6 in a MiG: 'Scuse Me While I Kiss
   the Sky   235

Acknowledgments   241
Index   243
About the Author   253

Foreword

"Life is not a dress rehearsal," my father Malcolm would say with an urgency and seriousness that left no doubt. He meant it. And for him, one of the keys to a life fully lived was adventure. Flying a Sphinx-shaped hot air balloon over Cairo, riding a Harley-Davidson on Pakistan's Karakoram Highway, these were the sorts of experiences he most relished. That same spirit, it seems to me, pervades this book, animating the people who populate it, including, in particular, the author. Through accounts of his own adventures in the mountains, on race tracks, and at the polar regions and through his interviews with adventurers of many sorts, Jim Clash explores how the human spirit is molded and uplifted by extreme pursuits.

In the process, he also suggests how the lessons of such experiences link back to the pragmatic world of business. Such connections are more common and often more direct than one might initially suppose. Listen to Sir Edmund Hillary on his and Tenzing Norgay's pioneering ascent of Mount Everest: ". . . We had challenges to overcome, which had never been seen before. Nobody had ever been to the top. It meant that during the whole expedition we had to establish the route ourselves . . . and we had this constant concern that we didn't know if it was physically possible to reach the summit." Change a word here and there, and he could be describing the struggles of an entrepreneur in a new field. That, too, is an adventure of sorts, and many of the qualities of character that make for success in a start-up business are likely similar to those that mark a Hillary or some of the others represented here. But that is not particularly why these stories are worthwhile reading. Rather, it is because they shed some light on the nature of adventure itself and its irresistible appeal to the human imagination.

Adventure today is essentially sport—albeit of the sort that risks life and limb. As such, it is generally divorced from immediate practical purpose. This was not the case historically, however. To try to scale a large mountain or cross an ocean simply "because it is there" is utterly and exclusively modern. In the past, an adventure had tangible reasons to be undertaken or it didn't happen. Ambition, along with the prospect of fame and personal fortune, probably animated individual adventurers; trade, conquest, and expanding the reach of the Church typically prompted patrons to fund their expeditions. There is perhaps no greater adventurer in history than Columbus, no more remarkable adventure than his 1492 voyage, and none with more far-reaching consequences.

The rise of science, exploration and the pursuit of knowledge justified the call to adventure. When Lewis and Clark set off in the hope of finding a northwest passage to the Pacific to facilitate trade and transportation, President Jefferson was explicit in his charge that they fully explore this unknown wilderness, report on its Indian tribes, catalog the flora and fauna, and so on. By the early twentieth century, there was another impetus as well: national prestige. The famed Shackleton expedition to cross the Antarctic continent was authorized by First Lord of the Admiralty, Winston Churchill, just as World War I began. Britain had recently lost the race to both the North and South Poles. With success, Shackleton's expedition would restore Britain's sense of paramountcy in exploration. Such nationalist sentiments would help propel many of the great adventures of the last century, including the first ascent of Mount Everest and the race to the moon in the 1960s.

With industrialization and the rise of affluent leisure in the nineteenth century, it began to be possible for individuals to pursue adventurous goals with no direct practical purpose, but doing so was generally frowned upon. To take risks without necessity or apparent reason was seen as reckless and morally suspect. Edward Whymper's famous first ascent of the Matterhorn in 1865 ended tragically when four of the climbers, including young Lord Francis Douglas, died in a fall. This and other mountaineering incidents caused an uproar in Victorian England. There was a public outcry denouncing this waste of the flower of English youth and much hand-wringing over the degeneracy that such frivolous risk taking implied. Pursuing the interests of the empire despite obvious danger in, let's say, the Sudan was worthy of a young gentleman, but climbing in the Alps while on holiday was not. This view did little to blunt the continuing development of mountaineering and other risky pursuits, but these activities remained for the most part the province of a relatively few, unusual souls often regarded as eccentrics.

It is only quite recently, in fact, that it has become both acceptable and practical for individuals on a large scale to seek adventure for its own sake. Today, we are free and able to climb and race, dive and sail, ski and surf with no more motive than personal satisfaction. Still, those who don't share the desire to chip their way up frozen waterfalls or thrill at the thought of running the whitewater of a narrow gorge in a kayak wonder why others would want to. It is a good question, and in the absence of practical reasons, it is hard to explain and quite impossible to justify. Herein lies another of this book's appeals. Amateurs and the less accomplished join history-making greats in its pages, vividly explaining why they seek adventure. Their shared passion for what they do is palpable and it makes the appeal of adventure more accessible to everyone.

With the world explored from pole to pole, with its highest

peaks scaled and its depths plumbed, the heroic age of adventure may be over. It is true that, as Hillary says, "Once we got to the top, of course, and showed it could be done, it made it somewhat easier for the people who followed." The search for adventure nevertheless remains a powerful urge, and today's great mountaineers do more than simply follow. They create new routes with new difficulties and barriers to overcome. In fact, there seem to be endless new firsts to attain. It may not really add much to the sum of human endeavor to climb Everest solo by a difficult route without supplemental oxygen, but it is testament to the deep human need to push ourselves higher and farther. For some elite climbers, like my friend Jack Tackle, that means putting up first ascents on elegant lines in clean, high-alpine style on remote mountains; they can still go where literally no one has been before. For others, like myself, it can mean simply climbing where we have not been before. And this, it seems to me, is the heart of all adventure, risking something new and, by so doing, perhaps to better ourselves.

In reading this book and thinking about the attraction and the meaning of adventure, I was put in mind of Edward Whymper's poignant and pointed reflection on climbing in his book, *Scrambles Among the Alps:* "There have been joys too great to be described in words, and there have been griefs upon which I have not dared to dwell, and with these in mind I can say, climb if you will, but remember that courage and strength are naught without prudence, and that a momentary negligence may destroy the happiness of a lifetime. Do nothing in haste, look well to each step, and from the beginning think what may be the end." That is good advice, it seems to me, whether you ever set foot in the mountains or not.

So, go, ahead, risk a little time. Read on!

Tim Forbes
December 1, 2002

Introduction

Ernest Hemingway once said, "Auto racing, bull fighting and mountain climbing are the only real sports . . . all others are games." The great American writer and adventurer had a point. He reckoned that the element of risk is an integral part of the sporting life, perhaps the very essence of the experience. Indeed, if you double-fault on a serve in tennis, you lose a point. Land in a sand trap on the golf course, the penalty is a few strokes. But strapped into an Indy race car or scaling Mount Everest, well, in those places, your life is on the line. To be sure, misjudge the exit of a corner at 200 miles per hour, and the race-car driver careens into a concrete retention wall—at best, destroying a $500,000 piece of precision machinery; at worst, snuffing out a life. Or consider the consequences of losing your footing while climbing massive peaks where a single misstep can result in paying the ultimate price for adventure.

Interestingly, by exploring the mind-set and motivations of adventure seekers, the stories in this book help identify and define character traits that translate into boardroom success. In fact, many chapters chronicle the exploits of top business-people who have an insatiable thirst for adventure—whether they are sitting in the corner office about to close the deal of a lifetime or in a remote corner of the world drinking in their achievement.

The book isn't limited to Hemingway's universe of racing/fighting/climbing. In fact, the chapters are flush with many of life's more unusual adventures and profiles of the folks who became part of history through those adventures. Perhaps more interesting, the book draws subtle parallels between the experiences of a lifetime and everyday business. Since most of the adventure treks are offered commercially, details on how to book them are provided whenever possible.

Along the way, the reader will discover that adventure and pushing limits isn't just physical. Splitting the atom in the first half of the twentieth century, for example, went way beyond the perceived limits of nuclear physics. For centuries, conventional science had considered the atom the smallest particle in the universe. Similarly, eclipsing the four-minute-mile barrier in 1954 was a tremendous physical act for Roger Bannister, for sure, but perhaps even greater psychologically. For almost a decade, athletes had come close, only to miss by a few seconds.

In the 1960s, fusing the music genres of rock, jazz, classical, and blues didn't seem palatable—or possible—until an iconoclastic trio called Cream, the lead guitarist of which was Eric Clapton, did it to perfection. Such feats will also be chronicled in the coming chapters. Finally, in their own words, we will hear what adventure means to some of the great pioneers of the twentieth century including Edwin "Buzz" Aldrin, Sir Roger Bannister, Sir Edmund Hillary, Dr. Edward Teller, and Rick Mears.

Again, following in the Hemingway tradition, this is a book about doing, not preaching, so I, too, will strap myself in for the ride.

Some analogies between business and adventure will be obvious. For example, former Fiduciary Trust chairman Larry Huntington contrasts the role of a high-altitude climber with that of a chief executive; Clinton Group hedge fund manager George Hall compares managing the risks of hedge funds with racing cigarette boats; COSI chief executive Kathryn

Sullivan talks about how her skills as a former astronaut have helped her with decision making in the boardroom; Foote, Cone & Belding creative director Robert Anderson, also a professional mountain guide, explains how he motivates executives while climbing the world's highest peaks.

Other comparisons between the two will be more subtle: the decision-making skills needed to drive a race car on the edge; the entrepreneurial spirit that's an innate part of Arctic discovery; the spirit of innovation that's linked to space travel.

As is the case for many, my own fascination with adventure started young, first by reading adventure books and watching science fiction TV shows like *Twilight Zone* and *The Outer Limits*. I also participated in organized sports, including football and track and field. What may have been most important, however, was an early interest in science, the ultimate study of adventure. In ninth grade, I won the junior high school science fair physics prize by building a laser. (In 1969, lasers were somewhat of a novelty. The judges had never seen one, so, I think, felt compelled to give me the prize even though I didn't do anything more than switch it on and off!) I also built and launched my own model rockets.

Then there was my experience as an amateur ham radio operator. As a 12-year-old and from the comfort of my bedroom in Laurel, Maryland, I was able to visit some of the most remote places on earth—Antarctica, Siberia during the Cold War, the Seychelles Islands, India, Kenya—all vicariously, of course, with radio kits I had built with my father and my best friend, Mike. After such contacts, ham operators exchange cards, which, not unlike postcards, often include beautiful photos and stamps. The ones I received only enhanced my desire to visit these exotic places. In fact, in the 1970s, I wrote a letter to President Richard Nixon requesting that I be considered for a summer tour at a U.S. Antarctic base as a ham operator. (In those days, satellite phones didn't exist, and the only way for members of the armed services at remote bases to communicate with their families was via radio.) Nixon's written reply stated that he had referred my request to a Dr. Quam at the Department of Interior. I never got to go then and am still waiting for Dr. Quam's reply. As an adult, I've the good fortune of living out many of my fantasies as a journalist for Forbes. Never underestimate the power of childhood dreams.

1

Commercial Adventure Today

The top of the world, the bottom of the ocean, the edges of space—all were virgin territory less than a century ago. Today, they are the destinations described in glossy brochures that tout extreme vacations and high-priced adventure treks. Chalk up the popularity of these adrenaline-pumping excursions to the collective midlife crisis of baby boomers and the tripling of the stock market during the 1990s, which created armies of millionaires intent on outdoing each other at work and play.

Indeed, when money was no object, the same type A personality and market hype that fed the Internet swell—and a general feeling of corporate infallibility—also compelled hard-charging executives to seek high-adventure fixes.

Lawrence Huntington, retired chairman of Fiduciary Trust International, a global fund manager in New York, reached the 28,000-foot mark on Mount Everest, the highest peak in the world, not once, but twice. Robert Williams, chairman of Genova Products, a plumbing supply company in the

Midwest, descended over two miles to the ocean bottom to view the wreck of the *Titanic*. And Dennis Tito, founder of Wilshire Associates, the West Coast stock index firm, entered turn-of-the-century history books when he hitched a ride on a Russian rocket and became the world's first space tourist.

Interestingly, the rocket from Russia is an example of how impassioned capitalism bolsters the adventure-trekking market. Using the 1991 collapse of the Soviet Union as an entrepreneurial springboard, gutsy communists-turned-capitalists invented ways to make a tidy profit off of adventure-seeking Americans, mainly by converting a wide range of sophisticated equipment—once used exclusively by scientists and the Red army—into tourist attractions. Today, the cash-strapped Russian government leases rockets, supersonic fighter jets, icebreakers, and deep-sea submersibles to thrill-seekers willing to fork over extreme amounts of cash for extreme thrills.

Space Adventures' MiG-25 ride to the edge of the earth's atmosphere, for example, costs $12,000; a jaunt to the International Space Station in a Soyuz rocket costs $20 million. Adventure Network International's flight to the South Pole has a $26,000 price tag, while Quark Expeditions' nuclear ice-breaker voyages to the North Pole start at $16,000; and Deep Ocean Expeditions' trip via submersible to the *Titanic* wreck runs $36,000.

The going rate for a good old-fashioned guided climb of Mount Everest is $65,000. For most adventurers who have the disposable income to satiate the call of the wild, however, the experience is—you guessed it—priceless.

The catalyst for much of the adventure travel boom traces back to 1986 and the publication of a book called *Seven Summits*. In it, Snowbird Ski & Summer Resort owner Richard Bass and the late president of Walt Disney Company, Frank Wells, chronicle their efforts to become the first to conquer the highest mountain on each continent (Mount Everest, 29,028 feet, Asia; Aconcagua, 22,834 feet, South America; McKinley, 20,320 feet, North America; Kilimanjaro, 19,340 feet, Africa; Elbrus, 18,481 feet, Europe; Vinson, 16,067 feet, Antarctica; Kosciusko, 7,316 feet, Australia.) What really prompted many corporate risk takers to pack their bags and follow in the footsteps of Bass and Wells was the idea that both men were in their fifties when they made the trips and that neither was really a climber. Amazingly, Bass made it up all seven peaks—Wells managed six. The Disney chief, after two Everest attempts, was killed in a 1994 helicopter crash while on a ski vacation and never got the chance to knock off his seventh summit. Nevertheless, the feat quickly caught the attention of armchair adventurers worldwide. "Our book definitely helped," admits Bass from his resort in Utah. "Before that, there were relatively few guiding services. It grew from there into a sizable industry."

What an industry it has become. Adventure travel revenues (including supplier sales) now run in the tens of billions of dollars annually and are growing at a 10 percent clip, says Geoffrey Kent, founder of Abercrombie & Kent, the largest adventure travel company in the world. "People have enough Ferraris in their garages," quips Kent. "What they really want today is an experience." (Kent got a chilly one himself recently by swimming among seals and icebergs at the North Pole.)

Call it basic instinct, but the correlation between corporate risk takers and adventure travelers may date back to our prehistoric ancestors. Let's face it, evolution has extracted the primal excitement out of a workweek that used to include whale and saber-toothed tiger hunts. As a result, baby boomers who find themselves trapped behind a desk after exhausting the thrill of the corporate hunt are forced to buy excitement. "People realize there's more to life," Bass says. "I've been successful in business. If that were all I was chasing, it would be an empty

3

bauble of accomplishment. I know a lot of executives who suddenly wake up and think, 'My God, there's got to be more.' "

Adventure and business meet again on Madison Avenue. Advertising executives, who spend billions on identifying and shaping trends, are hoping to score big with campaigns that target consumers who tie spending to the spirit of adventure. Witness the automaker naming game that boasts the Honda Passport, Ford Explorer, Mercury Mountaineer, Toyota Tundra, and General Motors Denali sport utility vehicles; recall their ad campaigns shot in African deserts, in the high Arctic, and on snow-capped mountains.

All imply that buyers who choose these tough-as-nails SUVs make high adventure "job one." Or how about the Acura, BMW, and Mazda ads that compare acceleration, speed, and handling of their luxury cars to that of a high-performance race car? Downright silly? Perhaps, but myriad demographic studies suggest that high-income consumers are attracted to adventures—or at least pretend to be.

Regrettably, there are times when corporate denizens, clamoring for a piece of the action, tragically misread the risks of adventure travel. Think about the widely publicized 1996 Mount Everest disaster that claimed the lives of eight climbers—many of them amateurs—when they were surprised by a late-day storm. Some blame tragedies like that one on the irrational exuberance that swept the adventure world. It's the same type of misguided enthusiasm that inflated the Internet economy. What's more, hyperenthusiasm inflates more than expectations. Recall that travel catalogs during the 1980s offered guided treks up the relatively innocuous Mount Kilimanjaro for $3,000. By the 1990s, the same brochures suddenly screamed, "Climb Everest, $65,000." Furthermore, the new promotions never bothered to explain that there is a significant difference in the skill and fitness levels required to climb Everest.

Climbing suddenly became chic with the Martha Stewart crowd, and the unqualified lined up to scale the world's highest peak the same way they rushed to IPOs. To put the phenomenon in perspective, consider that in 1992, 32 climbers topped out on Everest on May 12. That's about the same number that reached the summit in the entire two decades following Hillary's historic 1953 climb. Amateurs, like disgraced socialite Sandy Hill Pittman, rocker Billy Squire, and actor Brian Blessed, became more the norm than a curiosity.

Remarkably, Hillary never got caught up in the hype surrounding his climb. "I had fears for quite some years that a disaster would occur," said Hillary, "and finally it did. Inevitably, when you've got a group that has paid a large sum of money, it puts added pressure on you and the guides to take risks you would not normally take to get to the summit." In 1996, the Everest mountaineers kept moving toward the summit way past the 2:00 P.M. turnaround time, despite threatening weather below. Eventually, a late afternoon storm hit the peak, killing eight of them. Jon Krakauer's *Into Thin Air* (Villard Books, 1997) provides an excellent account of the incident.

Deadly mistakes are not relegated to mountain peaks. With the increasing number of commercial adventures available, all companies (whether in auto racing, polar travel, whitewater rafting, etc.) must be more vigilant. In 1997, three parachuters mysteriously fell to their deaths in unison over the South Pole while jumping. Every year, dozens of clients die while whitewater rafting. What can be done to prevent similar occurrences? Dick Bass isn't a proponent of increased regulation. "I don't think you can legislate people out of their dreams," he says. But the father of modern-day mountaineering adventure travel does place most of the responsibility on the adventure companies. "You've got to get them to police themselves. The first thing to control is the number of people you take." Bass also says participant screening should be much more rigorous. "Before you get on Everest with clients, spend time with them up high to see how they react," he advises. "Altitude brings out either the best or worst in people."

All said, you can't eliminate risk entirely from commercial adventure—nor would you want to. As Hemingway implied, risk is a big part of the challenge. But you can be smart about it. I'm often asked if I have a death wish. I do not. But, like a savvy businessman, I weigh returns against risk. To do that, one must distinguish between perceived risk and real risk.

Correctly belayed, you're a lot safer traversing a ledge on the Grand Teton over a 2,000-foot chasm than free-climbing without a rope just 25 feet off the ground. A 60-mile-per-hour crash in a passenger car likely will do more damage to the human body than a wreck at twice that speed in a specially built race car with the driver wearing a proper helmet and a five-point seat harness. Bottom line: Everyone is dealt a fixed set of risk chips at birth. Cash them in wisely. The following chapters offer some great options.

2

Because They're There

Unlike in daily life, where challenges can be complex, mountaineering distills existence into a single task: putting one foot in front of the other. You become focused quickly; your life depends on it. The single goal is reaching the top—with the least amount of risk and discomfort possible. I'd suggest that scaling a mountain is a good metaphor for scaling the corporate ladder, but really, it's not. Here's why. For starters, mountains don't care about politics, cajolery, or duplicity. They also don't discriminate on the basis of gender, race, or socioeconomic status. If you have what it takes—stamina, smarts, and some luck—you'll achieve your goal. Otherwise, you won't. There's no faking it up there, no room for posers. Mountains represent, in an increasingly virtual and bureaucratic society, one of the last bastions of the puritan work ethic. Perhaps that is why climbing is so popular with executives, who are beaten down by a barrage of scandal-ridden, paper-shredding subterfuge that has them questioning why they even go to work.

GRAND TETON: AMERICA'S MATTERHORN

Few mountains in the United States are as beautiful—and as sheer—as the Grand Teton. Towering over the fashionable town of Jackson, Wyoming, its 13,771-foot snow-capped summit is the center of attention in a range of spectacular peaks. Many call the Grand Teton "America's Matterhorn." There is one big difference, however. A climb of the Grand is less dangerous than that of its European counterpart—and less crowded. Unlike the disorganized climbing that defines the Matterhorn ascent, only half a dozen guided parties per day are permitted on the Grand's popular Exum route, making the experience more pleasurable—and safer.

Like a first love, the mountain holds a special significance for me. The Grand was my first real climb. On a chance visit to Jackson Hole, I saw the peak and was instantly drawn to it. When I entered the Exum Mountain Guides hut on Jenny Lake to ask if anyone ever did "the big one," a fit young woman behind the desk looked amused. She asked if I had any climbing experience. "Nothing like that," I replied. As teenagers, my younger brother Dave and I had climbed Mount Washington in New Hampshire. At 6,288 feet, it is half the size of the Grand. Further, Mount Washington is a walk-up, meaning no technical moves are required to reach the peak. The New Hampshire landmark also offers city slickers and tired climbers an alternative to hiking: the 100-year-old cog railway, which Dave and I rode down the mountain. My experience back East convinced the woman at the Exum guides' hut that I needed climbing classes before I took on "the big one." If I forked over $200, the Exum guides would give me two days' worth of climbing instruction to prepare me for the two-day ascent.

It occurred to me that my mountain-climbing resume

needed work. I wondered if there was an equivalent to an alpine MBA. I soon found out.

Day one—the basic class—is a thorough introduction to rock climbing. First on boulders, then on gentle grades, my group learned to move like elongated spiders, using tiny bumps and cracks in the rock as hand- and footholds to propel ourselves skyward. At first, my movements were clumsy and I was frustrated by the glacial pace of my improvement. But by the afternoon, I was making progress. What in the morning had seemed like barely defined rock protrusions now seemed like small ledges. We learned what to do with a rope, the climbers' best friend. There was instruction in knot tying (figure eights, bowlines), belaying (anchoring the rope so you can arrest the fall of a partner who stumbles), and group travel while roped together. I learned that at high altitudes, a pitch has nothing to do with baseball. To climbers, a pitch is a section of belayed climbing between 50 and 120 vertical feet, usually determined by the length of rope between you and the others tied to it.

Intermediate class the next day was more dicey. The group practiced basic techniques on more challenging terrain, and my fear of heights kicked in when the session culminated in a breathtaking, four-pitch ascent called Tree Climb, with angles as steep as 85 degrees. Near the top, 300 feet up, I was so scared that I got "sewing-machine leg," a euphemism for when one's leg shakes uncontrollably from a combination of fear and fatigue. But this was real climbing and a preamble to our final test of the day: a rappel off a 120-foot cliff, backward, the way it's done in those Army of One commercials on television. The key is to concentrate on what you're doing and not look down any more than you have to.

After passing intermediate class, I had the option of signing up for a two-day climb of the Grand Teton (cost: $600). One of the reasons I started climbing was to confront my fear of heights. And although the fear was far from gone, the two days of classes had my adrenaline pumping, and I decided to work through the fear instead of letting the fear through me.

"Tired but fulfilled," is the way Al Read, Exum's co-owner, describes students who reach the summit, "a cross between joy and disbelief that they could accomplish something so intense with so little experience." He told me the Exum student roster included Max Chapman, former chief executive of Nomura International, Tom Brokaw, anchor of NBC news, and Tim Forbes, chief operating officer of Forbes, Inc. I wasn't going to miss my chance to see the world from atop the Grand Teton.

The first day of the climb—a six-mile hike with full pack to the Lower Saddle camp at 11,600 feet—boosted my confidence. No technical skills are involved, but the hike does tap your physical reserves. Luckily, I'm an ex-trackman, and the daylong trek played to my strengths. Once at the saddle, though, my advantage soon dissipated, probably at the same rate as the thinning air. I quickly became just one of a dozen excited, green climbers crowded into Exum's tents, pretty much oblivious to the night air that routinely dips below freezing, even in the summer. We choked down a freeze-dried dinner of Salisbury steak and rice, and then it was off to our sleeping bags to ponder tomorrow. I was nervous, but excited, too, and couldn't sleep. At 4:00 A.M., the wake-up call came from the guides. I didn't need it.

One of the most exhilarating parts of adventure trekking is applying newfound confidence and skills to other parts of your life. I just didn't realize I would be reminded of that so soon. Ironically, for this business reporter, the first real challenge came after an hour of rigorous scrambling to a place called Wall Street, an infamous ledge that starts friendly at 30 feet in width, then tapers to 10, 3, 2, 1—then none! There was no irony lost on my companion, Laurie Weisman, either, a New York banker who had never met a Wall Street experience quite like this.

There, in the dark, with a headlamp and a brisk wind whipping around us, she halted her climb, later musing, "You first pause. In front of you the world drops off, maybe 2,000 feet, into the early morning mist. You have to step across a three-foot void to a small foothold—maybe the size of your thumbnail—while resting your hand on a slippery ledge." In class we had done similar maneuvers—but at only 15 feet off the ground. This was different: The wind, the cold, a bulky pack, and thousands of feet of black abyss made it terrifying. Thankfully, the thrill of the climb was intact, which helped propel us into what can only be described as a brilliant, methodical, dance that sent the troupe—climber by climber—closer to the top. From Wall Street, it's a dozen near-vertical pitches to the summit. The rock is good and solid, and we came across just one other party, a foursome. They were a welcome sight in such an isolated world.

By 8:30 A.M., we were there. All of Jackson Hole and the lesser peaks in the Teton range—Teewinot, Owen, Moran, South Teton—spread out beneath our feet. It's a spectacular view—and the effort was a small price to pay for the reward. What had Al Read said earlier? "Tired but fulfilled." He was right, except that he forgot the word *humbled*. Mountaintops can do that to you.

TRAVELER'S NOTEBOOK: Book the climbs early, be in excellent aerobic shape, and arrive in Jackson Hole a few days before classes. The town is 6,000 feet above sea level, and the extra days will help acclimate you to the thinner air. Most of the gear is provided by local guide services, Exum Mountain Guides (www.exumguides.com) or Jackson Hole Mountain Guides (www.jhmg.com). Other equipment can be rented at the local stores. Moosely Seconds and Teton Mountaineering are two I recommend.

MOUNT ACONCAGUA: SHIVER AND PRAY

Shiver and pray. Pray and shiver. And wait. Trapped in my tent at 19,000 feet on Argentina's giant Aconcagua, the tallest peak in the Western Hemisphere, that's about all I could do. It had been snowing for five days straight, with winds gusting to 80 miles an hour and temperatures dipping to −30°F. Tomorrow was my last chance to make it to the top, some 4,000 feet above where I was. If the storm didn't clear tonight, I would be forced to descend, supplies exhausted.

I sat up, nauseated from altitude sickness, and looked at the tent walls, sagging from heavy snow. Then I groped for the plastic water bottle in my sleeping bag. Two hours earlier it was filled with boiling tea, a treat the guides had brewed up to help keep me warm. Now it was just a slushy concoction well on its way to becoming a useless chunk of ice. I tossed the bottle aside, as I had done each of the four previous nights, and wondered aloud just why was I there.

After climbing the Grand Teton, then reading Dick Bass's account of his ascents to the tops of the Seven Summits, I set a lofty goal for myself: Aconcagua, which thrusts 22,834 feet upward along the border where Argentina meets Chile. As the second tallest of the Seven Summits, it is challengingly high, but essentially a walk-up, requiring few technical climbing skills. Still, I knew I would need solid experience to try it. I noted with grim confirmation that more than 100 climbers had paid the ultimate price in their quests for its summit.

There are two general types of climbing: rock climbing and mountaineering. The first, ascending steep rock walls with ropes, harnesses, and rock shoes, which I had done on the Grand Teton, is similar to scenes from the Sylvester Stallone movie *Cliffhanger*. Falling is the obvious risk. Mountaineering, what the Aconcagua climb is more about, involves snow, cold-weather camping, and other tests of endurance (for a Hollywood description, think of the movie *K2*). Weather, avalanche, and mountain sickness are as much danger as falling—and potentially more perilous.

The first step to a serious mountaineering experience is undertaken far below the summit: getting into shape. Without conditioning, you become useless on a mountain and a danger to yourself and to those around you. To build leg strength, I became my apartment building's eccentric, marching up and down the hot back stairs of my 17-story building in New York three times a week with a 50-pound pack on my back. During these sessions, I routinely lost five pounds to perspiration.

To strengthen my cardiovascular system, I began distance running in Central Park. The thinner air at high altitudes, combined with long climbing days—often 10 hours or more—means lots of heavy breathing. In high school and college I had run track, but just the sprints. I found distance running very different and more difficult, something akin to pain management.

Finally, to strengthen my upper body for carrying heavy packs, I lifted weights. On a long expedition, a month's worth or more of life's essentials are strapped to your back, including food, clothes, and emergency gear.

Fitness is the first article of faith in mountaineering. Most accidents occur on descent, when climbers are tired and careless. Fitness also makes the experience more enjoyable and memorable. "I've guided people to the summit of Mount Rainier who are so out of it they don't remember being there," says Lou Whittaker, co-owner of Rainier Mountaineering, Inc. (RMI) in Seattle, Washington, and twin brother of Jim Whittaker, the first American to reach the summit of Everest in 1963.

One of the best ways to train for peaks like Aconcagua, and one of the best introductions to mountaineering, is a trip sponsored by RMI, which offers year-round ice-climbing classes and a two-day climb of Rainier, the lower 48's most glaciated peak. A one-day class covers the basics of snow climbing. Another key, though harsh, reality of Rainier is that the mountain has killed its fair share of climbers, so the risk factor is part of your training mission. But the lesson of how to use crampons—spikes worn for traction on snow—is invaluable. To be sure, the awkwardness of crampons is offset by the strong desire to avoid seemingly bottomless snow chasms.

My group began the Rainier climb from the Paradise base with a full pack—a 40-pound bundle comprising clothes, a sleeping bag, water, food, and crampons. Our first stop would be Camp Muir, at 10,000 feet. Conditions were terrible—a heavy downpour that changed to sleet, then to a full-blown blizzard. Wet and miserable, I spent the night in a hut with two dozen other novice climbers.

Treks like this could train CEOs for long days that start when other workers are still hitting the snooze button. The wake-up call at Camp Muir was for 3:00 A.M. sharp; time must be budgeted for getting up—and getting down. We still had 4,000 more feet to go before reaching the summit, which meant we had a 14-hour day ahead of us—that is, if the weather cleared. Surprisingly, when the appointed hour arrived, the sky was crystal clear, purged of the storm.

We roped up in teams of four as a preventive measure to counter a slip. When that happens, and it does, the other team members go into self-arrest, diving to the ground and planting their ice axes into the snow to break the downward slide of the unlucky climber. Team self-arrest is also an antidote to crevasses, deep cracks in the glacier often hidden by a thin layer of snow, which suck climbers into the white abyss.

Climbing with headlamps and the haunting light of the moon, we made good early progress to just below Disappointment Cleaver. Encouraged by the turn of the weather, we were all in a good mood. What happened next, though, has convinced me never to attempt a serious climb without a professional guide.

As far as we could tell, it looked like a demanding but simple ascent to the top. Our guides had a different perspective—that we were walking into disaster. Lead guide Eric Simonson pointed to a moderately steep section just a few hundred feet above us. A thin layer of ice had formed on top of the snow from the previous day's precipitation, he explained. If we slipped on that stuff, we wouldn't be able to dig in our ice axes for self-arrest because they would just bounce off the rock-hard ice. We'd slide out of control, rapidly increasing speed until we barreled off the mountain or into one of Rainier's giant crevasses. In other words, we were turning back—immediately.*

The group was stunned and somewhat rebellious, but did as instructed. On the way down, we encountered another group coming up, guideless. Our guides tried to persuade them to turn around, too, with the same warning, but they ignored the advice. Looking over our shoulders and

---

*Sadly, this is about the same place and altitude where *Forbes Global* founding editor Lawrence Minard died on August 2, 2001. He had been climbing Mount Rainier with his teenage daughter in a group organized by Rainier Mountaineering, Inc., when he suddenly complained of shortness of breath. Unclipping from his group's rope, he sat down in the snow but never got back up. Efforts by the guides to revive him at the scene were unsuccessful. An autopsy later showed that Laury had died of a heart attack. As I mentioned in the dedication, Laury was my mentor for many years, first as managing editor of *Forbes*, then as editor of *Forbes Global*. In 2000, he formally gave me a column, The Adventurer (www.forbes.com/adventurer), which recounts some of the experiences in this book. Laury was a fabulous editor. Other journalists thought so, too. Last year the prestigious Gerald Loeb Awards executive committee launched an annual editing award in Laury's honor, the first editing award presented under the Loeb moniker. Laury was also a good friend. I miss him, as does everyone whose life he touched. But I can't imagine him moving on in a more beautiful place or doing anything else.

grumbling, we continued down, bitterly disappointed. The following morning, we read in the local paper that one of the guideless party had been killed a few hours later, and another, a solo climber, shortly after that at the exact spot the guides had warned was so treacherous. The message was clear. As an amateur, you can look death in the face and not recognize it.

With the sobering Rainier experience under my belt, my next task was to start altitude training for Aconcagua. It's impossible to overstate how difficult it is to do anything—including think—at high altitude due to the oxygen deprivation. While Rainier, at 14,441 feet, sounds high, by mountaineering standards it is not. Accordingly, my first stop was Mexico, to climb its famous volcanoes—17,887-foot Popocatepetl and 18,851-foot Orizaba.

There's no substitute for experience, whether you're battling the elements on Popocatepetl or battling the board of directors from a corner office. However, the value of experience didn't hit home until I hit Mexico. There I learned what altitude sickness can do to your mind and body—and how quickly it can strike. Gratefully, I was in good hands: Ricardo Torres, the first Mexican to climb Everest, was my guide. After spending a few nights at the Tlamacas hut, 12,500 feet above sea level at the base of Popocatepetl, we ventured out on an acclimatization hike to 16,000 feet. The group members were all experienced, so I couldn't understand why they were climbing so slowly—what I thought was a ridiculous pace. In addition, few conversed, choosing instead to concentrate on a type of exaggerated pressure-breathing method that sounded like a locomotive.

Having trained hard for this, I was in the best shape of my life. And, being the rookie, I wanted to prove myself to the group. Why not show off my superior conditioning? So up front I went, right behind Torres, and started peppering him with questions about his Everest experiences. He smiled and told me to calm down, to conserve my energy, but I would have none of it. I felt fine and I wanted him—and the others—to know it. So when the group sat for a break, I didn't. Instead, I stood there, with my heavy pack, snapping photos. When the group drank water, I didn't—I wasn't thirsty. I found out later that they weren't thirsty, either, just experienced. It's important to drink a lot, and often, at altitude, before your body dehydrates.

As we approached 16,000 feet, I suddenly began to feel dizzy, then nauseous. Not long after, I was staggering. The group had to take my pack. In a matter of minutes, I became a basket case, needing assistance just to walk. On the way down to the hut, I could barely keep in a straight line because of the nausea, headache, and dizziness.

A few hours later, two gracious Canadian climbers dropped by my bunk to check on me and give me a pep talk. At altitude, they confided, the tortoise wins the race. The human body needs to acclimate gradually to the thinner air or risk acute mountain sickness (AMS), the official tag for my physical and mental collapse. By midnight, when the group prepared to tackle the peak in earnest, I felt good enough to try. I didn't think I would make the top, but I did want to see how far I could go. This time, I started dead last and within an hour had fallen a quarter mile behind the group. I took up pressure breathing, and concentrated on my rhythm. Sure enough, it worked. By the time we arrived at the crater rim, 17,000 feet up, I had caught up to the back of the pack. As we roped up near the top, I had taken my place behind Torres again.

A few days later, with my confidence returned and a newly found appreciation for the slow and steady pace, we summited the bigger, and colder, Orizaba. I haven't discounted the value of experience since.

The last leg of my Aconcagua training would take place in the Ecuadorean Andes, on a high-altitude climb up what many

17

Altitude Sickness

Acute mountain sickness (AMS), the mildest form of altitude sickness, is common among people who climb above 12,000 feet. The initial symptoms are flulike and fairly innocuous—headache, nausea, irritability, loss of appetite. But if a stricken climber continues to move higher too quickly, AMS can deteriorate to high-altitude pulmonary edema (HAPE) or high-altitude cerebral edema (HACE). Both are life-threatening and must be treated immediately. Unless a Gammow bag (which simulates higher air pressure) is available at camp, the only antidote is descent to a lower elevation.

The medical reasons for altitude sickness are not fully understood, but the chemistry and physics are clear. As a climber ascends, the oxygen pressure in the atmosphere is reduced. The body compensates by breathing faster and pumping the heart harder. This causes blood to become more alkaline, which pulls chemicals regulating the porosity of blood vessels out of balance. Fluid leaks through the vessel walls and into internal organs, causing them to swell. The effect is most pronounced in the lungs (HAPE) and brain (HACE). Interestingly, there is a genetic predisposition to altitude sickness, meaning that no matter how good an athlete you are, it can strike. The good news, however, is that following some general guidelines can help prevent it and/or reduce its debilitating effects. If you want to climb high, take heed of these six suggestions:

1. Get into excellent aerobic shape before you go high. While conditioning alone doesn't prevent AMS, it can minimize it. The better shape you're in, the less stress on the heart and lungs when you're climbing.

2. Climb slowly to conserve energy. On big mountains, the tortoise wins the race. In fact, on many expeditions, women consistently do better than men. Why? They tend to be more patient. Women don't feel the need to race to Camp 2 or 3 or to carry more in their packs than they can handle.

3. Spend a few days acclimatizing at each altitude before moving up. Shocking as it may sound, if a climber were to parachute onto Aconcagua's summit, he or she would die within a few hours. But by ascending a few thousand feet per day and building a series of intermediate camps along the way, the human body can stand atop a 23,000-foot mountain like Aconcagua in relative comfort (and safety). Acclimatization is a gradual, necessary process.

4. Drink more water than you think you need. The rule of thumb up high is eight quarts per day, or until your urine is continuously clear. This is harder than it sounds: Often you must melt snow for water, which takes time and energy. What's more, most of the time you aren't thirsty. Finally, the more you drink, the more rest stops you must take. Never mind all the inconvenience—just do it.

5. Consider taking Diamox (acetazolamide). A prescription oral diuretic, the drug promotes regular breathing during sleep and helps regulate the blood's pH balance. The downside (other than tingling in the hands and feet) is an increased urine output—annoying in tight climbing situations. I use Diamox, and the positive effects for me far outweigh the side effects.

6. Avoid alcohol, which dehydrates the body. The tendency on organized expeditions is to drink on the plane en route to the mountains, often in remote locations, and/or at base camp. Abstain.

call the Avenue of Volcanoes. The twin peaks that would serve as my training ground were the 18,997-foot Cayambe and 19,348-foot Cotopaxi volcanoes. In addition to slightly higher altitudes, these mountains presented my group with more technical climbing challenges. From my perspective, that meant that I would have to think as well as persevere. American Phil Ershler, the first American to climb Everest solo via the difficult north ridge, was my guide. Through heavily crevassed terrain, we eventually found the tops of both volcanoes without incident. There was no overeagerness or altitude sickness on my part. Amazingly, on top of Cayambe, directly above the equator, we experienced a whiteout blizzard, which brings up another good point about experience. In a risk-laden situation, forecasts will get you only so far. Experience prepares you for the unexpected.

On paper, I was ready to attempt a climb of Aconcagua. Could my body and resolve survive another 4,000 feet of altitude? There was only one way to find out. The following January, I packed my gear and headed to Mendoza, the wine capital of Argentina, with the adventure company Mountain Travel Sobek. From there, it was a winding four-hour bus ride to Puente del Inca, at the foot of the giant Aconcagua near the Chilean border. After a 26-mile hike into base camp at 14,000 feet, with mules carrying the bulk of our gear, the group began building a series of camps on the mountain, both for logistical purposes and for acclimatization. The weather, while cold, was generally clear, and within 10 days we had established ourselves at high camp (19,000 feet up) and were ready for a go at the top.

During the night, however, the weather turned on us. Just before sunrise, the crisp, cloudless −15°F morning played host to screaming winds that reached upwards of 100 miles per hour. The guides estimated the speed by listening to the primordial freight-train sounds emanating from the summit block.

Being part of a large, structured group, though, we had little leeway for bad weather built into our schedule. So we made an attempt in hopes that, as the day progressed, the winds would calm. No such luck. The higher we went, the more we were stifled. I remember literally hunching over my ice ax at one point to avoid being launched into space. Finally, just below Independencia, a bombed-out shell of an old hut serving no other purpose than to mark the altitude (21,000 feet), the guides halted our climb. Bitterly disappointed, we descended to high camp, then down to base camp, and that was that.

Back in New York, I was fixated on the peak that defeated me, and I knew that I would return. If I didn't have what it took to climb Aconcagua, I wanted to know that about myself. Being compromised by the elements wasn't a true measure of my resolve or strength. This was an internal battle, and in my mind, the externalities had to be stripped away so I could arrive at the truth.

So I reengineered my journey from the planning stage on. To avoid the problems of a fixed schedule and a large group, I hired two private guides—Steve Quinlan and Kris Ann Crysdale, of Jackson Hole Mountain Guides. Both had been with me on tough climbs in the Tetons, and I trusted them. We packed enough extra supplies for two weeks' worth of inclement weather, and then it was back down to South America for my second attempt. I spent another year in anticipation and in training, getting myself in better shape than I had been on my first climb. Now my second chance was here.

For the first time in a week, the morning breaks clear and cloudless, a sure sign that it is time to shove off. I dress warmly, using every piece of clothing I'd packed. The temperature is below zero and may drop as we ascend. By 11:00 A.M. we are nearing Independencia. As we approach, I'm moving slowly—a laborious three breaths per step. A once-dull headache has escalated into a migraine. I'm intrigued by a group of Russian climbers using the hut as shelter against the wind: They are attempting to light cigarettes. I can barely breathe, yet they want a smoke. How can there be enough oxygen to light a match, I wonder, let alone sustain the burning of tobacco? The paradox quickly becomes too complicated to ponder—I write it off as a hallucination from lack of oxygen. Instead, I focus on the fact that I am now higher than on my previous expedition a year earlier—in fact, higher than I have ever been—and into uncharted territory.

After a quick break for water, we slog on. From Independencia, we traverse a long snowfield, then up steep snow to the base of the Canaletta at 22,000 feet. Thinking that it's only been an hour since leaving Independencia, I begin to get excited. But when I look at my watch, despair sets in: It is already 2:30 P.M. Time is passing so quickly. I start to wonder whether we will have enough time and I will have enough strength to scale the peak. Even Everest veterans call the Canaletta one of the toughest physical experiences in all of climbing. I was forewarned, but no warning can adequately prepare anyone for this beast. The Canaletta is simply the hardest thing I've ever attempted, both physically and mentally. It is 800 vertical feet of loose scree and boulders, a kind of hell near heaven. I guess it's one of Mother Nature's paradoxes. Three steps up, then a slide or two back or a fall on my face—over and over, like trying to climb up a down escalator. It's now 5 to 10 gasps between strides—like sprinting an entire 50-yard dash with each step.

The key is not to look at the top, which, like a malevolent mirage, appears to be only a stone's throw away but which never gets any closer. My brain is hypoxic, depleted of oxygen and playing tricks on me. For a while, I feel as if I'm watching myself from 10 yards away, struggling pathetically, in some kind of ghastly slow motion, to ascend a rock gully. What's the point, I begin to wonder. Just what is the point? Another three-hour blur and I am within 50 feet of the top. There is no concept of time anymore. I just know I must put one foot in front of the other and soon I'll be standing on the highest patch of ground outside of Central Asia. In fact, at that moment I'll probably be the highest human on earth because it's January, winter in the Northern Hemisphere, when Himalayan expeditions rarely climb. My guides tell me it takes a full 20 minutes to cover that last 50 feet. Finally, at 5:30 P.M. I see the famous aluminum cross commemorating lost climbers. I am at the top of the pile of rock called Aconcagua.

Many say it is rare that a person comprehends defining moments. I'm not sure that's true. I comprehended this personal defining moment. All told, I spent two years preparing and six weeks on the mountain suffering to complete this climb, and I did my best to savor it. It was especially satisfying given my first failed attempt. I unearthed a camera from my pack and snapped off a full roll of film, capturing the surreal view. Next, I picked up some souvenir rocks. Just as I was getting used to the dreamlike state, my guides tell me that we must leave—in three hours we must descend what it has taken us nine hours to climb. We have no choice. If we don't get back to our tents before dark, we risk losing our way and freezing to death in the rapidly cooling night air. Maybe the journey really is the worthwhile part, I thought, until I realized my journey was only halfway over.

It's easy to see why more people die on the descent than on the ascent. Increasingly feeble, I literally stumble down the Canaletta in a semidrunken stupor. I am so tired that I imagine just crumbling to the ground and falling asleep right in Canaletta's arms. But my guides, in language not fit to print, relentlessly urge me on. By 9:00 P.M., I'm safely back at high camp—painfully tired but grinning ear to ear. At sea level, I know I'm no Sir Edmund Hillary, but on that particular night you would have had a hard time convincing me otherwise.

A few weeks later, still high from the climb, I struck up a conversation with a coworker in New York about mountaineering. As I rhapsodized about the stark beauty of high-altitude nature, she interrupted: "But can't you get the same view from an airplane window?" You bet, I replied, then quickly changed the subject. Some people will never understand the worth and meaning of experience.

THE MATTERHORN: CROWDS IN THE CLOUDS

Rush hour in most places begins at 7:00 A.M. On the Matterhorn, it starts at 4:00 A.M., when the lights come on in the Hornli hut. At 10,700 feet above sea level, Hornli hut is the start for most climbs to the summit. Like a giant shard of glass—beautiful but dangerous—the Matterhorn's peak juts 14,687 feet above the Italian/Swiss border. It is probably the most photographed of the world's great mountains and attracts so many climbers that it's even more treacherous than it was before climbing became trendy. That's not to say it hasn't always been dangerous: In 1865, Englishman Edward Whymper led his party to the summit for the historic first ascent. But of the seven who got there, four fell to their deaths on the descent. Their graves in the local cemetery in Zermatt are a constant reminder that beauty is only skin deep.

Crammed into the hot and stuffy Hornli hut with a pack of smelly climbers, I had slept fitfully for maybe two hours in anticipation of what I thought would be the best summit day of my climbing career. During an intense week of preparation on smaller peaks (including the Breithorn) in the Zermatt region, my Scottish guide, Kathy Murphy, cautioned me that the mountain would be crowded and emphasized the importance of an early start on summit day to secure a spot near the front of the climbing queue. Yes, like some perverse amusement park ride, you have to wait in line to climb the Matterhorn. More than 100 of us would ascend the same knife-edged Hornli ridge. There is room on the steep rock for safe passage of only one single-file group at a time. If there is any business lesson to be had on the Matterhorn, it's about the balancing act between patience and action.

The Matterhorn can be scaled with intermediate rock-climbing skills, but Kathy warned that if unexpected bad weather blows up, it tends to come from the back, or Italian, side. If that happens when you're near the top, it's real trouble because, unlike many peaks, there is no escape hatch on the Matterhorn. You must descend the same long, sheer face that you just climbed. Even in good weather, the descent takes longer than the ascent—six hours up, eight hours down. Thus, if you leave at 4:30 A.M. and all goes smoothly, you're back at 6:30 P.M., just before dark. Not much room for error, which is why, all told, more than 500 people have died there, more than three times the number of fatalities on Mount Everest.

Over a tasty dinner of soup and pasta the night before the climb, I chatted with Tony, a British mathematics instructor who had just scaled Russia's Mount Elbrus, Europe's highest peak. He told me he had always fantasized about the Matterhorn and was excited about the climb. He seemed an interesting character with a good sense of humor. A few hours later he would become a different person.

To climb fast, you must be very fit and travel light. After dinner, Kathy emptied my pack on the bunk, discarding what was not absolutely necessary. Camera, gone. Spare water bottle, gone. Extra gloves, gone. Kathy told me that for safety reasons we must reach the Solvay hut (elevation: 13,100 feet) within three hours of leaving the Hornli or turn around. No arguments, no exceptions.

In the morning, I dressed hastily and made my way downstairs to a breakfast of hot oatmeal. Some parties had already left the hut, their headlamp beams darting side to side. With so many people on the mountain, there was an air of urgency, unlike any early morning climb I had ever experienced. I looked for Tony, the schoolteacher, but there was no sign of him. I figured he must be on the mountain already.

It was a cold but clear morning without a moon. Because of the steepness of the grade, the client/guide ratio on the Matterhorn is 1 to 1, and Kathy and I would be roped together from start to finish. The theory is that if a client slips, the guide's running belay will save that person. But Kathy and I knew that if I took a good fall in a precarious spot, her 125-pound frame would be no match for my 175 pounds.

After an hour of rigorous vertical scrambling, during which some of the ruder parties elbowed their way past us, I

25

was so winded that I told Kathy I had to rest. She resisted, explaining that the higher we went the steeper—and tougher—it would get. Beginning to think I might not make it, I asked her for an altimeter reading: 12,000 feet. That meant we had ascended nearly 1,300 feet—or a third of the vertical distance to the top—in just over an hour. My spirits brightened. If we could keep up even half that pace, we had a good chance of making it. But she was right: The higher we went the harder it got. We arrived at the Solvay Hut in two hours and 50 minutes, just 10 minutes short of the turn-around curfew. We were nearly two-thirds of the way to the top, and there was plenty of light now, as the sun was rising. No clouds were in sight, which further encouraged me.

After another hour of climbing, we stopped to strap on crampons for the steepest part—the summit block and its treacherous snowfields. That's where I saw Tony again. He was descending on one of the fixed ropes babbling: "They got me up this thing, now they've got to get me down!" I tried to reason with him, but he prattled uncontrollably. Fear glazed his eyes, and for good reason. The fixed ropes that dangled above my head were an absolute nightmare, as climbers jostled each other for position. Since Kathy and I had gotten a relatively late start, descending climbers were bearing down on us. Others below were pressing us to move up. Our belay ropes were getting tangled with the fixed ropes and with other belay ropes. Snow and ice compounded the mess. Kathy kept screaming at me to ascend. Finally, I muscled my way up the mangled fixed ropes through the disorganized crowd. I was so tired that I didn't care anymore.

At 10:00 A.M. we arrived at the summit, and all the pushing and shoving immediately melted away. The knife-edged top of the Matterhorn is breathtaking. It's a mile straight down to Italy on one side and the same distance to Switzerland on the other. Massive Mont Blanc sparkled in the morning haze. I rummaged through my pack for a camera. Kathy reminded me that we had left it at the hut to save on weight. Two Swiss climbers sensed my disappointment and offered to take my photo and send it to me. For a split second, I instinctually went for a business card. Some habits die hard. Instead, I did manage to convey that my last name was Clash, like the rock band, and that I worked for *Forbes* magazine. Assuring me that they had heard of both, they took one shot of Kathy and me. Although I knew I'd never see the photo, I took solace in knowing that somewhere there would be a picture documenting my painful achievement.

The long descent was made easier by good weather, and we regained the Hornli hut by 7:00 P.M. Over drinks that night, Kathy confessed that she hated guiding on this crowded mountain. In fact, on her last Matterhorn climb, she saw one climber actually punch another in an argument over a fixed rope.

Back home in New York, when I logged on to my computer, I found an e-mail message waiting for me: "Are you the fellow who so desperately wants his photo from the summit of the Matterhorn?" I couldn't believe it. One of the Swiss climbers, Martin Laternser, had tracked me down via the Forbes web site. I'm glad I got the photo which, incidentally, graces the cover of this book, because I don't think I'd enjoy thrusting myself into the Matterhorn madness again. Others agree. Timothy Forbes, chief operating officer of Forbes, Inc., and an accomplished climber whose ascent resume includes Mount McKinley and the Grand Teton's north ridge, laughed out loud when I told him the story of the fight between climbers. "The Matterhorn is a beautiful mountain," he said, "well worth the effort to climb it—once. But I would never do it again." My thoughts exactly.

27

TRAVELER'S NOTEBOOK: Alpine climbers should book climbs early. The most popular climbing months for the Alps are July and August, so reservations with guide services should be made by early spring. Many suggest hiring a non-Swiss guide, and I would agree: The Zermatt people know their mountain, but are notorious for rushing their clients. Max C. Chapman, former chief executive of Nomura International, told me that during his Matterhorn ascent, he literally had to threaten his Swiss guide to slow the pace. Evidently, these guides like to burn out clients early, so they'll turn around, leaving the afternoon free to lounge in the mountain hut.

The International School of Mountaineering in North Wales (http//ds.dial.pipex.com/ism) is the guide service I used. ISM's cost for the climb and a week of preparation on smaller peaks (excluding air and train fare to Zermatt) is about $2,000. The Schwartzsee Hotel (41-27-967-2263) is comfortable, inexpensive, and 8,500 feet above sea level (versus 5,400 feet for Zermatt), meaning you'll acclimate to the thin mountain air faster than if you stay in Zermatt.

MONT BLANC: MONARCH OF THE ALPS

Most folks think that Mont Blanc is the highest peak in Europe. Not so. While it is called the monarch of the Alps and rises 15,771 feet above sea level, Mount Elbrus, 18,481 feet high, in Russia's Caucasus chain, is Europe's tallest mountain.

Mont Blanc's grisly distinction, however, is that more people have perished climbing it than any other mountain. At least 2,000 climbers have died while on this French Alps peak in the past two and a half centuries. In 1997 alone, more than 30 people died on its flanks. In contrast, less than 200 climbers have perished on Mount Everest in the past century.

One reason is that Mont Blanc is a lot easier to reach than many other major peaks. Chamonix, France, the eclectic, picturesque town at its foot, has been a haven for European alpinists for centuries. In the summer, the town swells to 80,000 people from just 10,000 (mainly skiers) in winter. Many of the visitors are amateur climbers—not quite qualified to tackle the peak but drawn to it by what looks like a deceptively simple climb. In addition to being the highest in the Alps, Mont Blanc's summit is a gentle snow dome, as appetizing as a vanilla ice-cream cone. The Romantic period poet Percy Bysshe Shelley wrote about the mountain's deceptively good looks: "[Mont Blanc] gleams on high, the power is there; the still and solemn power of many sights and many sounds with much of life and death." I'm glad I was forewarned. During the day, Chamonix is abuzz with helicopters. Our guide explained that if you get into high-altitude trouble on Mont Blanc or on any of the neighboring peaks (like the notorious Dru), the helicopters are used in the rescue. In fact, she said, it would do us well to sign up for insurance in case we got into trouble. We did; the $50 fee was worth the peace of mind and the potential $5,000 cost of an emergency evacuation.

Mont Blanc was first tamed on August 8, 1786, by Michel-Gabriel Paccard, a medical doctor, and Jacques Balmat, a hunter, using the now-popular Gouter route. While technically easy because of its gradual slopes, the Gouter is arguably the most dangerous path to the summit. Rocks, some the size of Volkswagen Beetles, fall randomly along a section called the Grand Couloir, and five to seven climbers a season perish there. Again, because of the relative ease of this route, inexperienced hopefuls tend to congregate along the Grand Couloir, which means if one mountaineer slips and topples down, the falling climber is likely to knock others off the mountain, too. Our guide refused to even consider the Gouter; the last time she attempted it, her client was struck by a falling boulder, which shattered his forearm.

Instead, we were led to the technically more demanding but less traveled Traverse route, where we would scale both Mont Blanc du Tacul and Mont Maudit before tackling the last 1,000 vertical feet on Mont Blanc proper. In mountaineering circles, the Traverse is considered an intermediate snow climb, defined as requiring the use of an ice ax and crampons. The altitude is also considered intermediate, reaching almost 16,000 feet at the top. That means your preparation must include a robust conditioning and training program before you make your trip to the mountain, and you'll need time to acclimate to the altitude when you arrive. As a warm-up, we ascended Aiguille du Tour, a mixed rock-and-snow peak.

The actual climb of the Traverse starts with a breathtaking tram ride to Aiguille du Midi, 12,600 feet above sea level. Many tourists who take this tram believe that when they exit they are at the top of Mont Blanc. If only it were that easy. From the tram, it's a 1,000-foot descent to the Cosmiques hut, as civilized an overnight spot as one can find in the Alps. In addition to the comfortable beds and running water, we were served a delicious dinner of lasagna, fresh bread, and red wine, with ice cream for dessert.

Not long after dinner, we went to bed; our 1:00 A.M. wake-up call would come soon. We would ascend most of the route in the dead of night, when the snow is hard and the danger of avalanche is minimized. The dead-of-night climb would also ensure that we were off the peak before afternoon thunderstorms hit.

After breakfast, the three of us roped up and left the hut at around 1:30 A.M. The headlamp beams produced a ghostly procession as we headed toward the base of Mont Blanc du Tacul. The snow was hard, making for good traction as our crampons dug into the semisolid snow. With a maximum grade of 40 degrees, du Tacul was just challenging enough. Our next obstacle—Mont Maudit—was another story. Maudit is a steep climb from the start. Near the top, we hit 60-degree snow, which required us to dig in with the front points of our crampons. A major slip here by any of us, despite being roped together, would probably have been fatal. We completed Mont Maudit without incident.

The final test was the rounded dome of Mont Blanc itself, which, after Mont Maudit, was a relief. Its 25-degree slopes glowed a beautiful orange in the early predawn light. But here, above 15,000 feet, there were new problems. The air was noticeably thinner and the wind a lot snappier. Combined with our growing fatigue, the pace of the climb slowed considerably. My breathing kept a snail's pace cadence: Step . . . breath, breath, breath, breath . . . step.

About halfway up this final section, my climbing companion suddenly faltered. Loss of mental resolve seemed to weigh more heavily on her than physical exhaustion. So our guide, a seasoned professional, convinced my companion to keep climbing toward the summit by telling her that our descent route was on the other side of the peak. Having studied the route I knew that this was nonsense, but we were too close to quit, and my companion too tired to sort out the facts. She trudged onward.

At 9:00 A.M., and at an ever-slowing march, we reached the summit. Its gift: spectacular views of France, Italy, and Switzerland. The weather had held, and a celebration was in order, although atop Mount Blanc, celebration is a relative term. We untied our ropes, took a quick water and snack break, and snapped photos. The Matterhorn, some 20 miles away, was reduced to just a notch on the jagged horizon of other Alps peaks.

By now, I was trained to appreciate and accept the dangers of the descent, but the knowledge that we had to retrace our steps to the Cosmiques hut in the warming, slushy snow didn't make the challenge any easier. On the way down, we kept tapping our boots with our ice axes, like a pitcher scrapes his spikes on a muddy baseball field, to dislodge the slush

31

accumulating on our crampons. Too much slush and a climber's crampons are rendered useless.

I misjudged the danger of the many crevasses that had gone unnoticed in the dark during our ascent. Most seemed bottomless and were frightening. So were the snow over-hangs, hundreds of feet high. One that looked particularly ominous had killed a few climbers two weeks before, our guide told us, when part of it had collapsed on them. My only comfort was that we traveled as quickly as possible through that 150-foot-long stretch.

At 2:00 P.M., elated but exhausted, we again neared the Cosmiques. The temperature had risen to 50°F, and our water supply was depleted. The reflection of the sun on the sur-rounding snow made it feel as if we were in an oven made of ice. How many people had died of thirst, I wondered? None, of course, but in my state of nervous exhaustion it seemed like a real possibility. I was relieved to hear the grinding gears of the tram coming up to meet us.

TRAVELER'S NOTEBOOK: High season on Mont Blanc is July and August. Prerequisites for the trip are intermediate snow-climbing skills and top physical conditioning. An excellent guide service is the American Alpine Institute, Bellingham, Washington (www.aai.cc). The cost for a four-day trip is about $1,400, for six days $2,000. The price does not include round-trip transportation to Chamonix, France, but does include one guide per two climbers.

MOUNT KILIMANJARO: WIDE AS ALL THE WORLD

"Pole, pole," the porters chant. In Swahili, that means "slowly, slowly." No one in the group is racing. At best, it's two breaths per step. We've been climbing the Western Breach of Mount Kilimanjaro for three hours; our guide, Scott Fischer, says

Climbing for Causes

In the 1960s, when the country was overtly socially conscious, world hunger relief organizations like CARE were in the forefront. As the "me" generation of the late 1970s and 1980s took hold, however, media interest in not-for-profits began to wane. Today, CARE quietly provides relief and development to more than 60 countries in Asia, Africa, Latin America, and the former Soviet Union. That's quite a ways from May 11, 1946, when the first little CARE package was unloaded at Le Havre, France, as part of Europe's rebuilding effort following World War II.

The term *CARE package* has gained generic usage today, describing everything from a box of Hershey bars and magazines sent to a Marine in Afghanistan to a carton filled with shampoo and macaroni and cheese headed to a college dormitory. As a result, the organization worries that the public, and especially the Internet generation, may not have the same awareness of CARE as did earlier generations. So CARE officials took a different tack, organizing a mountaineering expedition to celebrate the organization's fiftieth anniversary. Sponsors would donate up to $100,000 each to send a climber up a major international peak. Kilimanjaro was chosen because it's high, yet requires few climbing skills and no special equipment. And, being one of the famed Seven Summits, Kilimanjaro would attract media coverage.

Climbing for causes is not new. In 1993, the American Foundation for AIDS Research raised $430,000 through its "Climb for the Cure" on Mount McKinley, the Alaskan icon that ranks as North America's highest peak. In 1995, San Francisco's Breast Cancer Fund raised almost $2 million by putting three breast cancer survivors on top of Aconcagua, South America's peak of peaks. Was the Kilimanjaro climb as successful? You bet. The program collected $700,000 in pledges, and all the climbers reached the top. Media coverage included stories in *Forbes* and the *Seattle Times* and on the NBC and ABC television networks. Since the inaugural expedition in 1996, CARE-sponsored climbs have become an annual event. (For more information, check out www.care.org.)

we're above 17,000 feet. That's higher than some small planes fly. Those of us who are up to the challenge, like the Starbucks crew, sing "pole, pole" to the tune of the 1960s song "Wooly Bully." In my altitude stupor, all I can muster is a look around. Things are a bit out of focus. A light snow is falling, making the steep rock even more slippery. Clouds drift by; we're in them one minute, out the next. I hear someone vomiting behind me, another victim of acute mountain sickness. Fischer takes her pack. I ask if I can help, too, but it's really just an automatic response. There's nothing I can do, I'm just trying to survive myself. It seems as if we'll never get to the next camp.

This adventure trek has a loftier goal than my previous trips. My mostly American group is raising money for CARE, the international relief organization. Armchair adventurers—most through corporate philanthropy—have sponsored our excursion to Africa's highest mountain. The idea is to raise money and awareness for CARE's fiftieth anniversary. After expenses, CARE (Cooperative for American Relief Everywhere) expects to net more than $500,000.

Most of the expedition participants, while accomplished in business, are not climbers. It's a group of investment bankers, corporate lawyers, and senior executives who are obviously long on heart, but shorter on the kind of climbing experience that might have made them think twice about the rigors of this ascent. There's one major exception, our guide Scott Fischer* of Seattle-based Mountain Madness, an adventure travel company. A world-class mountaineer, with ascents of Everest and K2 (the world's two highest mountains) sans oxygen bottles, Fischer was contracted by CARE to lead the climbing neophytes to the top. Including CARE representatives, guides, and the media, 20 of us are participating in the summit-a-thon.

---

*Fischer died in a storm on Mount Everest in 1996, doing what he loved. See accompanying story, "Remembering Scott Fischer."

Remembering Scott Fischer

I admit it. My first impression of Scott Fischer was a classic case of judging a book by its cover. When I met Scott, I didn't think I'd like him. Sporting shoulder-length hair, an earring, and looks good enough to threaten Brad Pitt, the 40-year-old professional mountaineer looked like a Viking hero. In my experience, that meant I would have to contend with a horribly overblown ego. I was wrong.

Within an hour of our first meeting, Fischer's boyish enthusiasm and disarming honesty were a welcomed discovery. As a technical specialist, he was one of the best. But his true expertise was subtly guiding climbers in a lesson in self-belief that usually culminated in a dream come true. What an amazing gift to possess. A veteran who had literally been to the tops of the world—Everest and K2—he deftly struck a balance between being a self-assured leader and one of the boys.

Often, during long, difficult days on Kilimanjaro, he'd fall to the back, relinquishing leadership to assistant guides and choosing instead to encourage hikers who lagged the group. It was a horrifying surprise when, on May 10, 1996, after he guided his team of amateur climbers to the summit of Mount Everest, a storm closed in and claimed the life of Scott Fischer and seven others. None of the seven was from Fischer's expedition; he was the only one of his group to die. The disaster, the worst in Everest's history, appeared in a slew of press, including the cover of *Newsweek* and on *60 Minutes,* and raised questions about whether amateurs can really be guided on mountains as high as Everest, a full two vertical miles higher than Kilimanjaro.

Scott had set up a fund to provide financial assistance to his wife, Jeannie Price and their two children, Andy and Katie Rose, in case of his demise. I never imagined they would need it, though. He is missed, but not forgotten. (Donations can be made to Fischer-Price Children's Fund, Seafirst Bank, 4001 SW Alaska, Seattle, WA 98116. Donations can also be made to a special program that will help teach kids about the outdoors: Scott Fischer Memorial Scholarship Fund, National Outdoor Leadership School, 288 Main Street, Lander, WY 82520.)

Climbing with this kind of group is interesting, if a little precarious. You don't have to be experienced to climb Kilimanjaro, because the mountain does not require technical prowess or the use of ropes and crampons. Nevertheless, the 19,340-foot elevation is challengingly high for most people. At the peak, there's only half the oxygen that there is at sea level. Weather, altitude sickness, and exhaustion collectively converge on climbers near the top. Which is where we are now struggling, some six days into the Shira route.

Shira is Kilimanjaro's longest approach, which is precisely why Fischer likes it. The Shira will give us eight days on the mountain versus the usual five for the heavily traveled Marangu (or "tourist") route. The slower ascent gives the group more time to adjust to altitude, which increases our chances of reaching the summit. The Shira also offers a much more aesthetic experience, as the Marangu is littered and polluted.

Three more hours of this lumbering agony and we're suddenly at the crater rim, close to high camp. As we rest, I survey the group. It includes Paul Higgins, an institutional bond salesman at Merrill Lynch, and Catherine Walker, the former general counsel of Westin Hotels & Resorts. Peter Ackerman, once a Forbes 400 member, looks like a scruffy mountain goat with his six-day stubble. Back in the United States, he is managing director of Rockport Capital, an investment firm in Washington, D.C. In the 1980s, Peter was a top executive at the now-defunct Drexel Burnham Lambert and the number two man under infamous junk-bond king Michael Milken. But right now, high yield is taking on new meaning for Peter, who has never before camped outdoors, much less climbed a mountain, He's sound asleep, snoring loudly, and exhausted. We shake him: "Peter, wake up." The snoring continues. Suddenly, with a start, he blinks, then stares at us like we're from another planet. It's 20 more minutes to camp, we tell him. Disappointed and disoriented, he struggles to his feet and blindly trudges on.

High camp, perched at 18,500 feet next to the 80-foot-high Furtwangler Glacier, is the altitude of Gillman's Point, where most people on the Marangu route stop, thinking they have summited. However, the true top is Uhuru Peak, another 840 vertical feet up and, because of the altitude, the most difficult part of the ascent. That's what we have to look forward to in the morning. First, though, we have to struggle through the night.

Windswept, barren, and cold, the lava rocks and glacial ice of Camp 6 are a stark contrast to the lush vegetation and animal sounds of the jungle far below. Mountaineers call territory above 18,000 feet "the death zone," because human life can't permanently exist there. The body slowly deteriorates from the reduced oxygen supply and eventually shuts down. We're not going to be here long enough for that to happen, but the night will exact its toll. By 6:00 P.M. we're in our tents. As the sun sets, the temperature drops into single digits. Sleep is almost impossible, interrupted by the potent combination of altitude, a 40-mile-per-hour wind, and good old-fashioned excitement. Every so often I glance at my watch, swearing at least an hour has elapsed. Usually it's only 10 minutes.

We're a far cry now from what seemed like the baronial splendors of our first few camps. On those lower respites, we'd rise at 7:00 A.M., when the amiable porters brought tea, coffee, and hot washing water to our tents. Breakfast was served around 8:00 A.M., after which we'd pack our gear and hand it to the porters. Then we'd begin the day's hike—anywhere from four to six hours—while the porters dismantled camp. Along the trail they'd pass us. The agile, vigorous Tanzanians, some with 100-pound loads and torn sneakers, seemed superhuman. By the time we arrived at the next camp, they'd have the tents pitched and dinner cooking.

Camps consisted of two-person tents, a large mess complex for meals, three freshly dug toilets (complete with wooden seats) and a big campfire. At night, at the lower elevations, we congregated around the fire, told jokes, and swapped stories. At Camp 3, some 12,500 feet up, participants explained why they had come along and how they were linked with CARE. Cathy Lindenberg relived her attempt on the mountain 18 years ago and talked about her decision to turn back after reaching Camp 3. Pregnant at the time, Lindenberg had suffered complications and was forced to abandon her expedition. Now, with her husband Marc, she had the opportunity to try again.*

Menno van Wyk, the chief executive of One Sport, a Seattle hiking-boot maker, was the first executive to sign up for the climb. Van Wyk talked about his parents, poor immigrants from Holland, and how CARE had helped many of their friends just after the war. For him, the climb was a way of giving something back. Dave Olsen, a senior vice president at Starbucks and a major CARE supporter since the 1980s, felt a special affinity with the organization: Both he and CARE were turning 50.

Now I lie awake, wondering about tomorrow. How will the group handle the last 840 feet to the summit? "Piece of cake," Fischer had said earlier, with his usual brio. Piece of cake? In my physical state, a piece of cake doesn't sound appetizing. Plus, having been on other expedition climbs like this one, I don't believe him. But what's important is that the rest of the group is undaunted by the prospects of the final ascent. Half the battle in high-altitude climbing is mental, and Fischer knows it.

The 6:00 A.M. wake-up call doesn't bring warmth. It's still cold, so we layer on all of our clothes and depart around 7:30 A.M. Within 15 minutes, the sun rises, warming us and the mountain by 10 or 15 degrees. The air is thin, and we make slow, steady progress. Fischer was right; the extra three days of

---

*Marc Lindenberg passed away in 2002. We all miss him.

acclimatization have done their job. Most of us feel better than the day before. Within an hour, we're approaching the top. I glance ahead at Cathy and her husband Marc, arm in arm. She's made a triumphant return. Walker, Ackerman, and the rest of the CARE champions are close behind. It's a big moment for all of them and their sponsors. When we reach the top, CARE will be a half-million dollars richer.

We arrive. Stretched out before us is a wide football field of broken volcanic rock nearly four miles above sea level. In his famous 1936 short story, "The Snows of Kilimanjaro," Ernest Hemingway describes the mountain as "wide as all the world, great, high and unbelievably white in the sun." Sixty-odd years later, not a word of the description needs revising. It's all backslaps and handshakes for the group, with an airplanelike view for hundreds of miles around. I remove an altimeter from my pack to check the height. The reading: 18,800 feet. Not bad—it's off by only 540 feet. What's more amazing, I can still do math at that altitude.

From Fischer's pack, a football materializes. We throw it around for a few minutes (the altitude helps my distance), take some photos, and then it's time to begin the long trek down. The plan is to descend eight hours via the steep Mweka route, making camp at 10,000 feet. We know that 9,340 vertical feet is a lot to drop in one day, but with small packs it's doable. Moving with the easy momentum of a descent, we reach Camp 7 at 5:00 P.M. We're tired, but happy. Fischer is waiting at the camp for us. He's not smiling, and we know instantly that something is wrong. "We've got to keep going," he says. "There's no water here to make camp." At first, we think he's joking. But his tone is deadpan.

We quickly realize the unthinkable: We'll have to descend all the way to the roadhead—another four hours—that night. That's a total vertical drop of 13,000 feet—or the height of 13 Empire State Buildings—in one day. Complaints are rampant.

It's dark, knees are sore, feet are blistered, mud and mosquitoes taunt us. At one point, I even vow never to climb again. Finally, at 10:00 P.M., we're back at the trailhead where we first put in and have access to water. Immediately, we collapse into our tents. Sleep, for the first time in a week, is not a problem.

Two days later, we emerge from the bush and into Nairobi, Kenya, with the scaly grubbiness of eight unwashed days well rinsed off. We're civilians again, dining at a touristy but interesting restaurant called Carnivore, where the staff stuffs you with almost every exotic meat imaginable—ostrich, alligator, wildebeest, gazelle—until you surrender by sporting a little white flag. It's perfect, as we're ravenous for meat after eight days of starchy pastas, potatoes, and cereals.

During the evening, Cathy Lindenberg asks what my next climb will be. Without hesitation, I confess to possibly Antarctica's Mount Vinson or Mount Elbrus in the Soviet Union. Cathy laughs, reminding me of my recent pledge never to climb again. "Oh, I do that on every climb," I say, then explain about climber's amnesia, how you remember just the good parts of an expedition—never the pain. Cathy says she understands. She's already beginning to remember only the good parts, too.

MOUNT KOSCIUSKO: THE SEVENTH SUMMIT

They say that good things come in small packages. I found the cliché to be true on a trek up Mount Kosciusko, Australia's highest peak. I was informed that my grandmother, if she were alive, could climb Kosciusko, which, at a mere 7,316 feet, is the smallest of the Seven Summits—a mere quarter of the height of Mount Everest. If you're looking for a yardstick to measure the altitude of Kosciusko, consider that the city of Santa Fe sits 7,000 feet above sea level.

40

Still, on a trip to Australia in June of 1998, I couldn't resist booking the one-hour flight from Sydney to Cooma, then renting a car for the 60-mile drive into Australia's Snowy Mountains. The lack of hype associated with the peak appealed to me.

I checked into the Thredbo Alpine Hotel—not as fancy as Sydney's Regent, but cozy. I decided a mountain climber should rough it. A 20-minute ride up the Snowgums chairlift took me to Kosciusko's base. From there it's an eight-mile round-trip hike to the summit. The day I went, there were few folks making the trip. It was downright cold. During the Aussie winter—June through August—it's often near zero, not taking into account the windchill. Your grandmother won't need crampons or an ice ax, but warm clothes are a must. Even in the Aussie summer, temperatures on Kosciusko dip below freezing.

Kosciusko was first climbed in 1840 by Polish explorer Paul Strzelecki, who named the peak in honor of military hero Tadeusz Kościuszko. Apparently, the shape of the mountain reminded Strzelecki of the Polish general's tomb in Kraków. Today, you "climb" on a three-foot-wide metal grate walkway built by the Australian government to protect the region's fragile wildlife. After about two hours you're on a dirt-and-snow path for the remaining half mile to the summit.

Compared with the madding crowds on Mont Blanc and the Matterhorn, the simplicity and solitude of Kosciusko drew me. There was no altitude sickness, no garbage or obnoxious climbers on the trail, no guides. Just me. The top of Australia is a crumpled pile of boulders offering up lovely panoramic views of the New South Wales and Victoria provinces. It's reminiscent of the summit of New Hampshire's Mount Washington that my brother Dave and I trekked as teenagers—old Precambrian rock and gentle contours sloping lazily off in the distance.

41

If you're a potential Seven Summiteer, as are many foreigners who travel the route, you may want to climb nearby Mount Townsend, too. Why? Remember the controversy in the 1980s over whether Everest or K2 was taller? The same thing, on a lilliputian scale, is happening Down Under. Townsend proponents, who say that peak is a few feet higher than Kosciusko, would like the government to resurvey. Former deputy prime minister of Australia Timothy Fischer has led walks up Kosciusko every summer for a decade. "With all this business about the Seven Summits, it could be good for our tourism," he muses from his office in Canberra, pulling out a tape measure. Translation: If Townsend does turn out to be higher, all the past climbers will have to come back to summit it.

A final caveat: Some climbers don't consider Australia a separate continent; they lump the South Pacific into one expansive mass called *Australasia*. To these people, 16,023-foot Carstensz Pyramid, in remote Irian Jaya, Indonesia, is the seventh summit. Hmmm. We were taught as kids that Australia is one of the seven continents. Puny as Kosciusko is, it's still officially the tallest peak in Australia. And that's the way I'll remember it when I reflect on the satisfying solitude of my climb. After all, whether you wear the hat of an adventurer or businessperson, there is something elegantly raw and inherently healthy about reexamining the simple elements of a journey.

3

Everest, According To . . .

Throughout the world and down through history, a universal symbol of success has been mountaineering. It stands to reason, then, that conquering the world's highest peak, Mount Everest, represents the absolute pinnacle of achievement. In early 1996, Mountain Madness guide Scott Fischer asked me to join his upcoming Everest expedition that May. We had climbed Mount Kilimanjaro together and ended the trek as friends. Writer Jon Krakauer had already signed on to be part of an Everest expedition led by New Zealand guide Rob Hall, and Fischer was looking for a journalist to chronicle his attempt. I gave the offer serious thought and, much as I wanted to try Everest, I didn't feel I was ready. With eerie thankfulness, I look back at the ill-fated Everest trip that claimed Fischer's life, along with seven other mountaineers. In lieu of my own Mount Everest experience, I lived the climb vicariously, by interviewing some of the peak's most noted climbers. The interviews reveal some uncommon facts and riveting anecdotes about this exclusive group. And they draw some important direct and indirect correlations between mountaineering and corporate achievement. The list of peakers includes the following:

Sir Edmund Hillary: Dean of Everest. While history books and adventure writers have made Sir Edmund Hillary a household name, many don't emphasize his contribution to the Sherpa people of the region. That is, Hillary's historic 1953 climb eventually led to his current work developing modern schools and health care systems for the Sherpas. In addition, Hillary's discussion of the traits that successful climbers should possess reads like a primer on good business practices.

Dick Bass: Father of Mountaineering Adventure Travel. In 1985, Snowbird resort owner Dick Bass became the first to climb the highest mountain on each continent and in so doing became the oldest man (at age 55) then to scale Everest. His ensuing *Seven Summits* book greatly influenced the boom in adventure travel. He reflects on the 1996 Everest disaster, the conditions for which he inadvertently helped to create, and he offers insight into what can be done to prevent catastrophes in the future. Bass speaks candidly about identifying and understanding personal and business-related limitations and advises how to succeed in spite of them.

Conrad Anker: The Mallory Question. Conrad Anker has his own unique story about the history of Everest: In 1999, he found the body of legendary climber George Mallory, some 2,000 feet from the top, 75 years after Mallory had disappeared into the clouds. The discovery of Mallory's body so close to the summit still fuels one of mountaineering's biggest debates. Did Mallory reach the top of Everest 29 years before Hillary and Norgay? Anker doesn't think Mallory made it, but his experiences are a testimony to grace under fire.

Jamling Norgay: Like Father, Like Son. In 1996, Tenzing Norgay's son Jamling climbed in his father's footsteps to the top of Everest. In our interview, Jamling speaks about the connection he still feels with his father (Tenzing died in 1986) and freely discusses the summit climb from a Sherpa's perspective. His eye-opening insight is the equivalent of a CEO taking a closer look at a foreign operation by stepping back in an effort to understand the global perspective.

Ed Viesturs: 8,000 Meters or Bust! Ed Viesturs, star of the hit IMAX movie *Everest,* is reputedly America's best living climber. He is attempting to become the first American to climb all 14 of the world's 8,000-meter (26,248-foot) peaks without supplemental oxygen, a feat first accomplished by the world-renowned Reinhold Messner. Viesturs has summited Everest, the highest of the 14 peaks, five times, thrice without oxygen. In our interview, Viesturs talks about the physical, mental, and business challenges of being a pro climber.

Lawrence Huntington: When to Say When. Former Fiduciary Trust chairman Lawrence Huntington twice missed the top of Everest by just 1,000 feet. His expertise as a climber and businessman are melded here, where he skillfully compares the role of a high-altitude climber to that of a corporate chief executive.

Robert Anderson: The Art of Guiding. Finally, Robert Anderson, a creative director at Foote, Cone & Belding and a renowned mountaineer, looks at Everest from the other side: that of the guide. Just how do you manage people on the world's highest peaks?

SIR EDMUND HILLARY: DEAN OF EVEREST

When Sir Edmund Hillary and Tenzing Norgay made history by reaching the top of Mount Everest on May 29, 1953—

and returned to tell the tale—they doubted that the world's highest peak would still entice climbers. "We thought that since we'd climbed it, people would lose interest," says Hillary. An uncharacteristic misjudgment by one of the most famous adventurers of the twentieth century. According to the American Alpine Club, the summit has been visited more than 1,200 times since Hillary's climb; more than 160 people have died in the attempt.

Many wonder what Hillary, a former beekeeper and a native of New Zealand, did after that historic climb. Plenty. He drove tractors across Antarctica to the South Pole. He flew to the North Pole with astronaut Neil Armstrong, the first man to walk on the moon. He's been New Zealand's ambassador to Nepal, India, and Bangladesh. He even received a satellite phone call from the top of Everest, in 1990, placed by his son Peter. But what Hillary is most proud of is his work in Nepal; he's quietly been building schools and hospitals there for the past four decades, enriching the lives of the Sherpa people.

CLASH: *Sir Edmund, how have the challenges of Everest changed since you pioneered the mountain?*

HILLARY: There obviously have been enormous changes. But I really feel that we were the lucky ones way back in 1953. In those days, we had challenges to overcome, which had never been seen before. Nobody had been to the top. It meant that during the whole expedition we had to establish the route ourselves. We had to cut the steps, fix any ropes. And we had this constant concern that we didn't know if it was physically possible to reach the summit. Because quite a lot of expeditions had tried before and had not been successful. So we had this considerable psychological barrier to overcome. Once we got to the top, of course, and showed it could be done, it made it somewhat easier for the people who followed.

CLASH: *How do you feel about the commercialization of Everest?*

HILLARY: I really haven't liked the commercialization of mountaineering, particularly Mount Everest. By paying $65,000, you can be conducted to the summit by a couple of good guides. Clients are spending a large sum of money just to trek up our route, mainly so they can go back home and boast about it. We just wanted to make the first ascent. But since then, it's become the first Englishman, the first American, the first woman, the first chap to go up backwards. Quite a few of the objectives I would call slightly gimmicky. I mean, they have to think up something that hasn't been done. Doesn't matter whether it's too sensible. If they think they'll get media coverage, they'll go ahead and do it.

CLASH: *Does that annoy you?*

HILLARY: Well, as I said, we were the lucky ones. We didn't need all those gimmicky things as reasons to do it. Another thing that's very different now is the publicity factor. When we climbed Everest, we had no concept of the publicity it would generate with the media. I thought that the mountaineering world would be quite interested, and that would be it. We also thought that since we'd climbed it, the public would lose interest. It was really a great surprise to me during our march out to Kathmandu when mail runners, on a daily basis, brought bundles of telegrams, complimentary letters, newspaper articles, and the rest of it. It wasn't until then we realized that the climb had become sort of a big deal.

CLASH: *What are your thoughts on the famous 1996 commercial disaster on Everest?*

HILLARY: I had fears for quite some years that a disaster would occur. And then, finally, it did. Inevitably, when you've got a group that has paid a large sum of money, it puts extra pressure on both you and the guides to get to the summit—to

47

maybe take risks you would not normally take. I'll always remember reading how very early in the morning, on their final day, the climbers looked down the valley toward India. They could see storm clouds and lightning flashing a long way in the distance. If I see signs like that I'm very careful indeed about keeping an eye on it and, if necessary, turning back. They, of course, didn't and were also very slow. Quite a number didn't reach the summit until three o'clock in the afternoon—very, very late.

CLASH: *Have we learned anything from it?*

HILLARY: I wish I could say yes. But I have the feeling that the urge to reach the summit by ill-equipped and inexperienced people is still there.

CLASH: *After the Everest climb, did you keep in touch with your late climbing partner, Tenzing Norgay?*

HILLARY: When I first met Tenzing, on the Everest expedition, we were friendly but communication was a problem. Tenzing spoke English but not terribly well, and I didn't really speak any Nepali. We were just able to communicate about mountains. But later on, when I was New Zealand's ambassador to India, I saw a great deal of Tenzing. He used to come to Kathmandu quite a lot. And by then, his English had improved dramatically. We spent many hours talking about the philosophy of life and our families.

CLASH: *Did you or Tenzing ever consider climbing Everest again?*

HILLARY: No. We agreed that neither of us had the slightest desire. We had done it first, and that seemed to be enough for us. I feel that one of the most exciting things in life, unquestionably, is to achieve a big challenge somewhere in the world, and to do it first.

CLASH: *Speaking of challenges: When you and Tenzing climbed, the equipment was much less efficient than it is today. Any thoughts on that?*

HILLARY: Yes, our boots were relatively primitive vapor-barrier boots, at a very early stage. Certainly nothing like the modern plastic boot, which is much better for steep climbing and more efficient in protecting against the cold. People still do get frostbite, of course. Complete solutions have not been found yet for core body temperatures at altitude. There are still people who die with monotonous regularity on Everest. The mountain is really littered with bodies. Every year there are people—particularly on the descent, when they are tired and their concentration is poor—who slip and come to grief. So climbing Everest may not be what it was 50 years ago, but it's still a big effort and can be dangerous.

CLASH: *What is your view of pollution on the world's highest peaks?*

HILLARY: I've always thought of mountaineers as being very much aware of the environment. But I regret to say that, on Everest, many expeditions have been careless indeed. It's understandable. Think about the stress you are under. Climbing at extreme altitudes is demanding work and isn't fun most of the time. You have the constant struggle against the lack of oxygen. Once you get to the top, or as high as you are going to get, your one ambition is to get down and back to mom and the family. I do think publicity by others and myself suggesting that the traditional national park attitude—you carry down what you carry up—is helping. But removing the backlog of rubbish is a pretty big job. The South Col, at 26,000 feet, is the highest rubbish dump in the world. Included in the mess of empty oxygen bottles, tin cans, torn tents, and the rest of it are a dozen dead bodies. So it may be quite a few years before, (a) all expeditions bring off everything they bring up, and (b) all the stuff from previous expeditions is cleared off and out.

CLASH: *Any ideas about how to do it?*

HILLARY: It should be absolutely compulsory for expeditions to remove all their extra gear. But, that's not easy, I have to admit. And it's almost impossible to supervise. If there's an expedition at 26,000 or 27,000 feet, there aren't many guards to check on what they're doing. So it really has to be a personal thing for the climbers; they have to be completely devoted to the concept that it's a marvelous mountain and that it must be kept clean and uncontaminated.

CLASH: *When your expedition was up there, did you pack out all of your gear?*

HILLARY: Of course not. Nobody had ever heard of conservation back then. We left our stuff on the South Col and probably started the first little piles on the ridge, which no doubt are still there.

CLASH: *Do you think George Mallory got to the top of Everest in 1924?*

HILLARY: I haven't the faintest idea. The only convincing evidence, really, would be if Mallory's camera were found with shots that indicated he had been to the summit. [It hasn't been.] There is, of course, the other very important factor, and all of the mountaineering world knows this: It's one thing to get to the top of a mountain, but it's not really a complete job until you get safely to the bottom. For 50 years I have been the hero of Mount Everest. I'm regarded as such, I've talked as such. So I couldn't really complain too much if, after all this time, I had not been first on top.

CLASH: *What advice would you give novice climbers?*

HILLARY: Well, my impression is that particularly the young don't like advice from old farmers like me. But if I had to give it, I'd advise young people not to start from the beginning by themselves. Hear what experienced climbers have to say, read about them, learn from their accumulated efforts. Take advantage of the years of pioneering efforts. They might find this boring, however, as the young want to rush head on, as it were.

CLASH: *What traits make a successful climber?*

HILLARY: You've got to have strong motivation—no doubt about that. Technical skills are also important. But if you have more of the first, you can get away with having a little less of the second. Good planning is important. I've also regarded a sense of humor as one of the most important things on a big expedition. When you're in a difficult or dangerous situation, or when you're depressed about the chances of success, someone who can make you laugh eases the tension. Suddenly, everyone gets a new lease on life, more confidence, and plows on.

CLASH: *Any personal examples that you would like to cite?*

HILLARY: We had a number of people with good senses of humor. I've got quite a good sense of humor myself. I remember on one occasion we were crossing a 20,000-foot pass, one that had never been done before. We came to the crest, and down the other side was extremely steep snow and ice. I had four others with me in the party—Eric Shipton, a very famous mountaineer, and three Sherpas. So I started cutting steps with my ice ax, the old-fashioned way, down this very steep slope. When I'd get down the full length of the rope, the Sherpa I was with would climb carefully down in the steps. I had him belayed, of course. Then Shipton and the other two Sherpas would follow. Well, we got about halfway down to a

51

particularly difficult area, and I went to some trouble to cut deeper steps. When I got down as far as I could, I called to the Sherpa on my rope, "Be very careful, Ang Rita, this is quite a steep bit, this."

So Rita climbed down carefully, but about halfway down he fell. He shot past me, in midair really, and finally came to the end of the rope with a great twang. Fortunately, my belay had held. There he was, over the steep slope below, just swaying back and forth. My feeling was that the other two Sherpas above would be petrified at one of their companions almost losing his life like that. But I was absolutely wrong. The Sherpas on top, seeing their companion in a predicament worse than theirs, thought it was jolly funny and started laughing. So here we were, spread out over this slope with all three Sherpas—including Ang Rita—laughing. And then Eric Shipton and I began laughing, too. From then on, we all climbed more effectively down the equally difficult section to the bottom. Before the accident, we had been very careful and cautious and rather afraid of the slope, but the laughter shook all that out of us.

CLASH: *Quietly, you've done a lot of charity work in the Everest region. What led you to it?*

HILLARY: When I was climbing I built up a close relationship with the Sherpa people. It was obvious to me that they lacked things we take for granted, like education for their kids and medical care. So, after a number of years of working with them, I finally decided that instead of just thinking about it, why not give them a hand? More than anything else they wanted a school in the village of Khumjung [in Nepal]. I was able to raise the funds—with the help of Sears, Roebuck and Company and another company in Chicago, Field Enterprises. We're not talking about vast sums of money. I imagine that the whole project cost no more than $20,000 in 1961. So we built Khumjung School and hired a Sherpa teacher from

Darjeeling. We started off with 40 children from the local village. They looked pretty scruffy in those days. Now we have over 400 children at Khumjung, and they wear jeans and down jackets. We've established over 30 schools and a dozen medical clinics and hospitals. The locals contribute their effort and labor, and we raise the financing with international lectures and through public appearances. The result is that this district probably has a better education and health system than any other area of the Himalaya.

CLASH: *Is there any student of yours that you are particularly proud of?*

HILLARY: Ang Rita, one of the first students at Khumjung in the 1960s, directs our Himalayan Trust in Nepal.

CLASH: *What new projects are you working on?*

HILLARY: We've been aware for years that in all of the primary schools we've established, teachers haven't had any formal training. They're mostly kids from high school. A few years ago we decided to establish a primary teacher training program and were able to get support from a Boston company. We started with three experienced New Zealand teachers and four experienced Nepali teachers. I honestly expected that we would have had 30 or, at most, 40 come for the training. But in the first year we had 180 teachers from 47 schools. We have more than 200 trainee teachers now. We feel that it's one of the most worthwhile things we are doing. It means that the children in these remote areas are going to get much better education and will be able to carry on to a higher level of training as they study at university in Kathmandu.

CLASH: *What do you want to be remembered more for, Everest or the work you've done in Nepal?*

HILLARY: I don't know if I particularly want to be remembered for anything. I personally do not think I'm a great gift to the world, I can assure you. I've been very fortunate. I have enjoyed great satisfaction from my climb of Everest and my trips to the poles. But there's no doubt, either, that my most worthwhile things have been the building of schools and medical clinics.

CLASH: *For a minute, go back to 1953. What were your feelings on the way up Mount Everest?*

HILLARY: In the early stages of the expedition, I was never confident that we were going to make it. Lots of people had tried before us. It wasn't until I got to the top of what is known now as the Hillary Step, quite close to the summit, that I realized I was going to set foot on top of the world.

CLASH: *What did you see above the Hillary Step?*

HILLARY: A corniced ridge, and we kept down the left side of the crest. It did seem to go on and on forever. Although there's not much gain in height, it's still quite a long way from there to the top.

CLASH: *How long did that take you?*

HILLARY: Oh, gosh, that's one question I've never been asked before. I don't know, probably a half an hour. We were tired, of course, even though we had growing confidence. And we sort of kept looking rather anxiously to identify the top. And then I noticed the ridge ahead was dropping away. And up to the right was a rounded snowy dome. So I just hacked my way up the last 40 feet or so, cutting steps, and we were on top.

CLASH: *Were you exultant?*

HILLARY: Well, I think my major feeling was not one of exultation. I didn't jump around and throw my hands up or anything like that. My feeling was much more one of considerable satisfaction, because people had tried before, without success, and we'd worked pretty hard at it. Here, finally, Tenzing and I were standing on top of the world. It was a pretty good feeling, actually. But, sort of subdued. I was still very much aware that we had to get safely down again. Tenzing was, too. I put my hand out to shake with Tenzing in a rather typical old Anglo-Saxon way, but that wasn't enough for him. He threw his arms around my shoulders and gave me a hug. We had a warm moment, if you will, on the summit of a cold mountain. I think he was more excited than I was.

CLASH: *Any memorable words exchanged?*

HILLARY: We really didn't say anything. We had oxygen equipment on. I took mine off and got my camera out. I knew it was pretty important to have a record of Tenzing standing on top, or of someone standing on top. But also to take shots down the leading ridges of the mountain just to give absolute, irrefutable proof that we had gotten there. I did realize how skeptical the world was.

CLASH: *What do you remember most vividly today?*

HILLARY: There are two other things I remember clearly, even in the short time I was there. One is that I did look around a bit to see if there was any sign of remnants of Mallory. I didn't expect there to be, of course, after all those years. And there wasn't. The other thing is that while standing on top of Everest, I looked across the valley, towards the other great peak Makalu, and mentally worked out a route about how it could be climbed. That was the route the French first climbed it by some years later. But it showed me that even though I was standing on top of the world, it wasn't the end of everything for me, by any means. I was still looking beyond to other interesting challenges. I'll always remember doing that. I found it quite interesting.

DICK BASS: FATHER OF MOUNTAINEERING ADVENTURE TRAVEL

When Snowbird Ski & Summer Resort owner Dick Bass climbed to the summit of Mount Everest on April 30, 1985, completing his quest to become the first person to stand atop the highest mountain on each continent, he had no idea the achievement would help spawn an industry. He was 55, the oldest man to scale the world's highest peak at the time.

Bass and his partner, Frank Wells, former president of Walt Disney Company, had come up with the idea five years earlier. Neither was really a climber. Undaunted, they knocked off one peak after another: Aconcagua (South America); McKinley (North America); Kilimanjaro (Africa); Elbrus (Europe); Vinson (Antarctica); Kosciusko (Australia). Then Bass scaled Everest, on his fourth attempt. Unfortunately his partner never did—Wells was killed in a 1994 helicopter crash after two failed attempts on Everest.

In 1986, Bass and Wells published their account of the climbs in the book titled *Seven Summits,* and mountaineering adventure travel took off. Whereas there were only a handful of guiding services in the 1980s, there are now hundreds.

CLASH: *How has mountaineering adventure travel changed since Seven Summits?*

BASS: It has expanded dramatically. When Frank and I climbed, there wasn't much of an industry. We learned the basics with traditional guides on Rainier and McKinley, then paid world-class climbers to accompany us to more distant peaks. They were just thrilled to have the opportunity to go to such remote places.

CLASH: *So you just paid for their trips—they didn't make money?*

BASS: That's right. And we got the benefit of their expertise. That's how it really started. It grew from there into a sizable industry of professional guides worldwide.

CLASH: *Where did you find your climbing companions?*

BASS: They were some of the world's best mountaineers. We got Chris Bonington and Rick Ridgeway to go with us to Vinson. They were eager because they had never been to Antarctica. That one cost us $125,000 for all the logistics. Reinhold Messner wanted to go, too. But we didn't take him because it would have been his seventh summit, and he would have beaten us. Wells cut him out! On Aconcagua, we had Jim Wickwire. He was thrilled to death. On McKinley, it was Phil Ershler, then a guide for Rainier Mountaineering, Inc. I was surprised later when Phil told me, "Bass, since your book, we're chockablock full. Any expedition I want to lead, we've got plenty of people."

CLASH: *So your book influenced the growth of mountaineering adventure travel?*

BASS: It definitely helped. Before that, there were relatively few guiding services. But in addition to Seven Summits, people also began to realize that there's more to life. I've been successful in business. If that's all I were chasing, it would be an empty bauble of accomplishment. I know a lot of executives who wake up and say, "My God, there's got to be more." That's why they want to climb mountains at an older age. They want to win the self-respect that comes from doing something that really lays it on the line.

CLASH: *Let's spend a few minutes on the famous 1996 Everest disaster.*

BASS: Having been there myself, I know exactly what happened. It was a matter of too many people up there. You take that bottleneck on the Hillary Step. If you're standing around for an hour or more waiting your turn, it's cold; you're not moving, you're using up bottled oxygen. It's one thing to be moving and generating heat inside your Gore-Tex; it's something else to be standing around. Those "ice worms" wriggle in fast.

CLASH: *What happened with the guides, Scott Fischer and Rob Hall? They both died, and they were two of the strongest climbers in the world.*

BASS: The guides were drained from the anxiety of nursing people up the mountain for so long. The anxiety was a tremendous additional drain—I don't care how strong they were. Those guides were conscientious; they felt the responsibility. I also think they were carrying a lot of stuff to the higher camps for some clients who weren't carrying their respective shares. They had Sherpas, of course, but the guides also did more lugging. It isn't just the added weight, but going back and forth between camps to make sure it was all there.

CLASH: *Whose fault, if anyone's, was it—the guides' or the clients'?*

BASS: Both. But I almost hold the guides more responsible. They must carefully choose who and how many people they take. In this case, it was strictly a matter of too many up there too long, and starting down too late in the afternoon. When David Breashears and I went up Everest we, along with our Sherpa, Ang Phurba, were the only ones high on the mountain. So whatever difficulties we had, we could address them immediately. I had a one-to-one response with one of the world's great climbers.

CLASH: *How about experience levels? Were the clients sufficiently prepared?*

BASS: Climbers should have high altitude experience before they attempt the really big mountains. People don't realize the difference between a 20,000-foot mountain and 29,000 feet. It's not just arithmetic. The reduction of oxygen in the air is proportionate to the altitude alright, but the effect on the human body is disproportionate—an exponential curve. People climb McKinley [20,320 feet] or Aconcagua [22,834 feet] and think, "Heck, I feel great up here, I'm going to try Everest." But it's not like that. The point is that there's no way in advance a guide can know how someone will do up high. If you're a guide with one or two people, you can make adjustments. But to have to administer to eight or more, that's too many.

CLASH: *So a better guide/client ratio is key?*

BASS: Yes. There wasn't any margin for error. I can picture it now, the physical discomfort waiting at the Hillary Step. Then they get to the top late in the afternoon. When they start down, the typical late-afternoon Everest storm comes in and reduces visibility, and then it turns dark with nightfall. They were overly ambitious and pushed too hard—something we've all done. I've certainly done it. So far, I haven't had to pay with my life, thank goodness.

CLASH: *When you climbed, were you ever pulled up any mountains as Jon Krakauer alleges of socialite Sandy Hill Pittman in his famous book,* Into Thin Air?

BASS: No, I was never pulled up any mountains.

CLASH: *Part of the thrill, I would think, is to get to the top on your own?*

BASS: Oh, completely. I put implicit faith in my climbing companions. I didn't question them. But I darn sure had to get myself physically up—and down—the mountains.

CLASH: *I read that on your summit day you and Breashears weren't even roped together. You certainly weren't hauled up.*

BASS: It was straightforward. We got up around midnight. It took us two hours to get hydrated and gussied up with all our gear. Now, at the time, I'm just trying to get my equipment together and remember everything. David looked over and said, "Dick, we're not going to rope up." And I said, "Fine," and went about my routine. After several minutes, David again said, "Dick, did you hear me? We're not going to rope up." And I said, "Yeah, I heard you." I was totally preoccupied with the moment. If I was going to climb Everest, I had to do it this time. Finally, right before we took off at 2 A.M., he said, "Dick, I hope you know what that means. I've been up there. It's icy. There are places where I don't think I can stop you if you start sliding. And I know you can't stop me. It's better we lose one than the both of us." I said, "Yeah, you're right, David," and went back to getting all my gear pulled together. That's the last we talked about it.

CLASH: *What, if anything, can be done to prevent future tragedies on Everest. Regulation?*

BASS: I don't think you can legislate people out of their dreams. The main thing is to have articles written—good level-headed critiques by people who know what they're talking about—and don't try to sensationalize or grandstand, like *Into Thin Air.* The articles get discussed in mountaineering circles. You've also got to get guide services to police themselves. The first thing to control is the number of people you take. Also, before you get on Everest with clients, spend time with them up high to see how they react. It will show their acclimatization ability, strength, endurance, and mental attitude. Altitude brings out either the best or worst in people.

CLASH: *Do you consider yourself a professional climber?*

BASS: Definitely not. I'm a high-altitude trekker. I got into the Seven Summits because it was a challenge. Marty Hoey [a mountain guide for RMI and winter Snowbird employee who died during an ascent of Everest in 1982] threw down the gauntlet. She said that my hot air would never get me up McKinley. But all I did was put one foot in front of the other until I got there with a big pack on my back, reciting poems and getting psycho-bio feedback like Pavlov's reflex. We were hardly ever on technical pitches.

CLASH: *Are you planning another book?*

BASS: Yes, *The Eighth Summit.* That's the figurative inner mountain every person climbs in his own life. It's a lot tougher than the literal mountains. The main theme will be that it's not really that important what's happening to us, but it's all-important what our attitude is in coping with difficulties.

CLASH: *For you, is the eighth summit Snowbird?*

BASS: Well, Snowbird will be the longest and steepest pitch. But it's not the entire eighth summit. Like everyone, I've done a lot of things. My problems aren't unique. God has visited a good cross section of life with me. But it wasn't just God visiting—it's also been my own curiosity, enthusiasm, and adventure spirit that's exposed me to a number of challenges.

CLASH: *Unlike some horror stories you hear today, you and Frank were gracious to your expert climbing companions. Tell me a little about that relationship.*

BASS: I'm not a taker; I'm a giver. We were two laymen who got criticized by some mountaineering types who said we bought the mountains. But look, we got ourselves up on our own two feet. I don't feel I should apologize for paying my own way instead of seeking corporate sponsorship. Sure, we paid expenses for some great climbers, but I don't feel that was unethical. We were honest enough to know what we were. And we weren't experienced climbers. We had a dream, and were really rank amateurs, when you get down to it.

CONRAD ANKER: THE MALLORY QUESTION

Most people think the famous climbing phrase "Because it is there" was first uttered by Sir Edmund Hillary. Not so. Actually the Brit, George Leigh Mallory, said it three decades earlier as he prepared to scale the world's highest peak. We know that Hillary made it to the top of Everest because he survived to tell the tale (his famous words were, "We've knocked the bastard off"). But what about Mallory? He and his partner, Andrew Irvine, were last seen alive less than 1,500 feet from the summit—still pushing upward.

Conrad Anker, an Everest summiteer who works for North Face, the outdoor outfitter, is certainly able to give an informed guess: He found Mallory's remains in 1999 as part of the Mallory & Irvine Research Expedition (*The Lost Explorer: Finding Mallory on Mount Everest,* by Conrad Anker and David Roberts, Simon & Schuster, 1999). Here, Anker tells of his discovery and whether he thinks Mallory ever did reach the top.

CLASH: *How did May 1, 1999, unfold for you?*

ANKER: At 9:30 A.M. we fanned out from where we thought the Chinese's 1975 Camp 6 had been. A climber on that expedition, Wang Hongbao, had reported seeing "an old English dead" about 20 minutes outside of the camp. There was a large snowfield that led over toward the Great Couloir, and I was at the lowest elevation, about 26,900 feet, of the area we planned to search. I had never been that high before, so I was going with what my body could do but still trying to cover as much ground as possible. After taking a short break for hydration, I scanned right and saw something—an anomaly on the horizon, this odd color of white. So it was around noon when I came across the mummified remains of George Mallory.

CLASH: *What was going through your mind?*

62

ANKER: It was very humbling. You come across dead climbers. The mountains are a demanding, cold place, and they don't allow for mistakes. I've seen bodies on Denali and Everest, and with the vast majority, the upper part—the torso and head—is pointing downhill, just because we're denser on top than on bottom. The pose in which Mallory had come to rest said a lot about his final moments. His head was uphill, and his arms were in a grasping-type position, probably trying to arrest a descent that was out of control. Then there was the snapped rope around his waist and a broken leg. It seemed that he had died struggling. I was even more in awe when I saw his wool clothing. Any of the stores in Manhattan that sell camping gear could outfit someone better than what he had on in 1924.

CLASH: *How long were you alone with Mallory before the expedition came over?*

ANKER: About 15 minutes. I didn't touch the remains, just sat there. For a moment I thought of keeping quiet. To just look, bury him, and not tell anyone. But once I made the call on my radio, of course, everyone at camp knew that something was up, because they were tuned into our frequency.

CLASH: *What did you find, other than skeletal remains?*

ANKER: A watch, an altimeter, a penknife, a pair of goggles, among other things. And some letters. The information that needed to go between camps on expeditions was done with pen and paper back then. The letters contained the same type of communication we do now over radio, but they addressed teammates by surname—very formal. "Dear Odell: We need to send up so many days of rations, four Sherpas; this one Sherpa's strong," and so on.

CLASH: *Later on during that same expedition you went to the top of Everest yourself.*

ANKER: Yes, 17 days later. It was demanding. Anyone who says that it's not is wrong.

CLASH: *Do you think that Mallory made it to the top?*
ANKER: No. Everest on the north side is far more mountain than he was prepared for. Mallory was always lauded as an excellent climber, and part of being an excellent climber is good judgment. He probably had already turned around and was going down when he fell. More important, there is the difficult second step, above 28,000 feet. I had set out to free-climb it myself on the way to the top. And I couldn't. I ended up stepping on a rung of the ladder the Chinese placed there in 1975. I don't think that it would have been possible for Mallory to do that kind of move unprotected, especially with a novice partner like Sandy Irvine, whose body has yet to be found.

CLASH: *Also, developments in climbing make it easier today than in 1924, right?*
ANKER: Yes. The greatest leap is in communications—how one is connected to the rest of the world. All the first climbers had were mail runners who would go to the Royal Post. As soon as the mountaineers disappeared over the pass into Tibet from Darjeeling, they were in a country that very little was known about. It was really remote. Nowadays you can't get lost. There are so many options—satellites, infrared—they'll find you if they need to. The planet isn't as big, so it feels a lot less wild than it used to.

Advances in equipment have made it easier, too. The oxygen delivery systems are much better. They're lightweight aircraft systems. In Mallory's time, every clothing fiber was natural—wool and cotton. Now they're predominantly synthetics—nylon shells laminated with fluorocarbon—much lighter and more efficient. And we know more about the body. How to eat the right kind of food at altitude—high in fat, for example—and drink the right amount of water. If they ran out at one camp, they would go all day, then drink heartily at the next camp at the end of the day. Now we know that a steady intake of water really helps performance, and climbers carry hydration systems on their backs that help with this.

CLASH: *If you could talk to Mallory, what would you want to say to him?*

ANKER: I have endless respect and admiration for who you were as a man and a climber. Please don't be upset if I disturbed your resting place.

CLASH: *Of all the people in the world, you found Mallory. Do you assign any special significance to that?*

ANKER: It was just by chance. But then nothing's by chance, you know?

JAMLING NORGAY: LIKE FATHER, LIKE SON

Jamling Tenzing Norgay grew up in the shadow of his late father, Tenzing, who made history in 1953 by climbing Mount Everest with Sir Edmund Hillary. In 1996, Jamling himself reached the summit as part of the expedition that filmed *Everest,* the blockbuster IMAX movie. While at the top, Jamling felt the strong presence of his father. It's no surprise, then, that his autobiography, cowritten with Broughton Coburn, is titled *Touching My Father's Soul* (HarperCollins, 2002).

The fourth of six children, Jamling was born on April 23, 1965. By age six, he had already shown a penchant for climbing, scaling Sikkim's B.C. Roy—a training peak—with his father. He quickly became his dad's right-hand man on climbs that the elder led for the Himalayan Mountain Institute. But Tenzing was careful not to encourage his son to lead climbs for a living. "My father told me he had become a mountaineer so we wouldn't have to," says Jamling of the risky profession many Sherpa people undertake to support their families. In 1985, Jamling moved to the United States to attend Northland College in Ashland, Wisconsin, where he graduated in 1989 with a bachelor of arts in business administration. To help ends meet, he worked as a black-belt instructor in karate and Tae Kwon Do.

After Tenzing's death in 1986, Jamling's early dream to climb Mount Everest was rekindled. To be a lead climber on an Everest expedition cost $35,000 then—more than Jamling could save from running his late father's adventure company, Tenzing Norgay Adventures (www.tenzing-norgay.com). Jamling also had accumulated some responsibilities: His wife, Sonam Dorjee, was pregnant with his daughter, Sonam Deki.

In 1995, after a five-summit solo expedition in Sikkim (on peaks ranging between 19,000 and 21,500 feet) Jamling was invited to join an American expedition as assistant base camp manager. The expedition was to mark the fortieth anniversary of his father's Everest ascent. It was there that he met film director David Breashears, who was in Nepal to recruit participants for his upcoming Everest movie. "I was looking for a climber to define the culture of the Sherpa people," says Breashears. "Who better to do that than the son of the first Sherpa to climb Everest?" With the tremendous success of the eventual IMAX movie, Jamling has become a sort of celebrity. How has it changed his life? And who does he think was the first to put his boot print on top of Everest, his father or Hillary? I thought I'd ask him myself.

CLASH: *Did your father encourage you to climb Everest?*
JAMLING NORGAY: No. I even asked him to pull some strings so that I could climb with an Indian expedition, and he flatly said no. Because he didn't have an education, he felt he needed

to give us one. He also knew climbing was dangerous. But the most surprising thing was that after my Everest climb, my uncles told me that Tenzing had always said I would climb that mountain, that I would follow in his footsteps. He knew it all along but never encouraged me. He wanted me to do it for myself and by myself.

CLASH: *When you climbed with him as a child, did he ever let on that he was proud of you?*

J. NORGAY: He didn't say much on top. But there was something about his smile. You can see a lot by a smile, and I could see that he was proud.

CLASH: *Did he ever talk about his 1953 climb with Hillary?*

J. NORGAY: Most of the stories I heard were on treks. He would take Western clients to Everest base camp. Then, around dinnertime, he used to talk. People paid extra money to be with him and listen to his stories. At the time, I was young, maybe 10, so I didn't pay attention. You know how you are when you're a kid, you have no idea of the relevance of what your parents say. Now I wish I had listened more.

CLASH: *How did your dad and Hillary end up together? In a corporate sense, were the roles Hillary more the CEO and your dad the president?*

J. NORGAY: When the expedition started, no one was thinking that the two would be partners. My father was a sirdar—he handled all the Sherpas. Hillary was just another climber and the only non-Britisher, I think, on the team besides my father. As they started the expedition, my father and Hillary became friends. If Hillary went up, my father would go with him. And this was something John Hunt, the expedition leader, noticed. As far as I know, there was no CEO-president type of

67

relationship—they worked together. Of course, my father respected Hillary for being a sahib, which is "master." But I saw them as partners in this big company. The Sherpa view of climbing is different from the Western view. We believe that mountains are places where the gods live, especially on Mount Everest. Before we climb, we perform religious ceremonies to ask God for permission and safe passage. Sherpas don't have any interest in climbing mountains. Mostly they climb as a necessity, to make money. But the Western world looks at Everest as another rock and says, "Wow, this is the highest mountain. Let's go conquer it." You don't conquer Everest. You go on Everest just as if you are crawling into your mother's lap.

CLASH: *You were filming on Everest in 1996 when those eight climbers perished. What do you think happened on May 10?*

J. NORGAY: That was our day to go to the summit. But when we saw all the inexperienced climbers going up, we decided to wait. Mistakes were made. People were high on the mountain too late. At 3:30 in the afternoon [mandatory turnaround was 2 P.M.], guys were still climbing up. Through the telescope we could see a line going toward the summit. The weather played a major role, but it wouldn't have if they had gotten up and down faster.

CLASH: *Did we learn anything from it?*

J. NORGAY: I don't think so. There are still people climbing Everest because they have big egos. If you want to do something, do it with the right motivation. Climb with respect for the culture, the environment, the people. If you climb with no experience, you jeopardize your life and put the lives of Sherpas and teammates at risk.

CLASH: *Let's talk about your own summit day, two weeks later.*

J. NORGAY: My desire to climb Everest grew even more after my father died. I wanted to climb to understand him. Throughout the whole climb, I thought about him. And, at a lot of places, I imagined what those guys had been thinking, where they might have slept. On the final day, halfway up from the South Col camp, I felt really strong. I felt my father was in front pulling me or behind pushing me, because I didn't know where this energy came from. When I finally got to the top, I took my goggles and mask off and cried. Then I thanked Miyolangsangma [the goddess of Everest] and left photos of my parents and His Holiness the Dalai Lama and a toy that belonged to my daughter, Deki. I could see my dad there, right in front of me, with a big smile.

CLASH: *Same smile you saw on B.C. Roy?*

J. NORGAY: Yes, exactly. And he was telling me, "You know, you didn't have to come this far." And then I realized I really didn't have to climb the mountain to understand him. The irony was that I had to climb the mountain to find out that I didn't have to climb the mountain. It's the experience that matters, not the getting up there.

CLASH: *Your pose on the summit looks like the mirror image of your dad's. Did you do that on purpose?*

J. NORGAY: Ever since Hillary took the picture of my father in that famous pose—with one hand up holding the ice ax and flags—no one has taken another. I thought it would be nice to do the same photo of me. I tried to strike the same pose, but I had the wrong hand up!

CLASH: *I have to ask that age-old question: Who do you think got to the top of Everest first, your dad or Hillary?*

J. NORGAY: Hillary says in his book that he stepped up there first. My father also says, in his book, that Hillary stepped first. My father climbed the mountain because it was something he had wanted to do all his life. He didn't want to boil things down to who climbed first because it was not important to him. I think the reason he said that Hillary climbed first was just to get rid of the media and people asking him questions because he felt it shouldn't be brought down to that level. "Fine, yeah, okay, Hillary climbed first."

CLASH: *Did you ever talk to him about it?*

J. NORGAY: I did ask him before I came to the United States, and he said, "You know, it's not important, Jamling. We climbed as a team." I leave it to the world to judge. My father had tried six times to climb this mountain. On the seventh attempt they were able to make it. He had been up the route before, so he had a lot of high-altitude experience. For Hillary, this was his first time on the mountain. I don't know how high Hillary had climbed before, but I don't think it was more than 22,000 feet. It is for people to make up their own mind instead of me telling them, because I don't know. The Sherpas, Indians, Nepalese think that my father climbed first.

CLASH: *In your heart, was it your dad or Hillary who first stepped on top?*

J. NORGAY: Well, as far as I'm concerned, it was my father. First, because he was my father. Second, he had more experience on the mountain. But again, I'm no one to judge. He never told me that. My gut feeling says that maybe he was the one up there first. Those days, they were roped to each other. So the difference was what, only about three feet?

CLASH: *Were you the first in your group to set foot on top of the world?*

J. NORGAY: Nowdays you don't rope up. The summit is a big area. How can I say I got there before Araceli [Segarra] if we were together? There's no line that, if you cross it, you're on the summit.

CLASH: *Do you have plans to climb Everest again?*

J. NORGAY: I promised my wife that, after filming the movie, I would never climb it again. I will not break my word.

CLASH: *You're a movie star and author now. Are you wealthy?*

J. NORGAY: Just because you're famous doesn't mean you're rich. My father was famous but not wealthy. The IMAX movie didn't do it. We were given $25,000. We don't get a penny now, and it's grossed more than $100 million. For me, that's not important. The movie is a step. It has taught the world more about Sherpas and brought my father back to the Everest scene.

CLASH: *Did the movie experience affect your book deal?*

J. NORGAY: Before the movie, I didn't have an agent. For the book, I got one. We want to pick up royalties and all the things that come with a book. So the deal is better, and it has made me a smarter businessman, too. My brother Norbu—the smart one in the family—said, "You'd better think about this book. Make sure that you don't get screwed over this time."

ED VIESTURS: 8,000 METERS OR BUST!

Mountaineering is a big professional sport in international circles, and famous climbers like Italy's Reinhold Messner and France's Catherine Destivalle easily pull in seven-figure incomes with their prowess. In the United States, though, such rewards are reserved for pro football, baseball, and basketball players. Pro climbers, for the most part, don't approach one-third of what a rookie baseball player earns.

Even five-time Mount Everest summiteer Ed Viesturs, who's considered America's best living mountaineer and is a star of the IMAX movie *Everest*, must hustle to support his climbing habit.

"In Europe, climbers are household names," says Viesturs, who doesn't have a lawyer, agent, or public relations representative. "Occasionally I'm recognized, and usually referred to as 'the Everest guy.' But I'm certainly not rich." Ed says he grosses under $300,000 annually, out of which he pays for the cost of his climbs. His salary is paid for by sponsors like Expedia .com and Mountain Hardware, which give him an average of $25,000 annually to promote their products, and from companies such as Conseco and GlaxoSmithKline, which pay him $10,000 to be a featured speaker at corporate events.

With 12 peaks behind him, Viesturs may well become the first American to reach the summits of the world's 14 highest mountains (all more than 8,000 meters, or over 26,000 feet, in height) without supplemental oxygen, a feat first completed by Messner in 1986. Most climbers must use bottled gas at those altitudes, where oxygen levels are just one-third those at sea level—and where each step requires 10 agonizing breaths. The peaks he has yet to climb are Pakistan's Nanga Parbat and Annapurna in Nepal. In our interview, this native of Seattle, Washington, describes how he balances business and adventure.

CLASH: *You're attempting to become the first American to climb all of the 8,000-meter peaks without oxygen. Which has been your toughest climb?*

VIESTURS: People are saying I want to be the first American, but that's never been a personal goal. It's kind of by default: I think I'll end up being the first American. It's a project I want to complete, and whatever that turns out to be in the eyes of other people—that's what it is. Any way you slice it, K2 as a package is harder than Everest, even though Everest is higher. More than a thousand people have climbed Everest—maybe only a hundred have climbed K2. Physically, without oxygen, nothing compares to Everest. But on Everest, there's some terrain where it's relatively moderate. On K2 there's no easy way up. It is very steep—on average, about 45 degrees from bottom to top—and unforgiving. The weather is also unpredictable. It's one of those mountains that continually throws fences at you. I call it the full-meal deal of climbing.

CLASH: *You climbed K2 in 1992 with the late Scott Fischer. When you were filming* Everest *four years later, how did you feel when you passed Fischer's frozen body near the summit?*

VIESTURS: I knew he was going to be somewhere along the way, so I tried to set myself up for that. Here I am alone, climbing with my headlamp—it's two in the morning—moving the light along the slope above me, and boom, it hits this form. I get closer and see that it's Scott. Thankfully, his upper body was wrapped up. I didn't see his face or anything—I didn't feel I could, at that point. Then I climbed on. I had decided earlier that I would stop on the way down. Later, when I stopped, I just tried to take in the scene. I was crying. I wanted to ask, "Scott, what happened?" Just looking at this guy, you know, he had been so strong. I'd never lost a friend before. It's a tough thing to see, to just sit there and know that he will be there for a long time. You can't bring him down. It's hard for you to climb at those altitudes, let alone bring a 200-pound body down. To get six climbers to lift a person, then negotiate the steep terrain, is dangerous and physically almost impossible.

CLASH: *The movie* Everest *has grossed more than $100 million, the second-highest-grossing IMAX film in history, just behind* To Fly. *Why was it so successful?*

VIESTURS: The original idea was to bring the beauty of an Everest climb to the general public. Then we had this major event [the storm in 1996 that killed eight climbers] that the whole world heard about—and we were part of it. The disaster was integrated into our movie, and made it 10 times more dramatic. So people came for the drama and maybe to find out more about what had happened. They had heard our film crew was there—*Into Thin Air,* Jon Krakauer's book, talked about us. But sponsors are still not beating down my the door.

CLASH: *Why is corporate sponsorship so difficult?*
VIESTURS: With mountaineering, it all comes down to secondary marketing. How can they use you to test and develop their products, then use you as a spokesperson or use your image in their marketing campaign? There isn't a crowd watching us live on television. So, for example, you don't have a Nike logo that millions of people are constantly seeing. Climbing is a little more mainstream now, but it's still not a great spectator sport. It takes hours and hours—it's not fast enough for TV.

CLASH: *Do people recognize you more now, since the movie?*
VIESTURS: Occasionally when I'm at the airport, they'll look at my ID and say, "You're Ed Viesturs, aren't you?" It's not instant facial recognition. It's often name recognition. They say, "Are you the Everest guy?" Also now, with corporate events, I'm getting more business. I never really promoted or advertised that. People just started to call and say, "Ed, we saw the IMAX film. Can you come speak to our group?" Then [codirector] David Breashears hooked me up with a speaking agency, Keppler Associates in Arlington, Virginia. David was getting so busy that he would tell them, "Call Ed; he can cover for me."

CLASH: *You're obviously an adept mountaineer and businessman. Are there principles and tactics in climbing that you can apply to business?*

VIESTURS: I'm pretty judgmental about my own performance, whether it's climbing or lecturing. I hate being unprepared, because I know I will not perform at my best. The problem with being unprepared is that I let myself down as well as other people. So preparation is key. Being passionate about what you do is important, too. It shows in your work and in your sport. If you love what you do, you do a great job. If you work for money and hate your job, it will reflect in the performance and longevity of whatever you're doing. You'll be miserable.

CLASH: *What is your opinion of Reinhold Messner? Many consider him the greatest living climber.*

VIESTURS: Some people say that he's arrogant, but maybe that's the psychology you need to do what he did. He's right up there with athletes like Muhammad Ali. A phenomenal mountaineer—very driven. Messner was visionary, 20 years ahead of his time. You've got to admire what he and Peter Habeler did in 1978 when they became the first to climb Everest without oxygen. Later, he climbed it solo in three days. Completely alone. You hear about solo Everest climbs these days, but they're not really solo. There are other people around. Psychologically, there's a huge difference.

CLASH: *It's very difficult to climb at 8,000 meters even with supplemental oxygen. What it's like without it?*

VIESTURS: Some call it the art of suffering. You breathe 10 times and then must mentally focus and force yourself to take that next step. Then you take another 10 breaths. You keep looking at your next objective, which might be a rock. You can't just look up to the summit—it's too huge a concept. You must break it down into little stages, and then break those stages into individual steps. It's such a basic event: You're climbing up a hill. And you've got this beautiful view while you're doing it. How much simpler can it get?

The 14 Summits of 8,000 Meters or More

Mountain	Altitude in Meters
Everest	8,848
K2	8,611
Kangchenjunga	8,586
Lhotse	8,516
Makalu	8,463
Cho Oyu	8,201
Dhaulagiri	8,167
Manaslu	8,163
Nanga Parbat	8,125
Annapurna	8,091
Gasherbrum I	8,068
Broad Peak	8,047
Shishapangma	8,046
Gasherbrum II	8,035

LAWRENCE HUNTINGTON: WHEN TO SAY WHEN

Sometimes success is just failure in disguise. For three decades, Lawrence Huntington was the top man at New York's Fiduciary Trust International, a global investment company. In 1991, when he first attempted Mount Everest, he reached 28,000 feet, just 1,000 feet shy of the top. But he was behind schedule and the weather was iffy, so Huntington, then 55, thought it prudent to turn around. Three years later he returned to Everest, only to halt at the same altitude and again retreat. Michael Rheinberger, his climbing partner on that first ascent, kept going and reached the summit, but he never came back.

Now retired, Huntington, a world-class sailor as well as climber, sits on a number of corporate boards. He has no plans to return to Everest, although in 2002 he did knock off Antarctica's Mount Vinson. Huntington says that there are lessons to be learned on the world's highest peaks that apply to life—and to business. From his New York office at the Explorers Club, of which he is a member, he reflects on these issues as well as others.

CLASH: *How did you become interested in climbing?*
HUNTINGTON: As a college freshman at Harvard, I watched Sir Edmund Hillary and Tenzing Norgay give a slide show describing their first ascent of Everest. I was mesmerized and thought, "Well, I'll never get to do that." But I never stopped thinking about it. I didn't start serious mountaineering until I was 40. And, much to my horror, I discovered that regular climbers were quitting at that age. But with my sons, then teenagers, I started climbing several of the world's high mountains: Mont Blanc, the Mexican volcanoes, McKinley, Aconcagua. And 15 years later, at age 55, I felt that I was ready to try Everest.

CLASH: *What do you remember about your first time there, in 1991?*
HUNTINGTON: I was apprehensive about my age, because the group was between 25 and 35. But there was one wonderful Australian named Michael Rheinberger, then 50, attempting Everest for his sixth time. I took him aside and said that I was worried about my age. He said, "Listen, we're here for three months. By the end of two, these hotshots will be gassed out. They don't know how to pace themselves." That's exactly the way it turned out. We got to the mountain in March and spent two months acclimatizing and building camps. By May,

when it was time for the summit push, half of the younger climbers were finished.

CLASH: *Tell me about summit day.*

HUNTINGTON: We were late leaving Camp 6 [27,000 feet], so we didn't start until 4:00 A.M., at which time Rheinberger and the other climbers were still not out of their tents. So two Sherpas and I took off, unroped. We climbed to 28,000 feet, by which time the sun was up. I could see the others following a long way behind. Think of the north side of Everest as the inside of a giant bowl: The higher you go, the steeper it gets. The general grade of the last 2,000 feet doesn't get all the way to vertical, but it gets close. So when you look down between your feet, it's 10,000 feet of air. I put my foot on a rock and suddenly slipped about six inches. It was a slip a careful person would have avoided. That was enough of a signal that I wasn't climbing well. I was also watching the weather. The wind was beginning to blow, and we were way behind schedule. So, in an instant, I turned back. Eventually everyone else did, too.

CLASH: *It must have been tough to do, though, so close to the top?*

HUNTINGTON: I never had any regrets. The real lesson for life—and for business—is that at critical moments you can't expect anybody to decide for you. You have to be prepared to assess the evidence around you—not wait for others, no matter what their reputations or perceived competences. When I came back to New York, our business was in an expansion mode, and I had the instinct that we should go into Asia. Many of my colleagues were nervous, because the entry would be expensive. But I realized that if we were to get the business into that continent, we just had to step off the curb. We took the first step into Hong Kong. Not long after, we entered Japan. I just had to swallow hard. Both decisions, in hindsight, turned out to be wonderful for Fiduciary's business.

CLASH: *Compare the role of chief executive to that of high-altitude climber.*

HUNTINGTON: One of the curiosities of high-altitude climbing is that the clothing hems you in. You wear goggles, which limits vision. If you're using supplemental oxygen you're wearing an oxygen mask, which further limits vision—and dramatically muffles your hearing. You're in a little cocoon. The more you think, the tighter inside you get—and your peripheral vision disappears. Being a chief executive clearly has moments in which the decision you make can come only out of your own brain. Typically, that happens because advice from your most trusted colleagues is 50–50, pro and con. If it were totally clear, the decision would have been made at a lower level. In the end it's a solo moment. And if you don't decide, the business opportunity drifts away.

CLASH: *What made you return to Everest in 1994?*

HUNTINGTON: Having come so close, I was preparing to go back almost as soon as I got off the airplane. I had become very good friends with Rheinberger, by then 54. We agreed that we would climb together again. I went in 1994 looking forward to climbing with Rheinberger. When I got there, though, I discovered that because this was his seventh attempt, he was flat-out committed to making the summit. I concluded that he was going to push harder than was prudent and that therefore it would not be a good idea to climb with him. So I got myself into a different group. The beginning was like 1991, in that the younger climbers arrived full of energy and burned out early. When it was time to go to the summit, I was climbing the best of my life—confident, strong. Rheinberger was in a different group, plugging away, too. His group went to high camp first, and we proceeded up a day behind. We never saw them come down when we moved up into the high tents for our summit attempt.

We had decided to leave for the top early, shortly after midnight, so we had to awaken at 9:00 P.M. to start melting snow for water. While we were just waking up, the radio came on, and our leader said that Rheinberger and his climbing companion had gotten to the summit at dusk. But they had been whacked by bad weather while descending. He asked us to give up our summit bid and try to carry some extra oxygen up to help them. So we started climbing, strung out all over the mountain. Everybody was solo. It was blowing furiously— winds of 100 miles per hour—and bitter cold in the dead of night, 30 degrees below, Fahrenheit. None of us could get close to them. The next day the weather was still bad. Rheinberger was delirious, snow-blind, and not making any downward progress. Our leader got on the radio and told Rheinberger's companion to save himself. So he came down but lost all his toes. Rheinberger is still up there.

CLASH: *What are the lessons here?*

HUNTINGTON: You can overcommit to a goal. It seems pretty clear that Rheinberger had organized himself to die trying to make the top. I was fortunate to pick up those signals early and get out of harm's way. In business, people often over-commit to an investment theory. A friend of mine has been a convinced investor in gold for the past 20 years. Of course, if you did that, you not only lost money, but missed one of the great bull markets.

CLASH: *Earlier you said you had an anecdote about Mont Blanc. How about telling it now?*

HUNTINGTON: We went up the Gouter route, not particularly demanding, except that we did something pretty stupid. We were ascending in the wee hours of the morning in pitch dark. A couple of hundred feet ahead was another group with headlamps, so we just followed. I got into the rhythm of it, walking along on this big glacier and not really looking up. Suddenly I was clanking up a set of wooden steps before I realized I was walking through a door. The guys had taken a turn off the route to go to the next hut!

CLASH: *Is there a business lesson to be had here?*
HUNTINGTON: Well, to stay awake!

ROBERT ANDERSON: THE ART OF GUIDING

Everest veteran Robert Anderson has the distinction of being extremely competent in both business and adventure. As a creative director at the advertising agency Foote, Cone & Belding in New York, he leads the team that develops online advertising for blue-chip clients, including JPMorgan Chase and Hewlett-Packard. As a professional mountain guide, he leads teams of executives to the tops of some of the world's tallest mountains. What motivates Anderson? The executives he guides? This is his unique perspective.

CLASH: *Tell us about your Everest Kangshung Face climb in 1988 and its eventual outcome.*
ANDERSON: The luckiest thing about the climb was that all I lost were toes. I'd been to Beijing in 1986 and obtained a permit for the Kangshung Face, the remote 12,000-foot mountain face on the east side of Everest in Tibet. I wanted to put in a new route with a small team, without using oxygen or Sherpa support. Everybody thought we were crazy, as nothing like that had been done before on Everest's tallest, and most remote, side. The biggest initial success was getting the expedition off the ground at all. We raised just over $350,000 in

81

six months, due far more to what I'd learned running an advertising agency than from climbing. We managed to attract a group of inspired sponsors, including American Express, Bayer, Kodak, and Rolex that, in many cases, I've gone on to work with.

The strong financial support allowed me to handpick three other climbers who are among the most talented in the world. They had psychological makeups that committed them to doing something that, on the face of it, was either nuts or just plain impossible. Looking at a Himalayan face, which juts 2.5 miles high, while standing on a pass 20 miles away was a very humbling experience for all of us. On the climb, we routinely logged 12-hour days starting at 2 A.M. On our rest days, we'd get up a wonderful hour later and carry 50-pound packs up a few thousand feet to support the lead team. The weather was horrendous, dumping snow and avalanches on us regularly. But, after four days, we reached a point we felt that, despite the rocks showering down on our heads and the ice towering above—and our isolation—we were committed and could overcome the dangers.

After weeks of difficult climbing, Paul Teare, Ed Webster, Stephen Venables, and I finally reached the South Col of Everest, the first humans to that point from the east. There wasn't a soul in sight back then. All four of us had completed the new route to the South Col, and Webster and I went on to the south summit the following day. Venables then went on to the actual summit, becoming the first British person to reach the top without oxygen. This was really the start of the adventure. It turns out that while we were up high, the slopes between 7,000 and 8,000 meters had loaded up with over three feet of new snow. We spent the next few days, at times literally crawling, to get back down to base camp. After all that time with virtually no food—and no water for the last 48 hours—cold toes [eventually lost to frostbite] were the least

82

of my worries. That the climb has yet to be repeated in its original style [without Sherpas or oxygen] is an ongoing testament to its difficulty. It is the expedition I will always remember as my most satisfying, with its blend of business challenge and difficult climbing. The satisfaction has been heightened because each of the team members has become a lifelong friend.

CLASH: *When guiding executives on a big mountain like that, what are the most important things to keep in mind?*

ANDERSON: People who are successful in business have choices. They could be on the beach, they could be golfing, they could be sailing around the world with their families. Knowing the real motivation behind why someone chooses to go off for a month or more where there are no showers, the high temperature for the day may be minus 20, and getting up at 4:00 A.M. is common is the most important thing to understand.

Often, these people want something far different from their business experiences, which they feel they know and understand to the point of boredom. They seek that which puts them in a new environment, something that is a huge challenge, and something that is very personal, with success and failure dependent upon their own performances. When life and death decisions need to be made quickly, making the right one provides a feeling of power and control that no business challenge can. So, as a guide, I want to learn, as quickly as possible, what someone's specific climbing motivation is—as opposed to what motivates him simply to improve his golf handicap. The people motivated by a personal desire to stretch their limits and learn more about themselves are ideal. People who just feel the need to prove themselves are dangerous.

Which leads me to the second thing I seek—balance. Balance is important across physical, mental, and spiritual areas.

The importance of being physically fit is obvious, but often overrated. At high altitudes, the moral of the tortoise and the hare is played out frequently. Physical balance is literally that. A person's connection to the earth and how he moves over it is more important than actual physical strength. I can watch someone walk across a parking lot and tell most of what I need to know about how he will perform in the mountains just by his cadence and by the way he steps up and down a curb.

Mentally, I look for an ability to drill down and learn how to do the most mundane things quickly and efficiently. At altitude, putting on a pair of double plastic boots takes some people a half hour. It really is that hard. I've even seen people proudly complete the task and stand up, only to realize they had tied their boots together—literally! Yet if getting up and out of a tent earlier makes you safer, doing the simple things expeditiously becomes very important. At the same time, I don't want people to get so deep they can't keep perspective. I climbed once with an Olympic athlete. He was wound so tightly that at altitude he couldn't sleep properly because he was constantly "psyching up" for the next day's climb. He eventually got to 25,000 feet, but mentally had worn himself down and had to descend just as we were going for the summit.

The most difficult balance to discern and understand quickly is the spiritual. When I say that I don't mean religion, but the faith people have in themselves to accomplish something that physically seems impossible and mentally seems too painful. Spirituality in this context means that the ultimate realization of the goal will require a leap of faith. On an 8,000-meter peak, where physically and mentally anyone is going to feel lousy, taking a rational assessment of yourself and the situation will only make you turn around and go home. Reaching the summit requires transcending the rational. This is where an executive gets his biggest reward, through gaining and expanding on an internal belief in himself.

CLASH: *Any specific examples of how executives apply their skills in the boardroom to the mountain?*

ANDERSON: From a psychological perspective, executives who choose to climb peaks are highly acute and very quick learners, assimilating knowledge almost by osmosis. And while some might be more dominating in their own environment, I find them to be very good listeners on a mountain, accustomed to taking in new information quickly and then acting upon it. I had two executives on an expedition with very different business styles. One was hard-charging, aggressive, obviously accustomed to dominating the decision-making process. But physically, he just wasn't very strong. The second man was much more the English gentleman, used to building a consensus and rallying a team around him. Physically, he was much stronger. I teamed them up on a rope with me, so that the mentally driven but physically inferior man would be encouraged—or maybe he just refused to be beaten—by the physically stronger man. And the other man now had someone who was struggling to keep up, so it helped motivate him to keep moving.

They figured out each other's competencies quickly and, in areas where there was deep snow, the stronger one went out front to break trail. In the morning, when it is so hard to get up and get moving, the more driven personality came to the fore, pushing for an early start by rousing climbers out of their sleeping bags so that his slower speed didn't keep them from reaching the next camp on time. The two very quickly assessed their own strengths and were able to use them to create a stronger team by relying on their vast experience building teams in business. And, more interestingly, they had to use parts of their personality they didn't in business to make their team actually work.

CLASH: *You're an executive yourself. Compare and contrast that with guiding.*

ANDERSON: Sitting in a tent at 8,000 meters in the Himalayas with a blizzard raging outside and sitting at a desk in an advertising agency in New York City are about as far apart, physically and geographically, as you can get. The penalties for a climbing mistake are absolute, which hones the decision-making process as nothing else will. Business decisions tend to be more complex, and most of the time aren't life-and-death. In addition, I derive great satisfaction from both jobs because each one of them allows me to lead and interact with people and assist them in achieving goals. In that respect, guiding clients and working with teams of businesspeople are very similar. The employees who work in the creative department of an advertising agency, for example, are some of the most interesting I've found on this planet.

Success in both fields requires vision, empathy, courage—and a dose of reality. The excitement and the passion necessary to do anything well need to be inherent in the pursuit of the goal. Whether crafting a route up a mountain or crafting communication in an ad agency, many of the same human disciplines are brought into play: the joy of setting out on a journey; trying alternatives; formulating a plan and persevering to see it through; examining results to see what can be improved next time. I find joy in an expedition filled with absolutes. I think many of my clients, who are successful in business, find joy in that, too. You go to climb a mountain. You succeed or you fail. The decisions you make can push you to the top, force you down, or kill you. A month or so later you are back, journey complete. You've lived a whole life condensed into a very defined time frame, with a final outcome. Climbing gets to the root of human nature very quickly; there is little room for the soul to hide. Bringing that experience back to the workplace can be very valuable.

CLASH: *A guide is a cross between many things: babysitter, cook, motivator, doctor, athlete, logistics manager. What is it really like?*

ANDERSON: While your average adventure traveler might think visiting Kathmandu, then traveling overland via an 18,000-foot pass to Tibet to have tea with a yak herder is a big adventure, it is just a small part of a normal Himalayan expedition. Guiding is a lot like running a small business. You have to deal with myriad small logistics while in the shadow of a mountain—and you need specialized skills to climb. In the initial stages of an expedition, a guide's business skills are far more useful than his climbing skills. An expedition with 15 members can end up having more than 100 people involved—from a booking company in the West to cooks in the East—and each has to do a very thorough and professional job or an expedition can be ruined. The old adage, "You're only as good as your weakest link," certainly applies on big mountains. Ultimately the guide is responsible for the safety and success of the expedition, so the more he knows about every step of the process the better.

On very large expeditions, a guiding company usually handles the details. I work with Jagged Globe in the United Kingdom, and success on our last two 8,000-meter climbs (Shishapangma, Cho Oyu) was in large part due to the company's skill in ensuring that little things were in place. That left me free to look after my clients and concentrate on climbing the mountain. Thankfully, despite stories of incompetent clients, I've yet to have one that actually needed babysitting. A guide should be as careful about choosing clients and the companies he works with as a client is about choosing the company and guide.

CLASH: *Guiding an 8,000-meter peak is very different than, say, guiding a Kilimanjaro or Rainier climb, right? Yet the press would have you think they're the same.*

ANDERSON: Yes. On 8,000-meter peaks, clients must be far more self-reliant because the level of assistance a guide can realistically provide is minimal and, in some cases, nonexistent. A guide's ability to assess a client's abilities is paramount. The failure to do so has been borne out repeatedly on Everest, with disastrous consequences. But while a guide may be able to provide little actual physical assistance, his role and decision-making ability at altitude are extremely valuable. When I first started guiding in the Himalayas, I quickly realized that I needed to make people think more for themselves, no matter what the situation. I developed a graphic chart that corresponds to the sky, the earth, your team, and the climber. I teach everyone to work through what is changing in each of these areas so that they are aware of the larger environment and what may be dangerous. At altitude, if you are only reacting to circumstances, you are behind. Only by thinking ahead can you attain any degree of safety. The good thing is that executives in today's volatile business climate understand this implicitly.

Starting on the first day of the expedition, I discuss the four areas with the group. The sky is the weather—clouds, sun, snow—and its effect on us as we climb. The earth is the terrain—rock, ice, snow, glaciers—on which we climb. The team is how each member is doing and feeling, including the guide. As people tire, they forget things and make excuses. Knowing what is expected—that is, how much is normal behavior and how far someone can push themselves—is essential. Finally there's you, the climber. Most inexperienced climbers get so wrapped up in themselves at altitude that they forget about the first three things. It's natural; the overwhelming sensation is often one of extreme fatigue and physical exhaustion. But being tired rarely kills anyone. At altitude, it is easy to listen to your own heartbeat; it may be the loudest thing you hear. But doing an ongoing head-to-toe check, "How are the toes, how do the legs feel, is there any numbness or burning where the face is exposed, how is the headache today and why?" helps break the body down into definable answers. Usually when you get done with that head-to-toe checkup, you discover that the sum of the parts is still pretty strong and that taking a few more steps just might be possible.

Monitoring the sky, earth, team, and yourself makes everyone a stronger individual climber—and enhances the team. Also, if you are particularly strong in one of the four areas, pushing boundaries in the other areas becomes possible. Climbing through a storm, for example, but being on solid ice with a good team and feeling confident about your own abilities becomes far less daunting. Or descending from a summit when you are very tired, but having clear sky, good snow conditions, and being in close contact with teammates is an accepted part of reaching the summit on an 8,000-meter peak.

CLASH: *What do you think happened in 1996 on Mount Everest, and will it happen again?*

ANDERSON: Guiding 8,000-meter peaks is still in its infancy. There are few parameters for conducting expeditions in the safest possible manner up there. Being at an elevation where people can't survive without oxygen for more than a few days will never be safe, so safety above 8,000 meters is relative. Furthermore, the significant rise in the number of guides working on 8,000-meter peaks has only increased during the past 10 years. In 1996, after a few years with relatively strong clients and good weather, guides on Everest began relying more on luck than skill to reach the summit. Strong Sherpa support, coupled with bottled oxygen, exacerbated that. In almost no other sport are you allowed to go from couch potato to playing in the Super Bowl. With climbing, it is

possible to book a trip with some companies who simply col-
lect your money and take you right to Everest. Hopefully, a
little logic prevails on arrival, and your skills and the mountain's challenges become a recognizable dichotomy.

But sometimes people sneak through the lower-altitude
defenses and arrive at the higher camps against all odds.
Those climbers bunched up high on the South Col route on
Everest in 1996, for example, had a false sense of security.
They looked around and thought, "All these other people are
here, so we must all be okay." With no room for error, even
the smallest mistake—a change in conditions, a misstep by
teammates—can quickly spell disaster. The Everest disaster in
1996 was an accident waiting to happen when that storm
moved in on all those inexperienced teams. Is this a bad
thing? The alternative would be setting up climbing qualifica-
tions and/or rules, which goes against all tradition and would
be impossible to administer. I would hope if someone wants
to climb a popular route on an 8,000-meter peak in high season that the climber is prepared for the weather, the climbing, and is ready to run out of bottled oxygen waiting in line
for a fixed rope to free up. So 8,000-meter wanna-bes now
face a new caveat emptor—beware of the team you join and
the route you choose, all may not be what you expect.

CLASH: *What's the most satisfying part of guiding?*

ANDERSON: The best part about guiding is easy to define—getting
the team to the top and returning safely. That indicates that
all the little logistics—the minutiae that had to be looked
after, the team building, the climbing—were done success-
fully. The top signifies the successful completion of all those
plans. It is also possible to have the best and most memorable
experience of your life without reaching the summit. In that
situation, there will be innumerable smaller triumphs: learning and teaching new skills; seeing people accomplish what

a day before they thought was impossible; meeting new people; the simple satisfaction of a job well done.

CLASH: *How do clients react when they must turn around short of the top?*

ANDERSON: I've rarely had to ask a client to descend. One of my goals is to do everything in my power and within the bounds of safety to get them as high on the mountain as they can go. And, if there is a decision to go down, it is usually their own. But I did have a client once who insisted he could climb higher, despite his inability to keep up with the rest of the team. So I assigned him his own assistant guide. They reached 21,000 feet. The next day the client got up late despite a lot of prodding from my assistant. It's a real test of anyone's fortitude to get up early at altitude, but more than one of my clients has done it when he thought the extra time would help his chances. After the morning fades in the Himalayas, it is so hot on the glaciers that climbing becomes nearly impossible. There is also greater possibility of a storm. So once the sun reaches the center of the sky, it is time to be at camp or to be headed down. If you need to start climbing at 2:00 A.M. the night before to achieve that, so be it.

This particular client never seemed to want to help himself. He didn't get up earlier and insisted that he had climbed Aconcagua with the same slow step-by-step strategy. It always worries me when people compare mountains, as each is unique. In the case of Aconcagua—the regular route being nearly all rock—similarities to a snow-covered Himalayan 8,000-meter peak are minimal. It was obvious my client was endangering not only himself, but the rest of the team, so I had to order him down. Of the four things he needed to be thinking about, he had failed on every one. The weather was unpredictable and could move faster than he could descend. He was unstable on the ice that made up a large part of the

91

route. He consistently slowed the team. And he wasn't cognizant enough of his own shortcomings to counteract his weaknesses. You can occasionally move up and down the scale on a few of these factors, but missing on all four—and not knowing it—is a frightening combination. On my first Everest expedition, Pete Athans, a seven-time Everest summiteer, oft repeated, "There are two types of Himalayan climbers, the quick and the dead." He is right.

CLASH: *Have you ever experienced the death of a team member on a mountain?*

ANDERSON: Never guiding. I always maintain an extra couple of layers between my group's capabilities and what I think is our maximum potential. Often this will still mean people pushing themselves far harder than they ever thought possible. On 8,000-meter peaks, anyone who summits will be very tired, so on summit day I look to have a strong lead team, who knows each other well, is confident on the terrain, and watches the weather. That way, we have a buffer if anything starts to change. Personally though, like many climbers, I've had more close calls and lost more friends than I care to count. My first real experience with death was in the Andes, descending a new route we had just put in on an 18,000-foot peak. Some ice crumbled under my friend's foot in a vertical chute, and he fell 2,000 feet. When you are young and climbing difficult new routes, you start to feel invincible. The experience shattered all of that for me. Going from completing a great, if admittedly dangerous climb on a beautiful sunny day to having one of your best friends gone a few seconds later makes you understand how fragile life is, right down to your core. You never forget it. Since then, I've witnessed a number of times where dying could have been as much an outcome as staying on this side of it.

A few years ago I was on the north side of Everest and a Spanish climber was pulled off a neighboring mountain by an avalanche. My climbing partner, Mike Bearzi, and I climbed up and found his body. A few days later we attended a memorial service where we buried him on the mountain just below where he had fallen. This year, Mike returned to the same area to do a new route on a peak next to Everest and fell to his death while descending. I lost another close friend in the mountains. Speaking at his memorial, I asked two questions that, in a long search of myself, were the only things that made much sense to ask: "Did he have passion for life?" and "Was he loved?" Climbing fosters a large dose of both, and the climbers I've known who have died could have answered either question affirmatively and with conviction. Maybe they achieved all they needed in this life and moved on more quickly than most. I've yet to know anyone who started climbing young, did it for a long time, and for whom death is a real fear. Our priorities change; we move from rock to ice to mixed climbing, and from Yosemite to the Alps to the Andes and on to the Himalayas—but few ever quit. The types of climbers I know, despite whatever else they might accomplish in life, are climbers forever—they will always be drawn to it. Pushing the limits of life makes it a richer experience, not one from which to hide.

CLASH: *You are part of the Everest 1953–2003 Expedition to commemorate the 50th anniversary of the first Everest climb. What's the plan?*

ANDERSON: Jamling Tenzing Norgay and I were lunching in New York last year when he broached the idea of a 50th anniversary ascent of Everest. He wanted to honor his father and his father's team, as well as launch a Sherpa-led sustainable cleanup of the mountain. Peter Hillary agreed to join us, so we have the sons of both members of the history-making team. So much has happened on Everest in the past 50 years, and not all of it positive. We thought the best way to commemorate the historic first ascent was to try to return the mountain to a state somewhat close to what it was when Jamling's and Peter's fathers first reached the top. The expedition will not only look back at the past 50 years but forward to the next 50, with a focus on the environment. We will also utilize the latest communication technologies to monitor weather and keep the world updated on our progress. We are doing a film and a book, too, and have a web site so people can follow our ascent.

4

The Business of Adventure

There is a special type of hybrid adventurer who combines pure adventure with the business of it. These people won't necessarily bet the farm by climbing 8,000-meter peaks or racing 200-mile-per-hour cars full-time, but they hedge their bets with another risk—supply and demand. In short, they find a practical way to make a living at their life's passion.

This type of adventurer is especially dear to me. As a journalist, my main job is to report and write stories. In the process, I'm able to experience adventures I've only dreamed about. Part of this was a conscious career decision on my part. As a child, I remember hearing about participatory journalist George Plimpton and thinking: "Wow, there's a guy who does two things I would pay to do—professional sports and writing—and he gets paid to do them." The following profiles include some of the more successful entrepreneurs who've built thriving businesses this way: Abercrombie & Kent founder Geoffrey Kent; racing-school owners Robert Lutz and Dennis Macchio; island broker Farhad Vladi; and IMAX film producer Greg MacGillivray.

GEOFFREY KENT: MR. ABERCROMBIE, I PRESUME?

The sun has just slipped below the jet-black rock of the Ngorongoro Crater, spilling yellow, orange, and red light across Tanzania's western horizon. A private safari group, organized by the adventure-travel company Abercrombie & Kent, watches in silence. One member of the group interrupts the quiet by anatomizing the sunset—discussing how dust particles in the atmosphere reflect and refract the various light frequencies. Nobody hushes him; the A&K guides know better. Their job is to enhance a client's experience, whatever direction it takes, and if Bill Gates feels the need to explain the science behind the scenery, so be it.

"Each client is different, and we treat them that way," stresses A&K's founder and chief executive, Geoffrey Kent. And he should know. His client list includes some of the world's most influential people: Warren Buffett, Jimmy Carter, Prince Charles, Hillary Clinton, Gordon Getty, Ralph Lauren, David Rockefeller, the Pillsburys, James Murdoch, Ralph Fiennes, Gene Hackman. "Gates likes science and primates," continues Kent. "Buffett plays cards. Jimmy Carter is more interested in people."

Adventure travel is a big business, with billions in annual revenues and a 10 percent annual growth rate. "People have enough Ferraris in the garage," explains Kent while gazing over the Namibian deserts from the top of a sand dune. "What they really want today is an experience." With headquarters in Oak Brook, Illinois, and some 3,000 employees in 40 offices worldwide, A&K is providing plenty of excitement, running trips on all seven continents. It is 10 times the size of competitors Mountain Travel-Sobek, Wilderness Travel, and Geographic Expeditions.

All of this success is a far cry from its meager roots four decades ago when Kent, a native of Nairobi, Kenya, and his parents, Colonel John and Valerie, founded A&K with a single

Big Daddy: The Mother of All Sand Dunes

Sand dunes start small, with a bush, say, or a stone—anything that gets in the way of desert winds carrying sand. As the centuries pass, the currents deposit more particles and the sand piles higher. The longer this goes on, the higher the dune grows. Wait 25 million years and you get Big Daddy, one of the oldest sand dunes on the planet and thought to be the biggest. A ziggurat of red sand, Big Daddy rises 1,200 feet from the parched African earth of the Namib Desert. Above is the deepest of blue desert skies; at its base is a sea of golden, talclike clay. The sharp contrast of the three colors reminds one of a giant Rothko painting.

Climbing Big Daddy, however, is not like climbing a Rothko painting, which would have to be a great deal easier. First you have to get yourself to Namibia, sandwiched between Angola and South Africa in southwestern Africa. The obscure country gained independence in 1990 after a century of European colonial rule, and while it covers more acreage than the state of Texas, its population is less than 2 million—about two persons per square mile. I flew 15 hours nonstop from New York to Johannesburg, connecting there to a two-hour flight to Windhoek, Namibia's capital. From Windhoek it's still another hour in a small charter plane to Sossusvlei, but the ride, with the sea of dunes undulating below, is supernaturally beautiful.

Since shoes are clumsy and tend to fill with sand, you climb dunes in bare feet. You want to start early, then, before the sun heats up the sand to well over 120°F. Wake-up for the group was 4:30 A.M., as Big Daddy is a good two-hour drive from camp. Climbers ascend in one of two ways: along the long, gradual ridges leading to the summit or straight up the 65-degree slip face. Most of the few hundred people who try each year choose the former. I chose the latter and was teamed with an adventurous bunch. Geoffrey and Jorie Kent, owners of Abercrombie & Kent, and their son, Joss, were my climbing companions.

From the start it was tough going. Locals say that most climbers who quit do so within the first 100 feet. I can see why. It's frustrating. For every step up, you slide back at least half that. You quickly learn to go up on all fours, like a giant spider, using your hands as anchors so your feet slide back less. You also learn not to look up. Like on a mountain, the top never seems to get any closer.

(continued)

I took to counting steps. First I tried 40, then rested for a minute. Too many. Then I tried 20. Too few. Finally I fell into a rhythm of 30 steps, a rest, 30 steps, a rest, and so on. The local ascent record for Big Daddy is around 18 minutes. It took us close to an hour.

The view from the top looks like another planet altogether—the red planet, Mars, perhaps. For miles in all directions, hundreds of red dunes, all shorter than Big Daddy but still imposing, fill the horizon. Pitch-black shadows alternate with an intense palette of bright reds. Dune climbing may be like mountaineering in terms of the physical exertion it exacts on the way up, but not on the way down. Our descent was easy. A combination of dune surfing, sliding and just plain stumbling had us back to the base in less than 10 minutes. That, combined with seal-like sounds from our feet rubbing in the sand, made us chuckle even though we were thirsty, covered with hot sand, and occasionally pinching ourselves to make sure that it all wasn't just a dream.

Land Rover, running animal safaris in east Africa. The big development then was refrigerated trucks, which allowed travelers to have decent meals and cold drinks in the evenings after their long days in the field, and Kent seized upon it for his operations.

A&K's principle now is the same as it was in 1962: adventure by day—game viewing, trekking, climbing, fishing, whatever—plush comfort by night. "Any fool can be uncomfortable," says Kent. "I learned in the British army that it doesn't take much more effort to be comfortable than it does to be uncomfortable." Comfort means different things to different people. For A&K clients, comfort means a bed with clean sheets, hot showers, fresh towels, good wine, gourmet food, and accommodating guides.

Prince Charles, who's been on several A&K trips, likes to paint landscapes. On a drive across the Serengeti Plain, he asked the driver to pull over. A satchel of watercolors in hand, he then told the crew to carry on, leaving him there alone to paint; three hours later, the convoy doubled back to pick him up. "He loves the solitude of getting away and the beauty of nature," says Kent, who was present that day. "He's a very unassuming person."

Generous, too. A few years later, the painting was a surprise present. "Charles said, 'I have a little gift for you.' I opened it up and almost fainted," says Kent's wife, Jorie. "He knew I had always liked that one. He had the colors, the fields, miles and miles of that golden grass on the Serengeti." The watercolor hangs above the Kents' bed in Vero Beach, Florida. Gordon Getty, the eccentric oil heir, is another story. While on an A&K trip bound for Tanzania, he missed the view of Mount Kilimanjaro as they flew by. Eventually realizing this, Getty stormed up front and ordered the pilots to turn the lumbering 727 around. No problem, he was told. Getty got his view and his photographs.

Abercrombie & Kent's high prices and reputation for indulgence attract a somewhat older (average age: 55 or so) and well-heeled crowd. The prices are high enough for the company to own its own camps, much in the fashion of Club Med. "Many travel companies are just fancy catalog publishers," scoffs Kent. "They don't do much more than book your trip, and you never see them again."

There are two tiers of A&K trips. Custom trips range from a few thousand dollars for Hillary and Chelsea Clinton's three-day African safari to more than $1 million for Bill Gates and his entourage's three-and-a-half-week romp through Kenya, Tanzania, and the Democratic Republic of the Congo. Then there are catalog trips, which can cost as little as $2,000 for a quick jaunt to New Zealand's lake district, or $60,000-plus for a round-the-world excursion.

The privately held A&K is still very much a family affair. Jorie, the daughter of Paul Butler (founder of Butler Aviation), is vice chairman. In 1972 she bought out the 50 percent stake of Kent's parents. She pours most of her time and energy into environmental and eleemosynary causes, including the A&K Global Foundation, which provides charity in countries to which A&K runs trips, and Friends of Conservation, which funds Kenya's Masai Mara Game Reserve. She also designs a line of A&K clothing and jewelry.

Their son Joss, a 1997 Harvard MBA and former consultant at Bain & Company, joined in 1999 as chief operating officer. After the elder Kent suffered a near-fatal polo accident in 1996, he realized that he and Jorie couldn't do it all themselves. The younger Kent, based in London, is putting financial controls into place, upgrading A&K's web site and computer systems, and running A&K Active—a new part of the company that offers more extreme trips (whitewater rafting, mountaineering) geared to younger clients.

Abercrombie & Kent is doing well enough that the Kents have been included in the London *Times'* list of Great Britain's richest people, with a net worth of more than $100 million. And you might say this includes the Abercrombies as well. "There never was an Abercrombie," confesses Kent, "at least not here. We put that in our name because, in the beginning, it made us sound bigger and more prestigious than we really were. The *A* also put us on top of most tour operator lists." The extra name also evokes memories of that safari-outfitter-turned-casual-clothier Abercrombie & Fitch. Clients, when they book a trip, still occasionally claim that they are friends of the Abercrombies, laughs Kent. "They evidently want special treatment or a discount. We just smile and tell them we'll do what we can."

ROBERT LUTZ: HIGH ON SPEED

Indy cars are screaming past Robert Lutz at the California Speedway. Some of his students are hitting 160 miles per hour on the backstraight. This is fast track in every sense. Lutz (no relation to Bob Lutz, the vice chairman of General Motors) has hitched himself to a fast-growing spectator sport and a companionate boom in motor sports entertainment. His racing school experience, Driving 101, caters not to pros but to thrill seekers who want the rush of speed. "I'm interested in the looks on the faces of my students as they climb out of the car," says Lutz. "When they are smiling ear to ear, that's what makes all the hard work worth it."

Lutz's father, Glenn, owns five dirt tracks in the Northeast. By age 8, Lutz was helping out during the summer, stocking concession stands. At 12 he was racing go-carts and, in 1987, became the Northeast champion of International Kart Federation. He knew he was hooked on racing, but he also knew that the road to glory as a driver was dodgy. While studying marketing at Central Piedmont Community College in Charlotte, North Carolina, Lutz found his path. He took a job at Fast Track Driving (a school to improve the skills of pro racers) and thought, "Why not offer something similar but for the fan? De-emphasize the technology and driving physics and play up the thrills." Besides, he reasoned, "There are a lot more race fans than race-car drivers."

As at any racing school, safety is key. Lutz knew that a fatality could cost him his business, so he devised a novel lead-follow program. Unlike most schools, where students find their own way around the track, his instructors would lead by a few car lengths, thus controlling speed and the all-critical racing line. Next Lutz had to gain credibility—and customers. He approached a handful of NASCAR drivers who would give his school name recognition and attract sufficient seed capital to lease time at a large superspeedway oval, acquire liability insurance, and pick up a few used stock cars. "At first people looked at me like I was crazy," Lutz recalls. He finally convinced Richard Petty, winner of a record 200 Winston Cup races, and two other partners to chip in a total of $200,000 in cash and equipment. Each took a 25 percent stake in what became the Richard Petty Driving Experience.

After three years, Lutz was netting $3 million on revenues of $7 million. He'd sent 35,000 racing fans speeding through without serious mishap (mostly just bruises and shattered egos). One of his students was Leo Hindery, then president of TCI (now part of AT&T) and later chief executive of Global Crossing, who liked the sport so much he decided to buy Lutz's shares in 1997 for undisclosed millions.

Retirement lasted less than two years. "I thought, 'What will I do with the rest of my life?' " Lutz recalls. Easy: Start another driving school. Only this time make it the fastest in the world, relying on modified open-wheel cars instead of stock cars. Based on his record at Petty, Lutz persuaded Championship Auto Racing Teams (CART), a sanctioning body for top open-wheel drivers, to lend its name (he dropped the name in 2002). To launch CART Driving 101 (www.driving101 .com) Lutz invested $5 million—$3 million of his Hindery payout and a $2 million bank loan at 9.25 percent. Why so much capital? Indy cars are more expensive than stock cars and, because of the higher speeds, must be greatly modified for safety.

In June 1999, Lutz opened for business at the Las Vegas Motor Speedway and promptly lost $1.2 million on revenues of $500,000. Reason: Classes were only one-third full, not enough to pay overhead and marketing expenses. But the next year, as the concept caught on through word of mouth and a $300,000 advertising campaign (two-thirds in print, the rest on TV), Lutz earned a respectable $200,000 on $3.3 million.

Many clients come from corporations like GlaxoSmithKline and Nortel Networks, which use the courses to reward employees and to build confidence. Celebrities occasionally pass through as well. Country singer LeAnn Rimes and Adam Firestone, who heads Firestone Vineyards, have run laps; so have actors Sylvester Stallone and race-car driver Robby Gordon. A more typical customer is Lawrence Vail, owner of a Racine, Wisconsin, garage door business, whose wife, Angela, gave him the course for his fortieth birthday. "It was this or a big party," she says, trackside at Las Vegas. "I'm glad it was this," beams Vail, who got his car up to 164 miles per hour in the advanced course. Lutz limits those classes (cost: $3,000) to only 10 percent of business, even though they are more profitable than introductory classes ($375 to $1,500). "In advanced programs we significantly increase our risk of crashes," he says.

Because of all the safety controls, Driving 101's insurance is not as expensive as you might think—around $100,000 per year for $10 million worth of liability coverage. Of the thousands of students who've gone through the school, only a dozen have spun cars, and just four have hit the outside concrete wall. All but two were in advanced programs. (Average damage to car on impact: $10,000. Most significant injury: a broken leg.) Lutz has expanded operations and now operates at five locations in the United States—California, Chicago, Las Vegas, Nashville, and Texas. Where does he go from here? "My ultimate goal," he says, "is to run classes at the Indianapolis Motor Speedway."

FARHAD VLADI: ISLANDS FOR SALE

From 2,000 feet up in our noisy Helicopter Seychelles whirlybird, the island below looks small and compact, a commingling of greens, whites, and gray-blacks. As we descend, the whites become pristine beach sand, the greens meld into the leaves of palm and coconut trees, and the gray-blacks crystallize into sharp granite cliffs and rounded boulders. When we finally touch down, one of the boulders begins to move.

Purchase Plan

Want to own a racing school? You can start from scratch, as Bob Lutz did, or buy an existing school. Dennis Macchio, an economics consultant, bought Bertil Roos Racing in Blakeslee, Pennsylvania, for $500,000 in 1999. A former racer, Macchio knows he won't get rich from it. His annual compensation now is in the low six figures—far less than the $1 million or so he made full-time at his consulting firm. Like Lutz, though, he gets his kicks from watching the students' enthusiasm. Not to mention that he still gets to race once in awhile.

Running a racing school isn't all thrills, though. There are plenty of humdrum business problems. Take over an existing school and you may well find that it has been running on empty. When Macchio bought Bertil Roos (www.racenow.com), he got 13 Formula 2000 cars valued at $25,000 each, the Roos Racing name and clientele, plus six test cars. The Roos school was founded in 1975 by the Formula One driver Bertil Roos and is well respected within the racing community. Derrike Cope, a winner of the Daytona 500, and Michael Andretti, a runner-up in the Indianapolis 500, have trained there.

But like many ex-athletes, Roos was no businessman; with only 1,800 students a year, the school struggled to turn a profit. He had done very little marketing—most students came in by word of mouth. Macchio immediately pumped up the advertising budget from 4 percent of revenues to 30 percent. To attract drivers with professional ambitions, he ran ads in trade magazines like *Sports Car* and *Champ Car*. For the broader market, he went to publications that included the *New York Times* and *Maxim* and to cable television's ESPN2.

And he expanded from the school's Pennsylvania headquarters near Nazareth and Pocono raceways to two other tracks (which he also rents), in Texas and Virginia. By 2000, the Roos school had bulked up to 2,600 students and managed to turn a profit of $200,000 on $1.8 million in revenue. Unlike Lutz, Macchio targets the serious driver, someone who wants to know everything about the race car, from strategy to the physics of turns. Fortunately, Macchio still has a stake in his lucrative consulting practice to help out. To any prospective racing-school owners, he has this warning: "It takes a large fortune to make a small one in racing."

"That's Charlie," shouts Farhad Vladi, who is showing me the 593-acre North Island in the remote Seychelles. "He doesn't like the helicopter noise." Charlie is a giant turtle. "Whoever buys the island gets him with the deed," laughs Vladi.

He's not kidding. Vladi is the broker to see for real estate that ordinary folks can't get to; he's the world's foremost island peddler. In the past three decades, he's sold more than 600 of them. For Vladi, the inaccessibility of his parcels is a major plus. "Every island is different," he explains. "People feel a particular energy when they step ashore. I can tell within minutes whether someone will buy."

The island business is booming. With offices in Europe and North America, Vladi Private Islands (www.vladi-private-islands.de) could top $40 million in revenues this year. Vladi charges about 8 percent in commission, part of which supports his staff of two dozen in offices in Hamburg, Germany, and Halifax, Nova Scotia.

Vladi has always had a special affinity for islands and, for that matter, the Seychelles. As a young Ph.D. student at the University of Hamburg in 1971, he visited the chain—located in the Indian Ocean between India and Kenya—on a lark and discovered that 80-acre Cousine was for sale. He ferried over to the island and took some photos. Back in his hometown of Hamburg, the entrepreneurial half Iranian, half German found a local businessman interested in Cousine. Sale price: $100,000. The client bought the island solely on Vladi's description and photos and paid him a 5 percent commission. Thus began Vladi's island-broker career. Since then, he's sold property from Fiji to Cap Ferrat. His clients include Virgin Group's founder Richard Branson, actor Tony Curtis, singer Diana Ross, rock group U2, and Iran's royal Pahlavi family.

As with any real estate, prices hinge on location, location, location in the island business. Vladi's recent inventory lists

Cheno Island—27 acres near Valdivia, Chile, which includes a small log cabin. Asking price: a reasonable $360,000. Contrast Leaf Cay 2, a smaller (15-acre) gem in the tiny Exumas part of the Bahamas complete with harbor, airstrip and 18 houses. Asking price here: $20 million.

What's caused the boom in island real estate? Discounted airfares and vacation packages for one. It's just too easy to visit the watering holes of the rich, such as Tahiti and the south of France. To truly get away now, the extremely wealthy need a moat as big as, say, the Indian Ocean. In short, they need their own island. Vladi estimates the world has 3,000 purchasable islands, with the supply growing. The Philippines, for example, is particularly well stocked, with 7,000-odd parcels. Vladi figures 300 to 500 of them have paradise potential once the Philippine government decides to allow outside ownership. It is also a lot easier to own an island today. New technology—including desalination plants, solar- and wind-powered generators, prefabricated houses, and wireless cell phones requiring no ocean cables—have all brought down the cost of operating an island hideaway.

Islands certainly make money for Vladi (he now has two of his own, near Halifax and New Zealand), but are they good investments for the purchasers? If you have to ask, you probably shouldn't own one. As a pure real estate play, folks are probably better off on the mainland. While most islands do appreciate in value, the infrastructure—depending on how elaborate—can eat an owner alive. Often, the costs cannot be recouped, because the next owner wants to design his own private Eden. "Ego is very big in the island business," says Vladi. "If an island is too developed, it can actually hurt the resale price."

Still, if you follow simple rules, Vladi says, the investment potential is enhanced. Make sure the island is registered in its particular country and has a deed; that it has vegetation, including a supply of fresh water; that it's not too far from the mainland so it can be stocked (and visited) easily; that a building permit is obtainable (bird sanctuaries don't make the best investments); that the island is in a politically stable area of the world; and that it has good weather, preferably year-round.

If you want to avoid all that hassle, you can always rent. A lively island rental market has cropped up, and it's getting livelier. Vladi estimates that a third of his revenue now comes from rentals. Again, there is a wide range of inventory. That first island (Cousine) Vladi sold in the Seychelles in 1971, for example, now rents for $10,000 per week. Isola Galli, near Italy's Almalifi Coast, will cost you five times that.

Whether you buy or rent, however, Vladi says there's something about the romance of an island that can touch even the most hardened of hearts. Peter Huntley, an unsmiling English financier, sold Fregate Island, another in the Seychelles, to German industrialist Otto Happel in the late 1970s. When it came time for Huntley to depart his domain for the last time, he commanded his private pilot to loop back and dip the wings while he wistfully threw a single rose from the window. "He had tears in his eyes, a man I could never imagine with tears," recalls Vladi. "This you would never do if you sell your condominium in Florida." Then there is the case of Peter Ruester, who once owned Seychelles' North Island, and Charlie, the giant turtle. He commissioned Vladi to sell it for $5 million. Another emotion came into play there. "Peter's second wife didn't approve of the island because she considered it the love nest of the first," Vladi says.

GREG MACGILLIVRAY: IMAX MAN

To make *Everest*, his large-screen IMAX hit movie, producer Greg MacGillivray had to figure out how to get an 80-pound IMAX camera to the highest place on earth. So he and codirector David Breashears put their heads together and designed a lighter, 40-pound camera that could still inhale 65-millimeter film at the speed of five feet per second. Their effort was well worth it. The film's greater speed and surface area produce detail and clarity that far surpass conventional cinema, resulting in *Everest*, the haunting, beautiful, if utterly unconventional film that has broken box-office records.

Before *Everest*, MacGillivray's defining work was *To Fly*, a vertiginous epic about the history of airplane flight. Grossing over $150 million and still running, it's the most successful IMAX movie ever. But *Everest* is hot in pursuit: With more than $100 million at the box office, it's moved into second place.

As a fanatic surfer growing up in Newport Beach, California, MacGillivray was obsessed with the power and beauty of nature. His first films were low-budget surfing flicks produced while he was studying physics at the University of California at Santa Barbara. He didn't have enough money to link sound to picture then, so he toured college auditoriums with his *Beach Boys* cassettes, narrating the voice-over live. To produce his second film, *The Performers,* in 1965, MacGillivray anchored high-speed cameras under the waves, catching board and surfer both in and out of the water. Because of the film's speed, the slow-motion scenes look fluid. It was a revolutionary way of showing the sport. *The Performers* became an international cult classic and made a $35,000 profit.

"It dawned on me I could make a living at this," says MacGillivray. There followed 22 large-format films, including *The Living Sea*, about the ocean and its floor, *Sky Riders*, about hang gliding, and *The Magic of Flight*, about the daredevil Blue Angels navy pilots. Unlike conventional producers who just put movie deals together, MacGillivray will roll up his sleeves in pursuit of perfection: He produces, directs, and even works as a cameraman. Occasionally he does mainstream 35mm work, too. He filmed the claustrophobic outdoor winter vignettes for

The Shining and action sequences for *Towering Inferno*. "I'm the guy Hollywood calls when they want extreme stuff," he says.

Only about 15 percent of the population typically sees an IMAX movie, half that of the average feature film, and MacGillivray would like to convert another 5 percent, or 15 million people, in North America. *Everest* is certainly helping. It has also assured solvency for MacGillivray for the foreseeable future: It cost only $6 million to make, and his firm, MacGillivray Freeman Films, owns 90 percent of the movie. NASA approached MacGillivray once to shoot in space. At the time, he had reservations. But that was before his film company had conquered Mount Everest. "If they asked me to go now, I'd reconsider," MacGillivray smiles. Who can blame him?

5

Tops and Bottoms of the World

Extreme travel embraces a literal meaning for some executives in that it describes, for example, the North and South Poles or the very deepest depths of the ocean. Intrepid travelers, therefore, can test the boundaries of extreme locales by participating in any number of luxury or economy trips that take tourists to the ends of the earth—literally. Ready to swap hectic schedules for the solitude of arctic nightfall or the ghostly silence of the ocean floor, executives would be hard pressed to find sojourns that refresh and invigorate like extreme destinations.

In many ways, the exotic mixture of adventure and discovery inherent in extreme travel is the same thing that draws executives to their chosen careers—albeit the vacation experience fortunately unfolds at a pace more conducive to introspection and appreciation. Such thrill-seeking treks also furnish aggressive managers with a getaway tailored for a psyche that has just unplugged from daily deal making and empire building.

A more playful thought about extreme travel comes to mind with respect to the recent spate of corporate corruption that includes Enron, Worldcom, the dot-coms, and Martha Stewart. That is, adventure travel could be used to curb corporate crookery. Indeed, experts who test the psyche of high-level white-collar criminals confirm that greed is not the primary motive behind complicated extortion schemes and rogue malfeasance. Instead, it's the craving for bigger challenges and the loathing of the status quo that drives morally flexible executives to the brink—or should I say *clink*. Wouldn't it be nice to ship that adventure-starved lot to the Arctic Circle or plunge them into a watery abyss to visit the *Titanic*—as a preventive measure, of course.

Joking aside, if you're an executive looking to trade up your Martha's Vinyard respite for something a little more sporty, investigate the polar regions. The historic events that define the polar cap adventure are the stuff of Hollywood hits—yes, literally.

To date, no less than a half-dozen movies and documentaries have been made about Ernest Shackleton's heroic, three-year-long rescue in which he saved 28 crewmen after his wooden ship, the *Endurance,* became trapped in the Antarctic ice in 1915. Even more books have been published about the subject. "People are fascinated with the polar regions of the earth, and always have been," says George Butler, who raised $3 million from Morgan Stanley to produce the IMAX film *Endurance.*

In 1908 and 1909, Frederick Cook and Robert Peary endured frostbite, starvation, and mutiny in their efforts to claim the North Pole. Roald Amundsen and Robert Scott encountered similar obstacles as they raced for the South Pole in 1911. Amundsen won, and Scott paid the ultimate price for finishing second: his life. It's much easier to visit the polar regions these days, what with the help of nuclear icebreakers, planes, high-tech gear, and the like. Now you can choose how you want to go, in which season, and how much you want to spend. Of course, there are those who still do it the old-fashioned way—on foot or with sled dogs. But, increasingly, that's becoming more the novelty than the norm.

SVALBARD: THE LONG ARCTIC NIGHT

In early March, after five long months of darkness and a few weeks of twilight, the sun edges over the horizon in Svalbard, a desolate group of Norwegian islands some 600 miles from the North Pole. But the light also brings tourists who fill Svalbard's main hotels, the Funken and the Polar, in the high season. While the spring light may appeal to some, I wanted to try the Arctic in winter, when there's no sun and the temperature averages −25°F. Why then? Why not when the mercury hovers, however briefly, above freezing? Because, notwithstanding the crowds, this better resembles the way people live up there.

You may have heard of Svalbard before; its largest island, Spitzbergen, played a crucial role in World War II, serving as an intelligence base for the British and Russian navies in search of Nazi battleships hiding in Arctic waters. Svalbard has also been in the news for, of all things, the 1918 flu pandemic. A few years ago, Canadian researchers exhumed the corpses of six Svalbard coal miners who had perished from it. Since the bodies were largely preserved in polar permafrost, they could contain traces of the virus and offer a clue to its origin.

After flying to Oslo, I boarded the Norwegian airline Braathens for the final four-hour leg. At 78 degrees of latitude, Svalbard is the farthest north one can fly commercially. Anne Surnes, our flight attendant, has traveled the route many times. In 1966, when she first visited, there was no airport—just monthly flights to provide miners with food and mail in winter when ships can't get through the pack ice. To land the DC-6, she says, "They just put lights out on the ice." Upon a moment of reflection, she adds, "The landings were quite smooth, actually."

Our 737 landed smoothly, too, but on a paved runway. As we deplaned at 2:00 P.M., I got my first blast of Arctic winter, and it didn't disappoint: −20°F with 40-mile-per-hour wind gusts. It felt like a punch in the solar plexus—the kind of shock that leaves you gasping for air but also makes your adrenaline pump with excitement. And it wasn't just cold, it was eerie; it took a while to sink in that it was midafternoon and the sky was pitch black.

Svalbard was discovered in 1596 by Willem Barents, a Dutch whaler. Translated, the name means "the land with the cold coast." It fits: Two-thirds of the islands are covered by snow, and the permafrost goes as deep as 1,300 feet. Until 1900, whaling, trapping, scientific research, and polar exploration were the main occupations of the few Russians and Norwegians hardy enough to make Svalbard home.

At the turn of the century, coal was discovered. Longyearbyen, Svalbard's capital, with a population of 1,500, is named for American John Longyear (by means town), who in 1906 founded his Arctic Coal Company there. In 1920, the Svalbard Treaty gave Norway sovereignty over the islands. In 1975, when the airport was built, tourists started coming up—a trickle at first, but now tourism is a major revenue source. Through winter and into May, outfitters sponsor dogsledding, ice caving, and snowmobiling expeditions, complete with guides and equipment.

Longyearbyen, huddled on the fringe of the Arctic Ocean, is bordered by mountains on three sides. There is but one main street downtown, if it can be called that: an open space between building clusters that runs slightly uphill for a mile. During the Christmas season, when I visit, strings of lights form a kind of canopy between the buildings, giving the town a festive feel. If you want to shop, an enclosed collection of stores features liquor, clothing (authentic sealskin coat: $2,000), a cafeteria and—get this—the northernmost franchise of the Body Shop. In the food section of one store, shanks of reindeer sit in an open cooler next to cold cuts. Miners stock up with avaricious seriousness; matriarchs, in strident Russian, call to one another from different aisles. The air outside, pure and cold, is a sterile medium; the introduction of any smell is immediately detected in its undiluted state. The exhaust from a car has never smelled so acrid. Body lotions and perfumes, tolerable in the polluted cities, smell cloyingly sweet and artificial.

One night I visit one of only a half-dozen ham radio stations in Svalbard. By day, Mathias Bjerrang is an air traffic controller for the Longyearbyen airport. In his spare time, he manages the club radio station—JW5E. He picks me up in a four-wheel-drive Volvo at the Polar Hotel, and off we go into the darkness. En route, he stops just long enough to point out a road sign with a big *X* across a polar bear. The bears are an ever-present danger in winter, he says, and a loaded gun is a must for anyone leaving the city limits. He points to his in the back of the vehicle.

The small radio shack isn't fancy, but it's warm and bright inside. Without any fanfare, he fires up the radio, points the directional antenna toward the United States, and slowly tunes the transceiver dial. "Listen," he says. There is a fluttering of weak static, but it is audible—and unsettling. "That's the aurora," he explains. Spectacular but elusive, the aurora borealis, or northern lights, is the main reason tourists visit Svalbard in winter. Seeing it requires clear skies and the polar night. But you can hear it on the radio, when it's active, at almost any time. More often than not, though, it plays havoc with radio propagation. So while tourists like the aurora, Bjerring does not.

Bjerring hands over the microphone and encourages me to use it. A licensed operator myself, I find a clear frequency and begin calling for hams in the States. Within a few minutes, hundreds are responding at once! What a thrill; as a youngster I had tried to contact Svalbard many times in such pileups, but to no avail. Here I am, giving other hams the chance at the thrill that I never got.

Another night I hire a taxi-van to visit remote No. 7, one of the last operating mines in Longyearbyen. Its coal heats the town through a unique series of hot-water pipes. To get there, we travel up a dangerously curved and icy mountain road that has no guard barriers; sheer drops of hundreds of feet are common. Halfway up, I ask the driver to shut down the engine and headlights and let me out. I wander to the edge of a precipice and gaze over the mountains gently lit by the moon. This is truly the middle of nowhere, I think. There is no wind, and the overwhelming quiet is heavy, like the fog your breath makes in frigid air. I look for the aurora. But the moon is nearly full, so I can't see what I had heard on Bjerrang's radio. But the moon holds its own fascination. It never rises and never sets—just circles the horizon once a day, like a giant celestial clock.

Later, I dine at Nordic Huset, which boasts gourmet food and a 20,000-bottle wine cellar. I have grouse—indigenous to Svalbard—and reindeer. (They are out of seal.) Over a first course of Arctic scallops, I settle into conversation with the waitress, Beate Bergholm-Lindgard. Aside from a German couple, I am the only person in the place. Again, the subject of polar bears comes up. "Svalbard may seem tame, but don't become complacent," the waitress warns. To illustrate her point, she gestures at a huge polar bear skin decorating the wall. "They shot him on the steps of the church, I think." Monica Lewinsky? Svalbard has heard all about her. "You mean cigars and stuff?" asks Lindgard, blushing. "We have the Internet, you know."

116

A significant Russian coal mining operation still exists in nearby Barentsburg (population 1,000), a few hours away by snowmobile, and the bronze-black statue of a coal miner stands guard at the center of Longyearbyen. But the mines are giving way to tourism, keeping many locals busy. The Funken, a former boardinghouse for miners, is adding rooms. Another motel has renovated above the restaurant, Steakers. And trips booked through Svalbard Polar Travel, the local outfitter, are at record levels.

Upon leaving the magical place, I have an hour to kill before takeoff. I walk from the airport to an icy beach bordering the Arctic Ocean. There, on the permafrost, is a shack the size of an outhouse with an electric light shining inside. Turning toward the ocean, with my back to Longyearbyen, I know that in a few months the cruise ships will come, cluttering up the horizon. But for now, all that lies between me and the North Pole is pack ice and a few hundred polar bears—what Robert Peary and Roald Amundsen must have looked on nearly a century ago. That much hasn't changed, I muse. Turning again, I head back to the airport, where my 737 is waiting.

TRAVELER'S NOTEBOOK: Braathens and SAS airlines fly round-trip to Longyearbyen from Oslo. Outfitters: Svalbard Polar Travel for snowmobiling, ice caving, cross-country skiing, dogsledding, Arctic cruising (www.spitsbergentravel.no). Hotels include the Funken (47-7902-6200) and the Polar (47-7902-3450).

THE NORTH POLE: A DIFFERENT KIND OF COLD WAR

Closing his thumb and forefinger together, Victor Godovanik, a Russian pilot with a decade of Arctic flying experience, informs a passenger: "Go home, tell your friends you were this close to death. This close." After circling three times,

Godovanik has just bounced our 26-ton Antanov AN-26 military cargo plane onto a 10-foot-thick slab of ice 60 miles from the North Pole. According to Godovanik, the 900-yard runway upon which we'd landed was only half the length suggested for our aircraft, and we were two tons over its weight limit. "Another half ton," says Godovanik, "and we'd all be dead."

As it happens Godovanik, like many bush pilots, likes to tease a bit. I later consulted Jane's *All the World's Aircraft* and found that the AN-26's maximum load was more than we'd carried and, indeed, the strip was long enough to land on safely. But I didn't know that at the time, and the pilot's sense of humor reminded me of why the North Pole is now one of the most coveted spots in adventure travel. Not that I needed much reminding at that point. The trip, organized by Bernard Buigues, owner of a Paris-based adventure-travel outfit called Parallele 90, had begun four days earlier in Moscow. From there our group of 15 flew Transaero Airlines 3,000 miles northeast to Norilsk, then on to Khatanga on Siberia's Taimyr Peninsula. The group was made up mostly of Europeans and included six women. Several of my fellow adventurers were mountain climbers; one had even summited Everest. All had ponied up $9,000 for the trip.

Stepping off the Transaero plane in Khatanga, a city of a few thousand robust souls 550 miles above the Arctic Circle, we get our first blast of Siberian weather: −35°F without windchill. And this is April. I throw on my heavy parka and plod over to what passes as a hotel. The toilets have no seats and the shower is primitive. At least there's hot water. Cost per night: a whopping $16. The buildings in Khatanga are drab browns and grays and look as though they could be picked up and moved at a moment's notice. The land, as far as the eye can see, is flat; deep snow covers permafrost in all directions. Dressed in heavy fur coats and *shapkas* (fluffy reindeer-hide hats with earflaps), the residents view us as strangers from another planet—which is pretty much what we are.

We are slated to spend one day in Khatanga, then fly by AN-26 and helicopter the remaining 1,200 miles to the Pole. But bad weather and a magnetic storm, which disrupts radio communications, keep us in town a few days longer. We make the best of the delay, piling into a Russian MI-8 transport helicopter and thudding off in search of Dolganes—small nomad groups of reindeer herders north of Khatanga.

At first the Dolganes are hidden by thick fog covering the tundra, but by flying low our pilot spies animal tracks that eventually lead us to them. They welcome our group into reindeer-skin tents, offer us tea, and peddle their wares. One wizened gent shows me a snow-white *shapka*. Buigues, acting as a translator, says he wants $25. Dollars, not rubles? You bet. This guy has never met an American, but he knows ruble devaluation. Buiges explains that the Dolganes have contact with civilization maybe twice a year, and within that time period the ruble's value can be cut in half. I hold out a crisp $20 bill and buy a beautiful shapka hat worth 10 times that in Moscow.

Over a wretched meal (supposedly chicken) that night at Khatanga's only public restaurant, Buigues, an explorer and filmmaker from Paris, explains how he came to first organize trips to the Pole. In 1987, he began working with the Russians on polar research, but mainly down south, in Antarctica. In 1992, as communism crumbled, government officials in Dixon, another Siberian city, offered Buigues a chance to travel to the North Pole for $40,000. While his dream was to go to the Pole himself, the fee was too high, so he put together a group of a dozen others to share the cost. At the last moment another paying customer wanted to go, so Buigues gave up his seat.

The next year, 23 people signed up, but nobody went; Buigues's Dixon suppliers suddenly got greedy and tripled their fees. In 1994, Buigues found new suppliers in Khatanga and took 53 paying clients—25 cross-country skiers and 28 who flew in to and out of the Pole via helicopter. This time, he realized his dream. Buigues's entrepreneurial instincts are fully honed. He hires Russian military and science professionals, many of whom lost their jobs when the government collapsed. The year I went, Buigues pumped $165,000 into the ailing Russian economy.

As Buigues recounts his tale, a Russian jeep rounds us up. The weather has cleared. Time to head for the airport, where Victor Godovanik and his AN-26 await us. The twin-engine turboprop is devoid of creature comforts, including seat belts. Sitting single-file along the inside of the fuselage, just like in the World War II movies, we face the center of the plane. Luggage, fuel drums, Samoyed dogs, sleds, and food are piled high in front of us.

After three hours in the air, we stop on the remote island of S'redny to refuel. But, as we wait for the fill-up, the weather closes in and we cannot take off. At first, I think this will be fun—staying the night at a mysterious Russian scientific station high in the Arctic. But quickly the thought deteriorates as I see where we are about to sleep: in the mess room, and it is a mess. Cockroaches infest the place—on the ceiling, floor, walls. I've never seen anything like it, and I live in New York. In an attempt to avoid these indestructibles, we camp in our sleeping bags on the dining tables. It doesn't matter. Within an hour, the little nasties are crawling all over us. Thank God the next morning the weather breaks. Gleefully, we pile back into the cockroach-free aircraft and continue on our journey to the Pole.

After two hours, we bounce down the recently bulldozed ice station runway at 89 degrees north latitude—just 60 miles from the Pole. After stretching our legs a bit, we transfer the gear and sled dogs to an MI-8 helicopter for the final leg.

About halfway to the Pole, we land to drop off the skiers and dogs. They will then cross-country-ski the remaining 30 miles over the next four days, sleeping in tents along the way. Each will pull a small sled with personal equipment; the dogs will haul food and tents. Once they reach the pole, the skiers will radio the helicopter to take them back to the ice station.

Now there are just five of us in the helicopter with 30 miles to go. In 20 minutes, guided by a global positioning system, which uses satellites to pinpoint location, we are within 300 yards of the pole. We can't land directly on it, as the ice pack there is judged to be too weak. So out we climb to cover the last three football fields on foot. The snow beneath our boots makes musical crunching sounds, a slightly different pitch with each step. We don't say much, absorbed as we are in being at the very apex of the globe. Surprisingly, it is a balmy 10°F—quite a bit warmer than Siberia. I keep pinching myself. Suddenly Buigues stops. "This is it," he says, consulting his GPS, "the top of the world."

Arriving at the North Pole is not like reaching the summit of a mountain. The northernmost apex of the earth is just a navigational point, the convergence of 90 degrees latitude and an infinite number of longitudes. Unlike the South Pole, which is 10,000 feet of fixed, layered ice over land, the ice pack above the North Pole drifts constantly on the Arctic Ocean—sometimes four miles a day. To stay on the Pole, I have to walk in the opposite direction the ice pack is moving. The mementos I leave—including a gingerbread cookie my mom had baked—will travel over 10 miles before our skiers arrive four days later.

There is no clock time at the Pole, as all time zones converge there. To travel around the world, simply walk in a small circle—noon New York time is a few inches away from 5:00 P.M. London time. The sun, low-angled on the horizon, is present in the sky 24 hours a day and won't set until October, when it's

121

night for six months. Our Russian guide, Marina Myshkina, and I pose for a photo. "Ever think during the Cold War you'd be arm in arm with an American on the North Pole?" I ask. "Incredible," she says, tears in her eyes. Indeed, it is incredible.

That night, back at the ice station, we party in the Russian pilots' tent. American rock music—Metallica, Nirvana—blares on the boom box. I give them a cassette tape, *Blue Sky Mining*, by the Australian rock group Midnite Oil, and they oblige by feeding me. We wash down olives, fish, dumplings with a spicy caribou center, and raspberry strudel with shot after shot of Russian vodka. Best darn meal of the trip. And no sign of cockroaches. At one point Vaesili, one of our lead pilots, boasts he can guzzle a whole bottle of vodka to my one shot. I dare not accept the challenge: He very well may be at the controls of the aircraft flying me out the next morning. Unlike the load factor for an AN-26, for these jokers vodka is very serious business.

ANTARCTICA: CLIMBING WITH PENGUINS

My fingers are numb and stiff, in the first stages of frostbite. I am on a steep, frozen slope, 1,500 feet above Antarctica's Weddell Sea. The water below, peppered with icebergs, is cold enough to kill a man in a matter of minutes—but the fall would probably kill you anyway. While I'd climbed my share of big, cold mountains, my fingers never chilled like this. I am worried. This isn't supposed to be a dangerous climb, and normally wouldn't be. But whenever you challenge the elements, even a small mistake can have disastrous consequences. My mistake is wearing pile gloves with no protective overmitts. While ascending fixed ropes for the last steep section to the summit, my hands are flash-frozen by the combined effects of windchill on the outside and the cold metal of the jumar on the inside.

But above beckons the summit of d'Urville Monument, a virgin peak devoid of human footsteps, just 100 feet away. Through 40-mile-per-hour gusts of wind I hear our guide, the world-renowned climber Conrad Anker, screaming at me. He sees that I am having trouble with my hands and holds up a pair of spare overmitts. He presents me with a simple choice: Descend immediately or gamble that the mitts will protect my hands long enough to get me to the top, then down, without frostbite. Sheepishly, I accept the two red Gore-Tex shells. The trip has cost $10,000—I can't turn back now. Plus, when will I get another shot at an unclimbed peak? Anker smiles and sends me up the final length of rope. A few long minutes later, I balance myself on top. The howling wind does everything it can to blow me off my feet, and my hands have no feeling, but I am exhilarated. I am standing at a place where no human has ever stood, on a continent I'd dreamed about since I was a kid, with a view unmatched anywhere on the planet.

Until the mid-1980s, Antarctica was inhabited mainly by scientists manning research posts and braving temperatures that can descend to −130°F. Until recently, it wasn't easy to climb mountains there, either. In 1983, Dick Bass, on his quest to become the first to climb the Seven Summits (highest mountain on each continent) organized the first private climb of Mount Vinson, Antarctica's highest peak. That pushed the National Science Foundation, the continent's American governing body, to open the door for commercial expeditions like ours.

I began the journey in Ushuaia, Argentina, a five-hour plane ride from Buenos Aires. A Russian ship, the 236-foot MV *Molchanov,* took us across the notorious Drake Passage, a 600-mile stretch of water between the southern tip of South

America and Antarctica that is considered by sailors the most treacherous sea in the world. We were relatively lucky. On both of our 48-hour crossings, the heaviest seas we ran into churned up 20-foot waves—countered well by antimotion drugs like meclizine and scopolamine. But that's not always the case: The crossing before ours had encountered 35-foot waves. Needless to say, its passengers had wound up seasick, and many were bruised, too, from being slammed against the ship's inside walls.

The *Molchanov* is comfortable, but far from a floating Four Seasons. I share my 10- by 15-foot cabin with Michael Kennedy, the former editor of *Climbing* magazine. He takes the top bunk, I take the bottom. The food isn't fancy, either, but it is hearty—meat and potatoes, soups and berry pies— just what you want after a hard day of climbing. As on most ships that cruise these nether regions, there are lectures on Antarctica's history, geology, and wildlife to help pass the time. Still, a favorite pastime of mine is hanging out on the bridge watching the Russian crew thread our ship through icebergs the size of Manhattan apartment buildings.

The average age of our 19 climbers is 48. Many are business executives. The other thing they share is that most are experienced adventurers—and in good shape. Bradley Neiman, a real estate broker from Denver, has been to the top of six of the Seven Summits. Jerome Corr, another real estate man, skied to the South Pole and wrote a book about it. Susan Babcock, a Stanford MBA and member of the *Los Angeles Times* board, climbed Kilimanjaro and Aconcagua.

But you don't have to a climber to enjoy the coldest continent. Each year, thousands of tourists flock to the continent's fringes to see glaciers, icebergs, whales, penguins, seals, and other wildlife; to stand on a frozen continent where, when the wind dies, the silence is as intense as the rock-hard light. Most of the trips, on Russian research vessels retrofitted for passenger cruising, run between November and March—summer months in the Southern Hemisphere—when there is plenty of daylight and the temperatures rise into the 20s and 30s during the day. For mountaineering enthusiasts, though, the *Molchanov* is a civilized way to get where you're going. Says Susan Babcock: "On a big mountain, you sleep in tents, melt snow for water, and go for weeks without a shower. Here we're served breakfast in fancy dishes, climb beautiful peaks during the day, and then come down, not to more trekking, but to hot showers, a bed, and dinner aboard the ship."

By the end of our trip, we had retraced some of explorer Ernest Shackleton's route, with visits to Elephant Island, the Palmer Peninsula, and Deception Island. I also claimed three new summits: d'Urville Monument, Spigot Peak, and Mount DeMaria. The first two, previously virgin, turned out to be easier than the last one, which had been climbed before by the British. All in all, the experience provided 11 of the best days of my life. "It's not that the mountains down here are that difficult," says Conrad Anker, smiling. "They're just so remote, many remain untouched by man." And, for the record, hundreds more beckon.

TRAVELER'S NOTEBOOK: The adventurous can now go all the way to the South Pole, at the center of Antarctica. It was first reached in 1911 by Roald Amundsen, a Norwegian, in a dramatic cross-continent race with Englishman Robert Scott, who died after reaching the Pole a few days after Amundsen. Unlike its northern counterpart, the South Pole is stable ice—some 10,000 feet thick—over land, and scientists work year-round at the Amundsen-Scott station there. Adventure Network International in Boca Raton, Florida (www.adventure-network.com) operates commercial flights to the Pole from November to February for

$26,000. During the winter months, however, temperatures can plummet to −100°F, and aircraft cannot fly in or out because metal landing gear becomes so brittle it snaps.

THE NORTH POLE: SWIMMING WITH SANTA

As adventures go, Quark Expeditions' cruise to the North Pole, while exotic, is pretty cushy. You travel aboard a deluxe icebreaker in comfortable, heated cabins equipped with hot showers. The ship has a well-stocked bar and gourmet meals, such as roast loin of veal and dim sum with salsa. You're waited on hand and foot by the courteous Russian crew. There's even valet laundry service. Plus, Quark offers an (optional) swim in the Arctic Ocean at the very top of the world. Now that's what I call "high" adventure.

In August, 102 of us, mostly Americans and Japanese, with a smattering of British, Germans, and Italians, meet in Helsinki, Finland, then fly in a chartered 737 to Svalbard, the Arctic island group I had visited in winter. There we board *Yamal*, our floating hotel for the next 12 days. With 75,000 horsepower from twin nuclear reactors onboard, *Yamal* is the world's most powerful icebreaker and one of only a half-dozen ships capable of reaching the North Pole. In winter, *Yamal* is used to sweep ice for freighters plying the Northeast Passage. But in summer, rather than having it sit idle as in the days of communism, the Russians lease the ship to Quark Expeditions (www.quarkexpeditions.com), a U.S. commercial tour operator, and get a much-needed cash dividend. Since 1993, *Yamal* has made more than a dozen trips to the Pole, bringing millions of dollars into the Russian economy.

Our group is an interesting—and wealthy—mix. (You pretty much have to be wealthy to take this cruise; the cheapest seat is $16,000.) There's Brian Cooke, a television writer from Guernsey, in the United Kingdom; Martinn Mandles, chairman of ABM Industries; Rita Schutt, a senior economic policy adviser at the German Finance Ministry in Berlin; and Alfred McLaren (my cabin mate), a former submarine officer and past president of the Explorers Club.

At 81 degrees north latitude, still nearly 500 miles from the Pole, we begin to encounter ice. At first, there are just periodic sightings of lone bergs. Most are what you'd expect—a pristine white color—but others are painted in beautiful shades of yellow and blue. Generally, we learn, the older the berg, the bluer it is, because its more compact geometry refracts light of higher frequencies.

Soon enough we hit the heavy pack ice surrounding the Pole—thinner than the spring pack seen the last time I'd come, but formidable nonetheless. *Yamal*'s bow—24 inches of strengthened steel—smashes cleanly through this stuff, 20 feet thick in some places. There is a constant up-and-down movement as the ship's bow rides up on the ice, falls as the ice caves in, rides up onto it again, falls, and so on. The procedure creates a deep rumbling best described as rolling thunder. Unexpectedly, the hypnotic motion serves to induce sleep rather than to deter it. The real hindrance to sleep is the constant daylight. In summer, near the top of the world, in "the land of the midnight sun," the sun never sets—it just circles the sky at a low angle.

To break the monotony of endless light, we keep to a regular schedule. Breakfast, lunch, and dinner are served at their normal times. At night we try to sleep by pulling the curtains and wearing eye masks. During the day, we attend lectures on Arctic exploration from such notables as Victor Boyarsky, the famous Russian polar explorer, and tour the ship's atomic engine room with our captain, Alexander Lembrik.

When we near land, helicopter excursions are arranged. One is to Novaya Zemlya, a large, crescent-shaped island where the Russians did nuclear testing in the 1950s (and recently has been the subject of speculation regarding whether Russia will begin controversial new testing there). The place literally looks like the moon, with boulders strewn over a barren, windswept surface as far as the eye can see. Another puddle-jump is to Franz Josef Land, a group of high-Arctic islands from which early explorers embarked on their attempts at the Pole. Bleak and on the fringes of civilization, it was staffed by Russian scientists and military personnel during the Cold War. Not anymore—the haunting, empty buildings are just another testament to Russia's better days.

Sometimes our insomnia pays off. At three o'clock one morning in the Cambridge Strait near Franz Josef Land, a polar bear and her cub are spotted near the ship. The captain immediately shuts down the engines, and those of us lucky enough to be awake spend the next 20 minutes photographing the powerful—but beautiful—animals. The cub is particularly curious and hangs around longer than its mother wanted; it keeps sniffing at the air, our scent being one it has never encountered while roaming the pack ice.

On the morning of August 11, as we approach the Pole, an excited crowd gathers on the bridge to watch the ship's global positioning system. When it reads 90 degrees north, a loud cheer bubbles up, some expensive champagne is uncorked, and fireworks pop. Ah, the North Pole. Again. I look around. Still no sign of Santa Claus. But there is a mix of ice and open ocean surrounding the ship. The weather—unusually mild for this time of year at only a few degrees below freezing—seems to alarm some passengers, and there are mumbles about global warming. Later, in the *New York Times,* it is reported that we are the first humans to see open water at the Pole. Truth is, there's always open water up there in summer. In August, when the ice pack is thin and scattered, its movement occasionally leaves the actual Pole uncovered. (The *Times* eventually retracted its statement.)

After finding solid ice on which to anchor the ship, we disembark and spent a few hours wandering around a surrealistic world of largely black and white. For me, the big moment is the polar plunge. A makeshift ladder is fastened to blue ice near the back of the ship, and a call goes out for potential swimmers. During the cruise, there had been lots of big talkers, but when we get right down to it, maybe only a dozen of us are takers. No wonder: The water is some 14,000 feet deep and its temperature just 28°F.

I nervously remove clothes to reveal the fire-red bathing suit I have on underneath, wrap a tether safety line around my waist and perch on the ice. From my talks with Geoffrey Kent, who had done the swim the year before, I know that if I sample the water with my toes or try to climb down the ladder and enter gradually, I will never do it. So I dive, headfirst, into the black water. The first few seconds I feel nothing—it's such a shock to the system that I'm essentially numb. After a few strokes, though, I realize something is radically amiss. First, it feels like a thousand needles are pricking me all at once, then my brain starts to go fuzzy. I sense that if I don't turn around immediately and get back to "shore," I'll pass out. It seemed like an eternity, but I am in the water for all of 30 seconds.

When I'm safely back on the "terra infirma," a shot of Russian vodka and a chocolate are shoved into my hand and a warm towel is wrapped around me. Later, I am presented with a certificate that says, "Did brave the raw arctic elements by stripping off multiple layers of warm, protective clothing and, in semi-nakedness before a cheering crowd of less hearty souls, plunged headlong into . . ." As if I need a piece of paper to certify that I'm crazy.

Sadly, in the Barents Sea on our way to port in Murmansk, we get word that the Russian submarine, *Kursk,* sank a few days earlier. Because of our ship's enormous power and proximity to the site, there is talk that we might be called in to aid the rescue efforts. But calculations eventually show that even if divers did manage to attach cables to *Kursk*, our 75,000 horsepower would not be enough to drag it into shallower water. What we did do was hold an auction on our ship, raising $10,000 for families of the *Kursk*'s crew. That may not sound like much, but when you consider that the entire Russian city of St. Petersburg—home to many of the dead—was able that week to muster up just $6,000, it is meaningful.

On future cruises, Quark is planning an optional submersible dive to the North Pole. Since, technically, the Pole is at the bottom of the Arctic Ocean, a visit to that point would let tourists reach the "real" North Pole, which would put them in the *Guinness Book of Records*. But that will really cost you: an estimated $50,000 extra for the chilly eight-hour dive. Human nature, always pushing new limits made possible by surging technology. There will always be a market for that.

> **TRAVELER'S NOTEBOOK:** For the more adventurous, Northwest Passage (847-256-4409) of Wilmette, Illinois, offers two-week dogsled trips to the Pole for $26,000, departing from Resolute Bay, Canada, initially by air, then by sled. A good introduction to dogsledding is offered in Barrow, Alaska, by John Tidwell of Alaskan Arctic Adventures (907) 852-3800. His team of 10 dogs is one of just two in Alaska's northernmost city.

A *TITANIC* TRIP: VOYAGE TO THE BOTTOM OF THE SEA

Even though Robert Williams hadn't yet been born when the *Titanic* sank on April 15, 1912, he's spent much of his life fascinated by the disaster. At age 8, his grandmother gave him a book that kindled his imagination. As a teen, he built scale models of the ship. Later, after Robert Ballard discovered the wreck of the *Titanic* in 1984, Williams went to meet him and to revel in his stories. Imagine Williams's surprise when his wife, Jill, gave him a *Titanic* sweatshirt for his sixtieth birthday, then told him he would need it—on the chilly submersible that would take him 12,460 feet beneath the surface of the North Atlantic to visit the actual wreck. "I was speechless," says Williams, chairman of Genova Products, a plumbing supply manufacturer in Davison, Michigan, with $100-plus million in revenues.

Forget the sappy movie, this is where the real adventure begins. An outfit called Deep Ocean Expeditions (www .deepoceanexpeditions.com) runs commercial excursions to the *Titanic*. To take adventurers down, it uses the *Mir I* and *Mir II*—two Russian submersibles (miniature submarines) built to withstand the tremendous pressures of the ocean depths.

Fewer than 100 people have seen the wreck since the trip was first offered commercially in 1998—less than the number of astronauts who have flown in space. Buzz Aldrin, the second man on the moon, has done both. In 1997, he went down for a few hours. "It was crusty, like gingerbread cake," he says of the remains. One reason so few have gone is the cost: a prohibitive $36,000 per person. Another is claustrophobia. Each submersible holds a maximum of three people—a pilot and two passengers—and is just 25 feet long and 10 feet wide.

The oceans, which comprise more than 75 percent of the earth's surface, remain one of the most mysterious and unexplored areas of the planet. The deepest spot, the Marianas Trench in the Pacific, has been visited only sporadically by humans. In 1960, Don Walsh and Jacques Piccard (father of Bertram Piccard who, in 1999, became the first to travel around the world nonstop in a balloon) descended 35,800 feet in the bathyscaphe *Trieste* to set the world depth record. In 1995 *Keiko,* a Japanese submersible, bettered that record by descending 36,007 feet. Traditional submarines can go down only about 3,000 feet.

With the collapse of the former Soviet Union, special undersea submersibles became available for commercial expeditions. They don't go as deep as the bottom of the Marianas Trench, but they do dive deep enough to visit areas full of shipwrecks and thermal vents.

Williams set sail in July from St. John's, Newfoundland, on the ship *Akademik Mstislar Keldysh*. A day and a half and some 360 miles later, the *Keldysh* arrived at the *Titanic* site in the early evening. "That part of the trip really brought up the hair on the back of my neck," Williams recalls, "because conditions, I'm told, were similar to what they were that fateful night." The ocean was flat, the weather calm, and there was no moon. "You look off the deck and, maybe 300 yards from where your boat is, it all happened. You just imagine what it was like. That moment, more than anything, got to me."

For the next few days, the crew of the *Keldysh* circled the wreck. Most of the time was used for lectures from scientists on board and familiarization with the ship and submersibles. By the day of the dive, the weather had deteriorated and fog had closed in, adding to the drama. After breakfast, a nervous Williams was fitted into his special diving suit. The biggest danger in a submersible is the same as in a spacecraft—a flash fire—because of the oxygen-rich atmosphere and all of the electronic equipment. "I'm not sure the suit would have helped much," says Williams, "because your face and hands are exposed. But it is made of material that doesn't give off static electricity."

The 11-hour dive starts at 9:30 A.M. The moment of truth, of course, is when the hatch closes, because then the passenger is in for the duration. *Mir I* is launched first; an hour later, *Mir II*. The theory is that if one sub gets tangled up, the other will be in close proximity. Williams was in *Mir II*. Once clear of the ship, the actual dive starts. The color outside the small porthole changes from bright gray just under the surface to green to blue and then just to black. In the dark through the porthole, flashing lights are abundant. "It's like sitting in a field on an August evening watching fireflies," Williams explains. "It's all undersea life, much of which gives off luminescence. You see some pretty big stuff glowing and pulsating. They look like big sponges with all these little things flitting around."

Surprisingly, there is no feeling of pressure during descent. But there is moisture in the sphere—the condensation given off by breathing. "They tell you all that beforehand," says Williams. "Still, when you get a drop of water on your head and you're down 12,000 feet, it's disconcerting. You're thinking, maybe a leak, you know?" Truth is, a leak at that depth would easily cut a person in half because of the tremendous pressure—more than 6,000 pounds per square inch. To prove the point, standard-size, eight-ounce Styrofoam coffee cups are routinely placed on the outside of the submersible. When subjected to pressures near the bottom, the cups shrink to about the size of a shot glass. "We went through a lot of cups as souvenirs for our friends," laughs Williams.

After about two hours, the pilot turns on the outside lights and a moonscape slowly materializes. Surprisingly, a lot of traditional life—coral, fish, crabs, starfish—scurry along on the bottom. But there is the unusual, too. "One creature, a yard long with big black eyes and a tail like an eel's, was fascinated and came right up to the porthole to look in," says Williams. "Obviously it had never seen light."

As the *Mir* combed the bottom, Williams remembers approaching a big hill. "It was actually mud that had been displaced when the *Titanic*'s bow hit bottom and burrowed in about 60 feet. To move up above it, we used our thrusters and, boom, came right in on the base of the bow. It was awe inspiring. You know the ship is big, but when you come upon it, it's absolutely massive. Each link in the anchor chain weighs over 200 pounds. You can even see where the white shear stripes start on the side of the hull."

"I also saw shoes," continues Williams. "At that depth the water is very calcium-deficient, so even skeletal remains dissolve over a period of time. When you see shoes on the bottom, particularly if they are two of the same type and in reasonable proximity, you know they didn't just drift down 2.5 miles and end up there. Probably somebody was in them. I had mixed feelings. I was excited but I also realized that an awful lot of people died that night—more than 1,500."

Being in the business, Williams also checked out the *Titanic*'s plumbing. "There are more toilets than you can count," he says, lightening up. "It appears that all of the ship's plumbing was done in lead. We saw Captain Smith's cabin. His bathtub is there with all the piping still connected. There is also lots of crockery. I would have given my eyeteeth to pick up a plate." Of course, Williams couldn't; the RMS *Titanic* Group has exclusive salvage rights to the wreck.

After spending a couple of hours at the bow, Williams's party made its way to the stern, about 2,000 feet away. "It's so badly damaged that only when you get to the back and see propellers do you realize it is the stern," he says. To the southeast, there's a large debris field full of kitchenware and bottles. Champagne is stacked as though still in the case, but the wood around the bottles has long since disintegrated. The $36,000 question: Was it all worth it? Williams sums it up this way: "I've talked to people who say, 'That's a lot of money. I'd rather take a nice cruise or go to Hawaii.' The worst thing is to breathe your last breath saying, 'I wish I'd done that.' I've done something now that I've always wanted to do. The biggest challenge will be to find another fantasy that will equal it."

DEAD SEA: HOW LOW CAN YOU GO?

It's one thing to venture up high, into the thin air of the world's tallest peaks, or even farther, to the vacuum of space. It's quite another to visit the bottom of the planet. The lowest patch of land on earth has its own special peculiarities. At 1,200 feet below sea (ocean, rather) level, the shore of the Dead Sea is as low as you can go without burrowing into the earth or diving into the ocean. After a week of dusty, off-road driving in a Land Rover through Jordan, it is a welcome and strange destination for us.

Our caravan of sport utility vehicles begins in Amman, the capital of Jordan. We are on one of Land Rover's Adventures—a program offered to Land Rover owners that features off-road driving trips in 15 countries (www.landrover.com). The average cost for nine days is $6,000; vehicles are provided in each locale by Land Rover.

To respond to competition from such SUV makers as Toyota and Jeep, Land Rover in the mid-1990s began offering the trips. More than 1,000 owners took trips on six continents last year. "We needed to differentiate ourselves," says Howard Mosher, chief executive of Land Rover North America. "Customers expect a relationship; they want to feel as if they've joined a club." Land Rover, founded in 1948, was owned by BMW for a while, then bought in 1999 by Ford. Ford has kept the travel program going.

After leaving Amman, we wind off-road through Jarash, a city of Roman ruins called the Pompeii of the East; the painted deserts of Wadi Rum, where much of the movie

Lawrence of Arabia was filmed (and where we participate in silly camel races); the port of Aqaba, where we snorkel in the Red Sea; then on to the ancient, rose-red city of Petra—beautiful architecturally, but overrun with tourists.

If you're a fan of off-road driving, this is some of the best. In addition to the pleasure provided by the exotic locale, we get to drive our vehicles—the Discovery and Range Rover—at angles of up to 30 degrees on rock without tipping over and up 100-foot-high sand dunes without getting stuck. Along the way we meet local Bedouins, photograph camels, and observe machine-gun-toting border guards.

On the last leg, we drive down from Petra, several hundred feet above sea level, and watch our altitude (monitored by a global positioning system in each vehicle) fall steadily—first to sea level, then to minus 300 feet, minus 600, minus 900. As we approach minus 1,200 feet, some of us begin to wonder when we will reach bottom. Mosher observes that the lowest point on earth isn't a point at all, but the entire shore of the Dead Sea. Why? Because water always seeks equilibrium.

A few miles away, near the banks of the Jordan River, is where John the Baptist is thought to have baptized Jesus. The river drains into the Dead Sea, which has a uniquely high salt content (30 percent versus about 4 percent for the oceans), and makes swimming an esoteric experience. Believe it or not, because of the large amount of salt, you can extend your arms and legs out above the water and still float comfortably. But don't put your head in; the minerals will scorch your eyes.

The Dead Sea is also the safest place on earth to get a sun tan. Because of the 1,200 extra feet of atmosphere between earth and space—and the high relative humidity from evaporation—the sun's most dangerous ultraviolet rays are blocked, leaving the lower-frequency ones to do the job. You'd never know this, though: The oppressive heat, combined with the heavy air, makes you feel sluggish and sleepy the entire time you're there.

When Land Rover visits the Dead Sea this summer, participants will be able to go even lower than we did. The water is evaporating at a rate of about a foot a year, lowering the shoreline. Four decades ago, the Dead Sea was 50 miles long; today it is just over 30 miles. Eventually, the lowest point on earth may be the dry, salty bottom of the Dead Sea—2,200 feet below what we normally think of as the sea.

6

Racing with the Wind

Auto racing has become America's fastest-growing spectator sport. The Indianapolis 500, for example, draws more people to one place in a day than the Super Bowl, World Series, and World Cup Soccer finals—over 400,000 fans. NASCAR events, where southern boys bang fenders traversing tracks like Daytona, are regularly among the highest-rated sports shows on television and enjoy a following of an estimated 75 million fans. And Grand Prix racer Michael Schumacher makes more money than any athlete in the world, save golfer Tiger Woods. In *Forbes'* 2002 ranking of athletes' pay, Schumacher earned an annual $67 million (to Woods's $69 million).

Contributing to the popularity of motor sports has been a significant increase in speed. The typical Indy car, for instance, now runs laps in excess of 220 miles per hour on the big speedways like Indianapolis. Compare that to the 1960s, when top speeds were more like 150 miles per hour. There are more vehicles, too: Indy cars, stock cars, Formula One cars, vintage cars, dragsters, motorcycles, and trucks. And the drivers race their machines on a number of different track types—ovals, road courses, drag strips, 24-hour venues, dirt tracks. But all combinations have two simple things in common: They involve financial and physical risk.

To be sure, the parallel between business and adventure is drawn again, but this time with a trackside perspective. It's on these smooth black tracks, in precision racing machines, that risk management and driving profits take on raw and unvarnished meaning.

RICK MEARS: FOUR-TIME INDY 500 CHAMP

In 1992, at the age of 41, Rick Mears retired a year after winning his fourth Indianapolis 500. The win tied him with A. J. Foyt and Al Unser Sr. for the most wins ever at the Brickyard. But both Unser's and Foyt's victories spanned longer time periods, so many say Mears's feat (four wins in 13 years) was more impressive. Had he not retired, sports pundits argue, he would have won more. They're probably right: Foyt and Unser raced longer and were much older when they called it quits.

Not surprisingly, Mears still works with his team owner, Roger Penske, the man he raced for when he captured his four Indy 500s (1979, 1984, 1988, 1991). He's a consultant these days, not a driver. Interestingly, the questions that linger about Mears's career are the same ones that dog successful executives in similar situations: What makes him so good at his job? Why did he retire at the peak of his career?

CLASH: *Why were you so good on oval tracks?*
MEARS: The big thing on an oval is to be smooth. Smooth is fast. The faster the oval, the more it suited my natural driving style. On the Grand Prix road courses, especially the street circuits, it is more stab-and-steer driving. You throw a car

around, hustle it more. On the superspeedways, you do the opposite. I always tried to calm myself before a race. A lot of people try to psyche themselves up. I would use the first part of the race for getting my rhythm, building up to speed. No surprises. Because the first surprise can be the one that takes you out.

CLASH: *What's the fastest lap you've ever driven?*
MEARS: When we broke the closed-course record at Michigan in 1986: 233.9 miles per hour. We were out there on a cold, windy day. There was probably another 7 miles per hour left in the car.

CLASH: *What's it like to drive that fast?*
MEARS: That's the hardest thing to describe. Although our G loading is side to side rather than up and down, it's like being on a roller coaster when you drop off the first big run, hit bottom, and the thing goes into a corner and mashes you down in the seat. That's the way the corners feel, plus you have to drive the car at the same time. You can't see it. If they could ever get across on television what a driver goes through, this sport's popularity would go through the ceiling. The turbulence, the G loading, the tire condition changing every two laps. It all affects the handling of the car. You're hunting for different spots on the track to get grip, running on the limit. It's one thing to drive around the track, but another to drive on the limit.

CLASH: *How do you know when it's time to retire?*
MEARS: That question had been asked quite a few times during my career. I always had two answers: If I physically feel I can't do the job or if the fun goes away. And the fun went away. It was a slow process, little things. The first was not taking it home with me. I was always one of the last out of the garage.

141

I was also one of the first drivers to take a computer to my hotel room and start looking at telemetry data—steering angles, throttle positions. I'd come back the next day and say, "Okay, guys, last night I was thinking. We need to look at this." When I caught myself saying, "Okay, guys, where are we, what are we doing?" I knew the desire was going away. When that happens, you don't do the 2 percent more you need to beat the next guy. You've got a team of 50 to 75 people trying to put the best equipment under you. If you aren't giving the same effort back, you shouldn't be out there. Another indicator was that I would get closer to things—like the wall. I never did get close enough that it was a problem, and nobody else ever knew. But I knew.

CLASH: *Do you miss driving competitively?*

MEARS: To me, the fun was in the limit. If somebody says now, "Why don't you just jump back in the car?" there's no way I could go out and run on the limit. Everybody also asks if I'm a speed freak. Speed's got nothing to do with it. It's competition. I don't care if cars go through a corner at 33 miles an hour. If somebody else has done 33.1, the fun part's doing 33.2. If it's 233, I want to run 234. It's all relative.

CLASH: *As a consultant to Roger Penske, describe what you do now versus when you drove for him.*

MEARS: I've always been involved with the engineering aspects of the car. Having been there, done that, as a driver, one of the main things now is helping the team gel more quickly because I understand both languages. If a driver says, "In turn four it's doing this," the engineers will look at the telemetry and say, "Yeah, look at the wheel travel." But I can look at it and say, wait a minute, there's a bump there. I've hit that bump.

Our group reluctantly aborted a summit attempt high on Mount Rainier after guides warned of dangerous ice conditions; two climbers were killed in approximately the same area, just hours after we turned back. *(Photo: Jim Clash)*

Sam Schmidt (left) and Indy racer Robbie Buhl with me before my successful 200-mile-per-hour run at Texas Motor Speedway. *(Photo: Steve McNeely)*

Surprisingly, the world feels peaceful when you're flying Mach 2.6 in a MiG. Here, I shake hands with my pilot, Alex Garnaev. *(Photo: Eric Anderson)*

Bob Lutz runs his own racing school, Driving 101. Here, he runs on the California Speedway at speeds close to a football field per second with me following. *(Photo: Tim Rue)*

Lamborghini chief executive Giuseppe Greco accepted my dare to ride in a Murcielago as I drove it above 200 miles per hour. Below: the dashboard registers our top speed. *(Photos: Michael J. P. Oakes)*

I snapped this panoramic
view from the top of the
22,834-foot Aconcagua,
second highest of the
Seven Summits.
(Photo: Jim Clash)

A former Forbes 400
member and honcho at
Drexel Burnham, Peter
Ackerman stands
triumphantly atop
19,340-foot high
Mount Kilimanjaro.
(Photo: Jim Clash)

The summit of Argentina's Aconcagua is marked by an aluminum cross, a remembrance of the climbers who have died while trying to conquer the mountain. (*Photo: Steve Quinlan*)

A&K owners Geoffrey and Jorie Kent atop "Big Daddy," a 1,200-foot-high dune in Namibia; it takes an hour to climb, but only five minutes to descend. *(Photo: Jim Clash)*

Indy cars have no top or windshield, making a snug helmet key. I'm carefully fitting one just before my 200-mile-per-hour run at Texas. *(Photo: Andy Muzingo)*

The Dolgane nomads, Siberian reindeer herders, come into contact with outsiders only a handful of times per year. *(Photo: Jim Clash)*

An ominous sign marks the fenced-in Trinity Site in New Mexico, where the first atomic bomb test was conducted in 1945. *(Photo: Jim Clash)*

CLASH: *Any lessons that you've learned racing that apply to business?*

MEARS: The harder you work, the luckier you get. You've got to be knocking. If you aren't, the door will never open. It's just like winning races. If you're running in the back of the pack, you never get to knock. You've got to get up front, and eventually the door swings open.

CLASH: *What about risks?*

MEARS: If you take a risk, the reward is greater. If I hadn't gone around Michael Andretti on the outside at Indy in 1991, we wouldn't have won. But I'm not a gambler. I say that, and people look at me. But I've never been. I learned a long time ago, that to win the race there's only one lap you have to lead. I talk about this with our new drivers. I ask them if they want to set a fast time qualifying. Then I tell them that there's only one way you can do that: complete the lap. It's not rocket science. If you want to win the race, you've got to spend the first half getting to the second half, and then the second half positioning yourself to lead the last lap.

CLASH: *Did you think much about death when you were racing?*

MEARS: Not really. You always know it's there, it can happen. But, again, that's where reward outweighs risk. I'd say it is the same in mountain climbing. If you love what you're doing, you take that risk. The risk is part of the fun.

CLASH: *Which Indy 500 win meant the most to you?*

MEARS: The first, in 1979, was only my second year there, so I didn't really appreciate it. I didn't understand what the place was all about. You get a little older and wiser and realize it may never happen again. You look at guys who have been there for years and have never won or who won it once. What

143

makes you any different? So each time gets better. The fourth in 1991 was incredible. I never dreamed of going to Indy, let alone winning it.

CLASH: *Your daring outside pass of Michael Andretti in the closing laps in 1991 is one of the most famous in Brickyard history. What went on in those final laps?*

MEARS: As it turned out, Michael, who was quickest all day, was still there at the end. That geared us up for the shoot-out. We didn't show our hand until after the last pit stops because, after that, nobody can make an adjustment. I got through turn four flat, with a pretty good run on him down the front straight. I think it surprised him because I hadn't run that strong all day. We got down to turn one and I'm following, in his tow, waiting to see where he's going to go. I've got to make a choice—left or right. He stayed down long enough to allow me to go to the right. So, I thought, that's my opening. I get beside him as we go into the corner. I don't know if I can make it through flat because I've had the last lap to build up speed. But I knew my tires were cool, and I was just going to pick up more understeer the longer we ran. I'm also thinking that I'm going to be hung out to dry on the outside. The higher I am, the more it's going to understeer, to push. But just as we turn into the corner, he dives to the apron to get his understeer out, which allowed me to come down just enough to keep my understeer out. Then it was a matter of being able to keep my foot in it and hope I'd make it out the other side. And we made it.

CLASH: *How did you feel when you knew you won?*

MEARS: I'm not a speech giver. When I get in front of a crowd, my knees get weak. I remember thinking, "If I win, I've got to give a victory speech, again. I'm going to get up there and make a fool of myself."

CLASH: *Any tips for me when I try it myself at Nazareth?*
MEARS: Stand on it and turn left!

NAZARETH: TESTING MY OWN METTLE

Nazareth, Pennsylvania, an hour's drive from New York, is home to the fastest one-mile tri-oval racetrack in the world, one on which Rick Mears had raced often. Bertil Roos Racing (www.racenow.com), one of the world's few oval racing schools, also makes its home there. What better place, I thought, than Nazareth, to take racing lessons? The two popular styles of open-wheel racing, road (Grand Prix) and oval (Indy), shouldn't be confused. While both use formula-type cars, the road courses combine shorter straights with several tight corners. Oval tracks (also known as speedways) intersperse longer straights with just a few sweeping left-hand turns. Because of fewer corners, average lap speeds are much higher on ovals—and, in the event of a mishap, less forgiving. The added risk is the reason you find fewer racing schools devoted to ovals.

Before I even stood on the hard asphalt at Nazareth Speedway, I spent a morning in the classroom. Forget the macho stuff, Bertil Roos owner Dennis Macchio told us. Racing is mostly physics: turning radius, apexes, G loading. The goal is to drive a line around the track that scrubs the least amount of speed possible. Hitting all the apexes right—the sweet spot on the inside of each of the corners—is key to conserving momentum.

As is the case with most racing schools, after class we toured the track in street cars. The *groove*, or line that hits all the apexes perfectly, felt slow—but we were cruising at only 50 miles per hour. Soon enough we'd experience firsthand why that line, periodically marked by orange cones, is critical to building speed—and to avoiding a crash.

Once you climb into the car, you're pretty sure that you do not want to crash it. With no top or windshield, and not much bigger than a go-cart, the Scandia Formula 2000 is essentially an Indy car with much less horsepower. Donning a driver's suit and helmet, I tightened the claustrophobic five-point harness straps and fired up the engine. Unlike street cars, the machines are loud and incredibly responsive. Sudden movements on the steering wheel or throttle, and the car jerks wildly.

Much was going through my mind as I shifted into high (fourth) gear for the first time. The air rushing through the open cockpit, combined with a car so low to the track that you can practically file your nails on its surface, greatly heightens the sense of speed. Even my initial laps, run on the slow side (75 miles per hour), felt fast. Within 50 laps, I had brought my times down to 40 seconds per lap. But my goal was 37 seconds, considered respectable by the school. (The instructors can do 35.) But shaving my time wouldn't be easy. Turn a hair too early entering a corner and the car gets loose; too late, and you're in a frightening push toward the wall. Both conditions make a lap feel faster than it is (any time you slide, you scrub speed). To run a 37, I needed to get pretty close to the wall exiting all three corners, and I had to be smooth entering and exiting.

Suddenly I was Rick Mears, and it was the end of the race. I grimaced through turn one without lifting the throttle, the first time I had done so, but had to fight hard in turn two, with all that extra speed, to dial the car down to the inside of the track. I managed a rough apex two-thirds of the way through, though, where I should have. And on the backstraight, I knew I had a legitimate shot at 37. I had never carried that kind of speed before.

Okay, all you've got left is turn three, I thought, and that's been your best corner all day. Relax, back off the throttle . . .

light brake . . . set the steering radius . . . now back on the throttle and let the car go all the way out to the wall. I glanced at the timer as I flashed by the start/finish line: 36.4 seconds, or an average lap speed of about 100 miles per hour. Just a guess, but if Mears reads this, he'll have to smile. He's right—it is about running on the limit, and sometimes the limit is you.

SKIP BARBER: GRAND PRIX RACING AT DAYTONA

It's one thing to drive solo on a racetrack, to improve your lap times. It's quite another to run in a race—with aggressive, high-speed traffic just inches away. Skip Barber Racing School (www.skipbarber.com) founded in 1975 and now the largest racing school in the country, allows amateurs to do both in sleek, grand-prix-style cars. Before you can race, of course, you must be trained, and a three-day introductory course, during which you learn the basics of road racing, is the first step. Unlike ovals, a road course (on which Formula One drivers race) involves a wide range of driving skills—threshold braking, sequential shifting (an average of 50 times per lap), tight cornering (both on left- and right-handers).

After that, there is a two-day advanced school in more sophisticated Formula Dodge RT/2000 cars, the cars used in races, where the protocol of racing (passing, flags, pit procedure) becomes second nature. The five-speed sequential gearshift in these cars takes a while to master. Picture a static ratchet wrench: To upshift, just notch it back a click; to downshift, notch it forward. To complicate matters, you don't need the clutch on the upshift, but you do on the downshift. The latter, therefore, takes longer to master, as you must blip the throttle each time you downshift to match engine rpm to the lower gears. My biggest problem was losing track of which gear I was in. Nowhere on the dash does it register, so memory, the tachometer, and the whine of the engine are your only indicators.

Upon completing both programs, I chose to run my first race at Daytona International Speedway, where I had trained. The famous 24-hour course, 3.56 miles in length, combines the wide-open NASCAR oval, banked at 31 degrees in the corners, with the tight twists and turns of a road course in the center. (Skip Barber offers races at a dozen other famous tracks, including Lime Rock, Laguna Seca, Sebring, and Road America.) The cars, crew, and driving suits are provided by Skip Barber—you just bring your intestinal fortitude and a checkbook. An average four-day race weekend, with practice and qualifying days plus two races, costs about $3,500, excluding crash damage. This is a bargain, though, when you consider how much more it would be to own and maintain a race car of your own.

Your weekend starts with a day of practice. Not surprisingly, that is when most accidents occur, as drivers test their limits on an unfamiliar surface. After spinning four times in practice, I finally crashed—in the infield rounding turn five. Luckily, it is a relatively sharp (translation: slow) corner, taken at about 40 miles per hour in second gear. I exited wide, dropped the left-front and back wheels into the dirt, spun across the track and into the wet infield grass, then collided head-on with a red steel guard barrier. The collision, which tore the right-front wheel and wing off the car, certainly got my attention. In addition to having my bell rung, the right side of my body was pretty well bruised.

During the mandatory trip to the track medical facility for a once-over, my number 14 car was towed into pit lane and a repair crew was put to work. In the interim, I was cleared to drive again and given a replacement car. Normally, competitors who crash are required to write a check for damages up to $3,900. I was lucky: Because I was on assignment, they didn't collect the $1,500 in damages from me. Needless to say, for the remainder of the weekend, I never spun again.

So, you ask, how safe is it? Very safe, but not 100 percent. Of the 57,400 race starts since Skip Barber began the series in 1977, two deaths have resulted from race accidents—one at Wisconsin's Road America in 1995, the other at Connecticut's Lime Rock in 1999. Viewed another way, that's two fatalities per 7.7 million race-weekend miles. However, you do think about it. The first time I passed the big *D* in Daytona painted on the NASCAR fourth-turn wall, where Dale Earnhardt was killed in 2001, I got a queasy feeling. At that point you have been gathering speed on the oval for almost a minute, so you're running in excess of 130 miles per hour. The key is not to look. As a racer, you quickly learn that your car tends to go where your eye travels.

Of the 60-odd competitors among three race groups, only five of us were rookies. Mark Patterson, a vice chairman at Credit Suisse First Boston, took me under his wing. A veteran of two years on the circuit, Patterson had competed in more than two dozen races. His first piece of advice: Don't spin qualifying for the race. Other drivers, he said, inevitably will while trying for the "pole"—the best qualifying time. When you spin, the rules mandate that you start at the back of the pack. I took Patterson's advice, ran conservatively, and qualified 13 of 18 cars in my race group.

The rolling start is when all the tension climaxes. Two abreast, crawling at 40 miles per hour on the oval, you feel as if you're about to tip over or slide down the steep 31-degree banking. Exiting NASCAR turn four, the pace quickens as the pack anticipates a green flag. While I've seen this procedure many times on TV, it is entirely different behind the wheel. You know that if you touch wheels with any of 17 cars bunched up around you, it will likely take out more than just your car. But adrenaline is pushing you to take chances. Can I pass the

149

guy in front of me before the first turn? Again, Patterson had told me to be cautious. With 30 minutes of racing ahead, why risk everything in the first 15 seconds?

To prevent one driver from having a mechanical advantage, cars are identically prepared and powered by the same two-liter, 150-horsepower Dodge engines, meaning there's a difference of less than one mile per hour between fastest and slowest. You'd never know it as we took the green flag and screamed down the front straightaway into a very tight turn one. Like a pack of hungry bees, cars in front of me darted to my left, then to my right. Once it was sorted out, only one car passed me on the start—pretty good for a rookie—but it was intense, and I wasn't even being aggressive.

After the first lap, you settle into a rhythm. The more experienced drivers form a pack that quickly pulls ahead. My task became protecting my position from the cars behind me. Most of my work was watching my mirrors and driving defensively, particularly in the infield part of the course. On the oval, the fastest part of the course, I could generally relax, though. My experience is mainly on ovals, so I was able to hold my own.

Near the end of the race, car number 8, the driver of which shall remain nameless to protect the guilty, came out of nowhere and forced me off-line going into six, the critical infield turn before reentering the oval. I had to make a snap decision—keep my line and broadside him, which likely would have put us both out of the race, or let him through. I chose the latter, and nearly lost it locking up the front brakes. I was furious. The two cars I had held off for eight laps got by me as well. With just one lap to go, I couldn't muster enough momentum to repass them. But I did shake my fist at Mr. Rude on the cooldown lap. Later, I heard from Skip Barber officials that he was on probation for similar offenses. After enough warnings, you're asked to leave the series.

I didn't finish last, and I hadn't spun or crashed the car. But I was still a bit disappointed. Had it not been for Mr. Rude, I could have finished better than seventeenth. But that's racing. The big boys suffer idiots regularly, Patterson later told me, except with millions of dollars at stake. In my second race the next day, I was a rookie no more. Starting seventeenth, I gradually moved up through the pack, eventually finishing fourteenth. I also shaved four full seconds off my best lap time, running a 2:23.8. Mr. Rude? He spun out in front of me on the second lap.

FONTANA: 200 MILES PER HOUR OR BUST!

At extreme speeds in a race car, little things become larger than life. A loose crash helmet, overrevving an engine—even sneezing—can all lead to disaster. I was about to find this out firsthand. Ever since Tom Sneva had broken the 200-mile-per-hour barrier at Indianapolis Motor Speedway in 1977, I had lusted for his experience. What does it feel like watching the world flash by, the length of a football field per second, with your backside three inches off the ground in an open car?

Although I'd never been in a real Indy car, I had driven fast on ovals. After my Nazareth experience, I gradually worked my speeds up at other, faster schools. Buck Baker Racing, founded in 1980, is one of the oldest stock car schools in the country. I did my NASCAR training with them at Atlanta Motor Speedway, a 1.54-mile high-banked oval, where I ran laps at an average speed of 135 miles per hour. But, in a stock car, the sensation of speed isn't as great as in an open-wheel car, because the driver is farther above the ground and strapped into a cockpit with roof and windshield. Stock cars aren't as fast as Indy cars, either.

So it was back to open-wheelers for more speed training with Driving 101, the world's fastest driving school, which operates at tracks such as Las Vegas Motor Speedway, California Speedway, and Texas Motor Speedway. The school's 1,800-pound machines, with more than 500 horsepower, are as close to real Indy cars as you can get. At Texas, I ran an average lap in excess of 160 miles per hour, an all-time record for the school, following lead instructor Dale Kokoski.

Next step: a real Indy car. Theoretically, in one I could not only hit 200 miles per hour, but had a chance to average that speed for an entire lap, as Sneva had done. That would put me in an elite club: More people have climbed Mount Everest than have driven a 200-mile-per-hour average lap.

The car I would pilot, provided by Brayton Racing, had the stuff to bring me to that pinnacle. With 675 horsepower, it was capable of speeds above 215 miles per hour and had enough torque to spin wheels in any gear. It was proven, too: At the prestigious Indianapolis 500 in 1999, the car had finished fifth, piloted by the Indy Racing League (IRL) racer Robby McGehee.

Brayton Racing is well known on the open-wheel circuit. The late Scott Brayton won three poles at Indianapolis and had held the track record for a lap—233.851 miles per hour. (Brayton was killed in a 1996 Indy crash during practice.) His father Lee, through Brayton Engineering, has supplied Indy car engines since 1983 and was a champion sprint-car driver during the 1970s. Younger brother Todd, team manager of Brayton Racing, was the Skip Barber Midwest Series champion in 1984.

But first things first. The main reason we were at California Speedway in Fontana was to qualify Brayton's rookie driver, John de Vries, for the IRL, which sanctions 15 championship oval races annually, including the Indy 500. My 200-mile-per-hour attempt would be secondary to the de Vries mission. Following weather delays early in the week (you cannot run Indy cars in the rain or with high winds), de Vries finally managed to qualify, but not without some drama. After running requisite

10-lap sessions at average speeds of 195, 200, 205, and 210 miles per hour, his car couldn't muster enough speed—215 miles per hour—to qualify in the last session.

But the crew made adjustments, de Vries altered his driving line through turns three and four, and the wind died as the sun began to set. With less than a half hour before the track closed, de Vries ran 12 consecutive laps in excess of 215 miles per hour to complete his IRL rookie test. Thrilled with his victory, we all went out and celebrated. A huge weight was lifted as the Braytons and their sponsors—Pit Bull Energy Drink, Rhino Cleaning Products, and Sprewell Motorsports—knew their car would compete in the IRL that year. I was excited for John, too, but nervous, knowing my big test would be the next day.

Dressed in a fireproof racing suit and driving shoes, I arrived at the track at 9:00 A.M., but my car wasn't ready. Seems a steering flange had been installed backward, which would have made the car snap to the left in the corners—not a pleasant experience at 200 miles per hour. The crew spent several hours disassembling the complex machine, then putting it back together to correct the problem. All the while, I tried to stay calm, but found it increasingly difficult. Get used to it, I was told: A real driver goes through this hurry-up-and-wait routine regularly. To pass the time and to calm my nerves, I walked around the two-mile oval. At a brisk clip, it took me 40 minutes. To break 200 miles per hour, I would have to cover that same distance in under 40 seconds.

Once repairs were completed, 1999 IRL Rookie of the Year Scott Harrington, a consultant to Brayton, fine-tuned the car out on the track. At 3:45 P.M., with just over an hour to go before the track closed, the car was finally ready. I sat strapped into the cramped cockpit with five belts, tightened to the point that I had trouble breathing. Indy cars are claustrophobic inside; your feet are squashed way up into the nose. The clutch, brake, and throttle are all within inches of each other. Good thing there isn't much use for the first two. Unlike Grand Prix cars, once up to speed you rarely shift. And you use the brakes only when coming into the pits. To slow the car down in the corners, you just back off the throttle.

The plan was to follow de Vries' car by a distance of 10 car lengths; any closer and my car would become unstable in his wake turbulence; any farther and I would lose the draft. Although de Vries had radio contact with the pits, I didn't, so I would rely solely on his cues. Gradually, we would increase our lap speeds until we hit 200 miles per hour or until something went wrong. I would be as alone out there as you can be—just the car, the concrete wall, and my nerve to keep me company.

As soon as I left the pits, I knew something was wrong. My borrowed helmet, loose in the garage, was suddenly buffeting all over the place. The faster I went, the more the helmet rattled. It was so bad that, on the straightaways, I sometimes took my left hand off the steering wheel to hold the helmet down so I could see the track. The dancing helmet also kept me from reading the dashboard tachometer, which I was supposed to do periodically to ensure I wasn't overrevving the engine. Bottom line: I should have come in. Against my better judgment I stayed out, feeling the pressure of a late start.

Within five laps, we really began to fly. Each time around, my engine began hitting the rev limiter a little longer, and on more parts of the track, meaning we were approaching maximum speed in that gear. In racing-school cars, rev limiters keep students from going too fast. What I didn't realize, though, is that with Indy cars, the rev limiter protects the engine from too many revolutions per minute for just a few seconds. On lap 8, de Vries slowed dramatically on the backstraight and pulled low on the track. I followed, sensing we were coming in. Either we had hit 200 miles per hour (I had no dashboard speedometer) or were pitting for adjustments. Either way, I was relieved. If it was the former, we had accomplished our goal; if it was the latter, I could get my helmet adjusted. I shifted into neutral and coasted the half lap into pit lane. There was no engine rumble, but I figured it had just stalled.

Before I even had the car parked, three track workers ran toward me with fire extinguishers. "Don't panic," one said. Panic, I thought, why would I panic? As soon as I looked in my rearview mirror, though, I knew why. Smoke belched from the engine and, instead of smiling faces, everyone was grim. Then I got the bad news: I had blown the engine, running in excess of 11,000 rpm. My run was over.

It's difficult to describe my emotions. First, I felt like I had let everyone down. Todd and Lee Brayton were out $20,000 in engine damage, and all the crew's work had been for naught. On the other hand, I was glad I hadn't crashed. Often, when an engine blows, Todd explained to me later, oil spills onto the tires and you immediately spin. Telemetry showed I was traveling at 171 miles per hour when mine let go, so spinning would not have been a pretty sight. I was disappointed. While I did manage an average lap of 164 miles per hour (about 44 seconds around the 2.029-mile oval), the elusive 200-mile-per-hour barrier still lay untouched.

We learned some valuable lessons for the next attempt. First and foremost, we would ensure my racing helmet fit snugly. We would also have radio communication between the pits and my car. That would have made all the difference because the crew could have warned me that I was overrevving and instructed me to shift. The radio also would have allowed me to complain about the loose helmet. The advice from four-time Indy winner Rick Mears seemed to play like a broken record in my head. Before I took the California run he said: "Take small steps so there are no surprises. After you're 100

percent comfortable in the car, stand on it and have a blast."
The next time I will listen more closely. There's a lot at stake.

RACING FOR KIDS: SECOND CHANCE TO SPEED

It took seven months to secure another attempt at 200 miles
per hour. Brayton Racing, fully committed to giving me a second try, ran out of sponsorship money by midseason, so I had
to find another team. Such is racing.

In May at the Indianapolis 500 race, I met an interesting
character: Dr. William Pinsky, a pediatric cardiologist and former racer who, in 1989, founded the charity Racing for Kids
(www.racingforkids.com). His concept was simple: Celebrity
racers, on their own time, would visit sick children in hospitals
near the tracks they were driving, at the same time raising
money for medical research and equipment. "It's such a boost
to the morale of the kids," says Pinsky, "and all the money we
raise goes directly to Children's Hospitals."

Indy 500 star Robbie Buhl, the most prominent of RFK's
racers, has visited more than 10,000 sick children over the
past dozen years. I got to chat with Buhl—even stand next to
his car on the front row of the Indy 500 race (he had qualified
second at 231 miles per hour). I wanted to talk about racing—
he wanted to talk about his hospital visits. I was impressed.

After the 500 I got an idea: Perhaps I could couple my
next attempt at 200 miles per hour with a fund-raiser for Racing for Kids. I called Steve McNeely, one the charity's boost-
ers, and he was intrigued; I would raise the money and he
would approach car owners for potential equipment donations to stage the event, thereby ensuring all cash raised would
go directly to charity. Surprisingly, within a month I had
found $20,000 in pledges. But McNeely was having more trou-
ble securing a car and a track. News of my blown engine at

California Speedway had spread within the racing community, and some were spooked that I might repeat what had happened there—or worse, crash.

By July, McNeely had found a team and crew willing to let me try at Michigan International Speedway, one of the fastest tracks in the world, on the day after the IRL race there. I was psyched; Michigan's two-mile oval is a carbon copy of California, but with more banking in the corners (18 degrees), meaning it is faster. At the last minute, though, the speedway quashed our attempt.

That left just one more track on the IRL circuit fast enough to make a reasonable run at 200 miles per hour: Texas Motor Speedway. I knew this track well from Driving 101, but it is a tighter oval—just 1.455 miles around. The 24-degree corner banking would help, but a 200-mile-per-hour average lap would mean getting around in just over 26 seconds. For perspective, the fastest lap ever turned by a professional NASCAR driver at Texas was just under 28 seconds. While Indy cars are faster than stock cars, I would definitely be flying!

After checking my credentials, Eddie Gossage, manager of Texas Motor Speedway, decided to give me the green light. The idea was to do the run on Monday, September 16, the day after the IRL race because the car and crew would already be there. McNeely approached IRL team owner Sam Schmidt for use of one of his cars, and he agreed—providing the machines survived the race and that we donated part of our $20,000 to his Sam Schmidt Paralysis Foundation (www.samschmidt .com). (A former Indy racer himself, Schmidt is paralyzed from the neck down from a crash in January 2000 at the Walt Disney World Speedway in Orlando.) The Treadway Racing crew agreed to stay on to prepare the car, but because all had flights Monday afternoon, my run had to be scheduled for the morning—and the earlier the better. Buhl stayed on, too, to be my driver "coach," as did McNeely, John Martin (Buhl's engineer), Driving 101's Bob Lutz (for moral suppport), and the staff of RFK, including executive director Patrick Wright.

The race on Sunday was a barn burner. Penske's Helio Castroneves, who had won the Indy 500 earlier in the year, and Panther Racing's Sam Hornish Jr. were neck and neck for the 2002 IRL points championship going into the event—the last of the season. After 190 laps, the two traded for the lead just inches apart at 220 miles per hour. Finally, on the last lap, Hornish went high and Castroneves low while exiting turn four. The crowd was on its feet as the two touched momentarily; then Hornish edged Castroneves at the start/finish line for the win—and the championship—by just nine-thousandths of a second.

All of this was exciting, for sure, but I nervously watched Schmidt's two cars throughout the race. When number 55, driven by Will Langhorne, faltered on lap 135 with gearbox problems, I held my breath. My last hope now was number 20, the Dallara/Chevrolet driven by Greg Ray and qualified at 217 miles per hour. I prayed Ray would finish the race—and he did, in fourteenth place. I had my ride!

At 8 A.M. Monday, we all met in gasoline alley, but the track was far from ready. Seems a miscommunication had occurred: Gossage thought we would start at 1 P.M.; we envisioned 8 A.M. It's not like you can just go out and drive. The track's asphalt surface was littered with debris from the race (pieces of carbon fiber from wrecks, oil, trash, etc.), potential hazards to the special Firestone racing slicks at extreme speeds. Ambulance and fire crews also must be in place in case the unthinkable happens—the car hits the wall—and they were nowhere to be seen.

I had been through this hurry-up-and-wait before, at California, so I tried to relax and make the best use of time. First, the crew meticulously fitted me into a molded driver's seat loaned by Indy racer Scott Harrington. I was also given my pick of Buhl's driver's suits (he's about my size). I was particularly careful about hunting down a snug helmet equipped with a radio. I didn't want a repeat of the buffeting fiasco at California. Once the track was blown clean, Buhl and I drove a few laps in a rental car, he giving me pointers on the racing line. There would be no lead car this time, so I would have to find my own groove around the track.

Then it was time for me to get into the car. My heart was pounding, but further delays once I was strapped in had a calming effect. To talk on the radio, I was told, just push the green button on the steering wheel. A digital speedometer was smack in front of me on the dashboard. Not that I would have much time to glance at it, but you never know. I was also told to move the sequential shift up to only fourth gear (there were six gears) during my run, then leave it—the car was capable of 210 miles per hour in that gear without any danger of hitting the rev limiter.

With the thick helmet padding and fireproof suit in the cramped confines of the car, I couldn't hear much other than sporadic radio communication. An umbrella was put over the cockpit to keep direct sunlight off of me. I closed my eyes and tried to envision the configuration of the quad-shaped oval I was about to drive. Because of the extreme heat—140°F in the car—I was quickly drenched with sweat and almost fell asleep. When the ambulance and fire crews finally arrived at 12:30 P.M., it was time. The starter tool was inserted into the back of the car, I flipped up the ignition switch, depressed the clutch, and put the car into first gear.

I ran my first three laps slow—just 120 miles per hour—to get a feel for the car and to check the track for debris. When I came in, some adjustments were made and I went back out for a few more, faster laps. On the fourth lap I brought the car up to 185 miles per hour on the backstraight, and it felt solid—incredibly fast, but solid. My helmet felt secure, too, with just a tolerable amount of buffeting. I experimented with my racing line, finding that the low one best suited my driving style. I came in again, more adjustments were made, and then it was time for the run.

I figured it would take me at least 10 laps to work up to 200 miles per hour, if I could do it, so my plan was to pick up the pace by a second or two each lap. That way the speed comes gradually, almost hypnotically. On the fifth lap, I saw the speedometer flash 200 miles per hour at the end of the frontstraight. That boosted my confidence. But the goal was to average 200, a much more difficult proposition, and that meant keeping the speed all the way through the tight corners. I squeezed the throttle a little more and had a moment in turn one where the car got high on the 24-degree banking. I didn't panic, though—it had happened to me before with Driving 101, and I kept the higher line through turn two.

After a few more, faster laps I heard the words, "199.4—Clash, don't do this to me again," crackle over the radio. From the speeds I had seen on the dashboard—over 205 miles per hour—I knew the number was an average lap speed, so I was almost there! I matted the throttle between turns one and two and held it down the backstraight and well into turn three. It was now or never, I thought. What a ride! I was on the absolute edge and had no time to glance at anything but the videogame-like track ahead rushing toward me. After flashing by the start/finish line I heard the words, "Pit, pit, pit—you did it!"

I backed off the throttle, and a powerful combination of joy and relief overcame me. "Thanks guys, you were great," I managed into the radio as I coasted down the backstraight. Those few moments alone in the car were some of the best in my life. As with my return to Mount Aconcagua, I had worked hard at this second attempt, and I couldn't help but contrast it with the bitter disappointment at California in February. Not just that, but because of our efforts, deserving charities were $20,000 richer.

In the pits, everyone was smiles as I brought the car to a stop. Wright looked relieved, Buhl gave me the thumbs-up, and McNeely was clicking off photos. I was so excited that I purchased a stopwatch that had captured 201 miles per hour on it from John Martin—I didn't want it to be used again. I also had the entire Treadway crew, including chief Skip Faul, sign my T-shirt as a souvenir.

My dream had begun in 1977 when, on television, I watched Tom Sneva run the first lap above 200 miles per hour at the 2.5-mile oval called Indianapolis. Who would have believed that a quarter century later I would run a lap slightly faster—and on a track a mile shorter? (Computer telemetry showed my fastest lap was run in 26.034 seconds, or 201.2 miles per hour, and that my top speed was 207.7 miles per hour. Sneva had averaged 200.5.)

A few weeks later at the U.S. Grand Prix Formula One race in, of all places, Indianapolis, I met a number of racing enthusiasts: Sarah Fisher, the world's fastest woman Indy driver and a spokesperson for Tag Heuer; Tony George, owner of the Indianapolis Motor Speedway; Prince Andrew; and the racing legends Mario Andretti and Jackie Stewart. But it was my chat with the city's mayor, Bart Peterson, that put it over the top for me. When my host, Ginger Kreil of the Indy Partnership, mentioned my Texas run, he suddenly became childlike. "You're the first 'normal' person I've ever met who has driven above 200 miles per hour," he gushed. "What was it like?"

I thought about it for a second. "It was like being a big kid," I said politely, smiling. "A big, fast kid. And some day I want to do it at your city's speedway, too." He grinned and said, "Hey, you never know."

ITALY: LAMBORGHINI AT 200

You hear about the eye-popping speeds of Ferraris, Lamborghinis, and Maseratis, but nobody ever gets to drive them that fast—at least legally. My goal was straightforward: I wanted to take Lamborghini's new Murcielago production car to its top speed of over 205 miles per hour.

When I approached the company staff in Italy about it, they surprisingly agreed to let me try. Why would anyone in his right mind allow a journalist to attempt something so dangerous, you ask? "There's a slight doubt in the customer's mind as to whether our cars can really go that fast," says Giuseppe Greco, Lamborghini's chairman, "because there are very few places where it can be done. If we let an auto industry journalist try it, he might be perceived as not totally objective. But you, being from a critical business magazine, are perfect."

Well, I wouldn't say *perfect*. As you know, I've been to a number of racing schools in the United States and have driven fast before, but I am far from an expert. To run over 205 miles per hour in a passenger car—well, that's dangerous no matter how you slice it. Unlike in a race car, you are toast if anything happens because production cars are not built to withstand the extreme impacts at such speed.

It is practically impossible to do something like this in the United States. Believe me, I tried. Red tape and potential lawsuits in the event something goes wrong will discourage the most persistent speed freak. Even if you can finesse a production car, only a few test tracks—owned by the Big Three automakers—are large enough to try it on, and they won't let outsiders in. In Europe, however, there's a more relaxed attitude. As with skiing or mountaineering, if you want to kill yourself—go right ahead.

After a few months planning the event, I met the Lamborghini staff at Nardo Prototipo—a four-lane, 7.8-mile

(12.6-kilometer) circular track in southern Italy where the exotic carmakers test. In addition to a support crew of half a dozen, there was Greco himself; Giorgio Sanna, the company's professional test racer; and Sergio Fontana, head of public relations.

Lamborghinis are exclusive machines. Less than 10,000 have been sold since the company's inception in 1963. All are handmade. The famous line includes the Miura, Silhouette, Urraco, Countach, and Diablo, but none (other than a few late-model Diablos) are capable of speeds of the new Murcielago. In fact, it is today's second-fastest new production model (only the limited-edition Ferrari Enzo is faster). A 12-cylinder, 6.2-liter engine produces 580 horsepower that pushes the Murcielago to a top speed of over 205 miles per hour and from 0 to 60 miles per hour in 3.7 seconds.

Audi VW Group, which purchased an ailing Lamborghini in 1998, has put $150 million into building up production capacity—and into research and development. A museum, restoration facility, and company store have also been built at the Modena, Italy, headquarters, which I toured. The company produced 420 cars in 2002 (up from 297 in 2001), a third of them for the U.S. market. (Price tag for the Murcielago: $280,000, excluding taxes.) This year, with the introduction of a smaller version of the Murcielago, the Gallardo, retailing for about $180,000 (to compete with the Ferrari 360 Modena), Lamborghini plans to quadruple production, to 1,700 cars.

The weather forecast for Nardo—strong winds and showers as a front approached—didn't bode well for high speeds on our scheduled test day. To run top speed, we needed a perfectly dry track and no wind. To attempt to beat the front, our plan was to get on track in the morning, as early as possible. Jet-lagged and excited, I slept fitfully for a few hours. When I looked out my hotel window at 6 A.M. it was overcast, but there was no wind—and no rain—yet. We had a chance.

Once at the track (and after a few high-powered espressos), I climbed into the Murcielago for my first time—a black one that looks like a spaceship when its winged doors are open—strapped on my helmet, and belted in. Racer Sanna explained from the driver's seat that to go top speed, I needed to be in the far outside lane because, of the four, it is banked the steepest—12 degrees. That meant the right side of the car (I would be traveling counterclockwise) would come to within a few feet of the imposing steel guardrail. Sanna knows this track well. In February 2002, he drove the Murcielago for an hour straight, averaging a record 199 miles per hour with refueling and tire-changing stops.

After a few warm-up laps, Sanna pulled over and we switched places. I put the animal (Murcielago is named after a famous bull from the nineteenth century) into first gear and slowly released the clutch. The muscle was there, for sure, but the car was surprisingly quiet—and smooth. I shifted up through the power band of five gears and into sixth, made my way to the outside lane, and gritted my teeth.

As I broke through the 180-mile-per-hour barrier, a kind of tunnel vision took over. You stare so intently at the road ahead—a wide but constant curve—that nothing registers peripherally except as a background blur. At 190 miles per hour, I was committed. For an instant, I thought about what would happen if one of the Pirelli tires blew—or if an animal scurried in front of us from the surrounding woods. We would never know what happened. An accident at that speed means instant death. But fear diminishes performance and there was no room for error, so I quickly put the thought out of my mind.

The pedal was now firmly planted on the floor . . . 195 . . . 198 . . . 200 . . . 205. Distance markers on the guardrail flew by at the rate of more than a football field per second. Oh, it was fast, all right—deceptively so. In open-wheel race cars, wind buffets your helmet and the noise is deafening. Nothing relaxing about it. But here, in a luxurious cockpit, I was able to enjoy the world above 200 miles per hour. If I had wanted, I even could have listened to the radio. It is deceptively intoxicating.

I ran above 200 halfway (about four miles) around the track, then backed off. Earlier, Sanna had explained that overcast skies and no wind make for a good top speed, but the air temperature, 83°F, was too warm to sustain it—the engine would overheat. Once I parked the machine, I glanced at the trip speed registered on the dashboard—208 miles per hour (335 kilometers per hour)—three-tenths of a mile faster than the top speed I had clocked in Schmidt's Indy car at Texas. Wow! Sanna said that's as fast as anyone has driven the Murcielago—including himself—and faster than any journalist has ever driven a Lamborghini, period.

"At 208 miles per hour, you have no friends but me," Greco laughed as I exited the car. Half jokingly, I asked if he wanted to join me—in the passenger's seat—on another run. Surprisingly, and to the audible gulp of PR man Fontana, he agreed. I took Greco to within a few feet of the guardrail at 205 miles per hour—and he didn't flinch. That's what I call faith in your product.

That afternoon it poured, flooding the small roads in Torre Lapillo, but we didn't care. During a celebratory lunch at our hotel, we all watched the Belgian Grand Prix on Italian television. Fittingly, Michael Schumacher, in a Ferrari, won his tenth Formula One race in a single season—a record. When the graphic showed Schumacher's top speed that day—319 kilometers per hour—one of our crew joked that I had just driven a Lamborghini 16 kilometers per hour faster. I winked at our waitress, Andrea, and she just laughed. Ferrari and Lamborghini—always competitors!

On my flight back to New York, I read writer P. J. O'Rourke's account of a California rally race in which he had participated. "The older I get, the faster I was," he mused. I won't have to worry about a pathetic line like that as I cruise through middle age. No matter how you serve it up, 208 miles per hour will always be 208 miles per hour.

VINTAGE CARS: LET THEM EAT DUST

Every time Wal-Mart scion S. Robson Walton turns a lap at Laguna Seca Raceway, he risks his $2 million 1958 Scarab Mk1 vintage race car—not to mention his $20 billion hide. At the Annual Monterey Historic Automobile Race, Walton's car, on the straights, approaches 150 miles per hour. He is separated from the track by six inches of air and one thin sheet of aluminum. "Let me put it this way," says a fellow vintage car racer and friend of Walton. "These cars killed a hell of a lot of people when they were new. The same cars are being run today by people who aren't as good, and they're being run faster."

After skillfully negotiating 10 laps of 2.2 miles each, Walton has built a formidable lead on the 16-car competition and wins easily. Fellow billionaire Bruce McCaw was supposed to be at Monterey, too, but scratched at the last minute. McCaw and his $3.5 million 1953 Ferrari 375 MM Vignale Spyder had won the coveted Monterey Cup the previous year.

Like Formula One, the vintage-car-racing circuit runs weekend races all over the world, from March through November. The difference: The cars are classic racers from another era and most of the drivers are amateurs. Why do they do it? Midlife crises are probably part of the answer. But there's a romanticism associated with great old cars that transports owners to another time and place. Many vintage collectors lusted after a particular car when they were young, but couldn't afford to indulge themselves. "You've got a group that grew up with *Car and Driver* magazine who now have the

166

money to spend, and they're buying all the cars that were their fantasies when they were kids," says grocery store magnate and billionaire Ronald Burkle, who's been collecting vintage Ferraris, Shelbys, and other classics for more than two decades.

You've got to be in love with these cars to drive them. Many are from an era before power brakes or power steering, let alone great sound systems. A driver must be in good physical shape to race one. Walton, for example, is a triathlete.

I'll attest to the physically fit claim. As research, I was given the opportunity to drive a 1961 Ferrari 250 GT Sperimentale, valued at $6 million, around the Willow Springs, California, racetrack. Without power steering or power brakes, it really has to be muscled through the corners. Most scary is the price tag. When I almost lost control in one corner, my first thought wasn't personal safety—only how much damage I would do to Steve Forbes's (my employer) presidential campaign coffers if I wrecked. (I didn't.)

There are three basic types of historic car events, ranging from the mild to the hair-raising. Tours, like the 1,000-mile-plus Colorado Grand, are driven at civil highway speeds over a period of days—mostly for owners to enjoy their machinery on the open road. Rallies—like Italy's Historic Mille Miglia, where participants cover 1,000 miles in less than three days—are timed competitions during which thousands of auto enthusiasts line the streets to cheer the drivers on. Races like Monterey or Coys International Historic Festival at the Silverstone Racing Circuit in England are purely competitive. To add a degree of safety, the rules declare that any driver who veers off course or causes an accident can be banned from competition for a year or more. Monterey is the crown jewel of the U.S. vintage race-car circuit, drawing more than 50,000 people over three days.

Some vintage car drivers are flashy. Others, like Rob

Walton and Bruce McCaw, are lower key. Without much fanfare, Bruce's younger brother John purchased more than $80 million worth of vintage cars in the late 1990s, more than any other collector. One collection of 10 Ferraris, acquired from Formula One maven Bernard Ecclestone, is rumored to have cost the younger McCaw $40 million. "It's clear that John amassed one of the world's largest Ferrari collections in the shortest amount of time," says Bernard Chase, co-owner of Symbolic Motor Car Company, a major dealer in vintage cars, who counts McCaw among his prized customers. Another rare car—a 1955 Mercedes Grand Prix W196—reportedly was purchased by McCaw from Frenchman Jacques Setton for $12 million (down from its $20 million price a few years before).

Describing Rob Walton's low profile, Symbolic's Marc Chase recalls selling the Wal-Mart heir a rare 1958 Ferrari 412 MI. "When [Rob] showed up outside, you'd never know this guy had any money at all," says Chase. "It was before we opened, and he was just sitting there on the corner in his shorts. The next thing you know, we were selling him a car for a couple of million dollars." On the other hand, Walton doesn't use a phony name when he's racing. In the 1960s, driver Jean Blaton—from the famous Belgian industrialist family—used the pseudonyms "Beurlys" and "Haldeaux" in race programs to keep his family from knowing he had entered. Ditto in the 1980s with German businessman Louis Karges, who went by the alias "John Winter."

Los Angeles Times Mirror mogul Otis Chandler is another collector and former race driver (he quit in 1983 at age 55). After racing Porsches in the early 1960s, Chandler started seriously collecting in 1968 with a single $25,000 Duesenberg motorcycle, one of only seven made; today it's worth over $1 million. He now owns one of the most important vintage collections in the world, with dozens of rare cars. Back in his racing days, Chandler, schooled at Bob Bondurant School of

High Performance Driving, routinely pushed his 1,110-horsepower Porsche 917-30 (bought from IRL honcho Roger Penske) to 200 miles per hour down the backchute at Riverside. Can you invite pals on that kind of road trip? Chandler says he took friends around the track in a small passenger seat built into the car. "If you work up to speed gradually, it's okay," he says. "But to be put in the seat like that—people are just blown away by the experience."

More recently, Chandler has focused on collecting American classics—he now has more than 30 cars made between 1930 and 1942. "They represent the zenith of American car production," he says. Some that Chandler purchased at Christie's Pebble Beach auction include a 1932 KB Lincoln Custom 12 Convertible Sedan, for $200,000; a 1931 Cadillac V-16 Madame X, for $110,000; and a 1938 V-16 Cadillac Towne Car, for $70,000. Chandler is also an avid vintage motorcycle collector. He owns 150 bikes—including that Duesenberg—that he keeps on display at his 45,000-square-foot museum in Oxnard, California.

Are vintage cars good investments? They can be, but bad timing hurts even millionaires. In the late 1980s, at the market's peak, Swiss bottle-cap magnate Albert Obrist leveraged up to purchase what would become a $70 million collection of vintage cars. When the car market crashed in 1990, his collection dropped to $25 million in value and he suffered a financial crisis trying to pay off his loans. "Cars, where there's a fairly good supply—like Ferrari Daytonas—haven't gone up at all," says Ron Burkle. "It's the really rare things that trade at premiums. People are very selective and much more educated now."

"I have a couple of cars worth over $1 million," says Otis Chandler. "But I don't collect to make money. I collect because I really love cars. But I think we're a minority. There's a very large group that speculates." Chandler says the most expensive

---

Seven-Figure Used Cars

Symbolic Motor Car's client list includes past and current Forbes 400 members Ronald Burkle, Otis Chandler, brothers Bruce and John McCaw, and S. Robson Walton. Gateway's Ted Waitt almost bought a $335,000 Bentley from Symbolic, but his wife thought it was ostentatious. Hong Kong billionaire Sir Michael Kadoorie bought a car from Symbolic, as did celebrity performers Nicolas Cage, Charlie Sheen, and Vanna White.

Founded by brothers Bernard and Marc Chase in their garage in 1985, Symbolic moves more than $100 million a year in high-end vintage car metal. The 25,000-square-foot showroom in La Jolla, California, houses some of the world's rarest cars. Whereas most vintage car dealers act as brokers between buyers and sellers, Symbolic buys for its own account. That requires significant amounts of money, but the Chase brothers say they have no trouble earning back the cost of their capital.

In 1996, for example, Symbolic picked up a 1967 Ferrari 412 P for $3 million. The car's provenance was outstanding: It had won the prestigious 1,000-kilometer races at Monza (Italy) and Spa-Francorchamps (Belgium) in 1966. After just a year of restoration, the car sold for $4.5 million to a prominent Japanese collector.

Symbolic Motor Cars has a philanthropic side. Bernie Chase, with the help of San Diego Padres owner John Moores, Portland, Oregon, cable mogul William Bauce, and Detroit builder Bernard Glieberman, raised some $60 million for Scripps Research Foundation's Institute for Childhood and Neglected Diseases in 1998. Some of the money came from expensive vintage car donations. John McCaw chipped in, too. He bought a 1967 Ferrari 275 GTS/4 NART Spyder at Christie's Pebble Beach auction for more than $2 million, all of which went to Scripps.

---

cars—more than $1 million—hold their value even in a down stock market because many are already in strong hands like Walton's and the McCaw brothers' or they have a strong history. Witness Walton's 1958 Scarab, built for Woolworth heiress Barbara Hutton's son, Lance Reventlow, and a winner of several important American races in the late 1950s. Symbolic's Bernie Chase sums up the investment angle best: "This is the ultimate of thin markets. One car may sell for $3 million, but try selling three of the same model at the same time."

GEORGE HALL: CIGARETTE BOATS AND HEDGE FUNDS

George Hall likes to take calculated risks. As chief executive of New York's Clinton Group, he runs billions of dollars in hedge funds full of complex mortgage-backed securities. For relaxation, Hall has raced boats—at 110 miles per hour. His wins include races in Virginia Beach, Virginia, and Ocean City, Maryland, and he has competed at the world championships in Key West, Florida.

In 1991, after receiving degrees from the Merchant Marine Academy and Wharton Graduate School of Business, Hall founded Clinton Group at about the same time he started racing boats. He has never had a serious accident, either in his boat or in his hedge funds. Since he opened his biggest fund, Trinity, in 1996, it has experienced negative returns in just a handful of separate months. Hall attributes the steady performance of his funds to his practice of taking lots of small, cautious bets, rather than big, risky ones. I asked George about his approach to risk—both on the water and in his funds. Not surprisingly, there are similarities.

CLASH: *The perception is that hedge funds are risky. True?*
HALL: Part of the problem is that there's no accurate definition of what a hedge fund is. *Hedge* implies risk management. But a lot of funds have gravitated toward taking large bets on market movements and have become quite speculative. The entire hedge fund universe gets tainted. In our view, a hedge fund should be an arbitrage strategy where you look for inefficiencies in the market and try to buy something that's

underpriced, then hedge that with something that's fair- or overpriced. The amount of money you make in these long and short strategies is not that large, but you can use leverage to enhance your return. That's where the problem comes in. If you use too much, it helps with gains, but also enhances losses if you're on the wrong side.

CLASH: *Is that what happened with John Meriwether of Long-Term Capital Management in 1998?*

HALL: Clearly, he had a lot of leverage and had difficulty getting out of positions when he had to. The fact is that the market is not inefficient to the point that it creates huge price inefficiencies, but there are enough of them that if you use a modest amount of leverage, you can get pretty good returns.

CLASH: *How much leverage will you take?*

HALL: In the mortgage funds, a debt-to-equity ratio of 2 or 3 to 1. We have a more liquid yield-curve arbitrage fund that is more like 10 or 15 to 1.

CLASH: *Did you get redemptions when LTCM crashed?*

HALL: We had some. Unfortunately, sometimes people have to redeem to fulfill other obligations because of losses. And sometimes the banks or brokerage firms that lend money panic—and decide that they don't want to lend to hedge funds anymore. We try to avoid that by maintaining a good relationship with lenders. As soon as we sense there's any kind of general market crisis, we meet with them and explain that we're in good shape and that they should just continue doing business with us as usual.

CLASH: *Do you think the bad rap the hedge fund business has gotten is fair?*

172

HALL: I don't think you can generalize. One good thing is that during the last few years many notable hedge funds that had recorded years of very high returns have either closed up or changed their goals. That, I think, is better for us. It makes the playing field more even. You don't have to compete against people advertising ridiculously high returns that aren't sustainable.

CLASH: *Let's talk about boat racing risk.*

HALL: Boats have come a long way. They are structurally pretty sound now. It's not like pre-1985 when boats were likely to break up if you had a mishap. Now we use canopies, so we're totally enclosed. If the boat flips over, you're pretty safe. Or if the boat submerges, you're protected. They have oxygen tanks. The real risk is making a mistake while driving. If you turn too fast, you can roll over or hit another boat. You take as many safety precautions as you can. Beyond that, it comes down to focus and judgment and not being careless.

CLASH: *Not to force it, but it sounds a lot like when you decide on which securities to buy and how to hedge them.*

HALL: You can get blindsided by some unexpected move in the market. A lot of it is trying to figure out what possible things can happen in the future. Same goes for racing: anticipating the water conditions, what other drivers are going to do. One big parallel is not to get feelings of infallibility, and to know your limitations.

CLASH: *What does it feel like at 100 miles per hour on the water?*

HALL: You're looking at markers, trying to navigate. You're look- ing at the water. You're looking in the mirror to see if other boats are around. What I find is that you start the race and then it's over. It goes by very quickly because you're so focused. But, you know, it's exhilarating, it's exciting, it's a little scary.

CLASH: *Compare it to driving a car.*

HALL: It's a lot bumpier. In a car you've generally got four wheels on the ground, so you feel more in touch. As a boat goes faster, less of it touches the water. When you're really going fast, the propellers and a little piece of the stern are in the water and the rest is flying. And it's over rough terrain. So, it's quite a bit different than going fast in a car. It's not just the sensation of speed—it's the bumps, the lack of contact with the surface.

CLASH: *What's it like to pass someone?*

HALL: Unlike with race cars, you generally pass on the outside. Smaller boats tend to stay on the inside, and the larger, faster boats pass on the outside. That's where a fair number of accidents occur. If a boat on the inside cuts to the outside while it's being passed, it's going to get run over.

CLASH: *What's the scariest moment you've had in a boat?*

HALL: One race we hit a wave and went up in the air, and it seemed like an eternity until we came back down. We wound up snapping one of the motors off. Nobody got hurt, but we took quite a jump. We started to take on water, and we had to have the boat taken out of the water before it sank.

CLASH: *What was one of your more satisfying racing moments?*

HALL: When conditions are rough and there are a few accidents, you're excited just to finish. I've had exciting races in Fort Lauderdale in rough water where you couldn't get much speed—just 60 miles per hour. The waves were so big—

you're really trying to go from the top of one to the top of the next—not getting caught in between.

CLASH: *How about a scary moment with your hedge funds?*

HALL: In 1994, around the time they liquidated the portfolios of David Askin of Askin Capital Management. We were a relatively small fund with $200 million under management. Askin was a large mortgage hedge fund. Rates had gone up a lot, and I guess their hedges weren't what they should have been. So the asset value of the portfolio went down. And then the dealers who had lent money to leverage the portfolio began making margin calls. Generally, when one firm is having trouble, the lenders assume that other firms are having trouble, too. So you have to worry about who is lending you money and whether they will continue. That was a tense period. Then, in 1998 with the losses of Long-Term Capital, there was a worldwide liquidity crisis, so there was anxiety again.

CLASH: *What parallels can you draw between managing risk in a hedge fund and in a boat race?*

HALL: The most important thing is to know your limitations. The one most likely to have an accident boating is the one being too aggressive, flying a little too high, turning a little too fast. And not understanding that you're on the edge, in a danger zone. There are times when it seems that the one who's most successful in boat racing is the one who has the least regard for safety. Because if you drive out on the edge, and if you're lucky enough not to have an accident, you can go pretty fast. I think there's a similarity with hedge funds. A lot of people can be very successful taking risks and getting huge returns for a while, but at some point you're going to have an acci-

175

dent. You have to be disciplined, because, in the long run, you're better off.

CLASH: *Meaning you wouldn't pass, you'd wait?*

HALL: Yes. In some cases, you lose the race if someone's driving too fast. But you've just got to let them go. If some competitor in a hedge fund is getting better performance but taking risks, you've got to say, "Well, I'm not going to compete with that, because I want to be in it for the long haul."

7

Adventures in Physics and Metaphysics

A dventure is often associated with the physical accomplishments and goals. But as in business, it's not only the mechanics that contribute to the victory. Often, it's imagination and creativity that introduces a breakthrough. Sometimes it's sheer drive or sweat equity that keeps a company on track. Other times, inspiration and passion drive a workforce.

So, too, are brains and brawn symbiotically joined in adventures that push the limits of human interaction. Why do some athletes suddenly rise above their past performance levels during the Olympics while others with far better credentials wither? What does it take to break a world record, or to push the absolute limit in physics against all conventional thinking? Where does the inspiration come from to form a new genre of music, to escape from the top of a fiery World Trade Center? From inside, of course.

NEW MEXICO: GROUND ZERO

I'm standing where the deep blue sky meets the parched white sand of the New Mexico desert, where physics changed forever the course of international politics. Today, it is bright and clear. There are no clouds, no winds, no disturbances. The circle of sand I'm visiting—maybe two hundred yards across—is fenced off by foreboding barbed wire. Had I been here on July 16, 1945, at 5:30 A.M., I would have been incinerated instantly by 10-million-degree heat from fissioning plutonium atoms. Not today, though. Flowers grow, mothers hold their children, a crew from a Japanese television network records a documentary.

Some say that modern history began on this patch of dirt 110 miles southeast of Albuquerque when the United States detonated the first atomic bomb on top of a giant steel tower 100 feet above where I'm standing. On my right is what's left of the tower today—melted tentacles of one of its legs. On my left is a patch of sand scorched so intensely that it was fused into a green glass called Trinitite.

It's not widely known, but twice a year—on the first Saturday of April and October—the U.S. government opens to the public the Trinity Site, also known as ground zero. There's no need to book a visit and there's no admission charge. Just turn up at Otero County Fairgrounds in Alamogordo, where a caravan of cars, complete with police escorts, departs at 8:00 A.M. sharp for the 85-mile trip across the normally restricted White Sands Missile Range. There were about 80 cars the day I visited.

Trinity is the place where the Manhattan Project ended and the nuclear era began. There, during World War II, the best scientific minds in the world toiled for three years at nearby Los Alamos to perfect a device they called "the gadget." With the force of 17,000 tons of TNT, that gadget broke windows 90 miles away.

At 10:00 A.M., after a sobering two-hour drive through the desert strewn with road signs that read "Danger, Unexploded Live Munitions" and "Peligroso! Missile Impact Area," we were suddenly within a half a mile of ground zero ourselves. Before you enter the fenced-in part, there's a tent with Geiger counters. Radioactivity? "Any out here can be blocked by your skin," Lisa Blevins, a White Sands employee, assures us. She says touring ground zero results in about two milliroentgens—less than the radiation absorbed flying from New York to London in a jetliner. To prove her point, she points her Geiger counter wand at display items that include a radium clock dial, some old Fiestaware pottery (which contains uranium dye for color), and the rare Trinitite glass. The Trinitite produces the fewest number of clicks.

Inside the fenced-in area there's a mock-up of Fat Man (the plutonium bomb used at Nagasaki) on a big flatbed truck. Attached to the north fence are historic photos that show, among other things, Los Alamos director J. Robert Oppenheimer and other scientists surveying damage just after the blast, the tower before it was incinerated, and the bomb in different stages of the explosion. There's also a jet-black monument erected in 1975 proclaiming Trinity a national landmark.

Deborah Bingham, another White Sands employee, has answered the questions of visitors from all over the world—England, Japan, Switzerland, Germany, Mexico—during her tenure at the site. She can attest to the mixed emotions. "You see lots of World War II vets who think it was a good thing we invented the bomb," she says. "But others say they wish the atom was never delved into."

I'm intrigued by the mix of people. Some seem clueless, as though they were bused in from Disneyworld. But others have a serious, inquisitive look. Vladimir Shapovalov, a Ukrainian metallurgist, says he has known about Trinity since

179

his childhood in Russia during the Cold War. Asked if he feels any irony standing here with an American after decades of nuclear arms buildup, he flatly says no. "It was only political," he smiles. "People are the same everywhere, I think."

At noon, I'm ready to join the caravan for the long drive back to Alamogordo. In a part of the circle of sand where nobody else has wandered, I spy a small purple wildflower. I bend down to inspect it, and there, on the desert floor a few inches away, are two little pieces of Trinitite, undisturbed and sparkling green in the sun.

> TRAVELER'S NOTEBOOK: The Trinity site, located near Alamogordo, New Mexico, is open to the public the first Saturday of April and October. A good book to read in preparation for the trip is the Pulitzer Prize–winning *The Making of the Atomic Bomb,* by Richard Rhodes (Simon & Schuster, 1986). For more information, check www.alamogordo.com/trinity.html.

EDWARD TELLER: FATHER OF THE HYDROGEN BOMB

An interview with the great physicist Dr. Edward Teller is a lot like a long, hard game of Ping-Pong: You hit the ball back and forth, back and forth, with Teller asking as many questions as he answers. None of it is chitchat. His direct queries about cloning and nuclear weapons leave you uncomfortable and invigorated at the same time. When the exchange has ended, you're not sure whether you've won or lost. But you certainly are on edge.

Even after suffering a stroke, the father of the H-bomb, though a bit wobblier in his mid-90s than in his prime, remains an undisputed genius. He lives in Palo Alto, California, splitting time between Stanford's Hoover Institute and Lawrence Livermore National Laboratories. As a young

Hungarian émigré physicist in the early 1940s, Teller helped develop the atom bomb at Los Alamos. But he is most famous (or infamous, depending upon whom you talk to) for pioneering the hydrogen (fusion) bomb—today's standard in nuclear weapons and hundreds of times more powerful than the atom bomb the United States dropped on Hiroshima.

Teller talks passionately about Japan—why, perhaps, we should not have dropped the bomb at all—and about his volatile relationship with J. Robert Oppenheimer, who had directed efforts at Los Alamos. In this interview, he answers some big questions: What's the greatest danger facing the world? (Hint: Teller doesn't think it's nuclear war.) Did Werner Heisenberg, Teller's former teacher, purposely stall Germany's efforts to produce an atom bomb in World War II? And would Teller's controversial Star Wars missile defense system ever have worked? Teller also offers insights into Albert Einstein, Presidents Harry Truman and Ronald Reagan, and mathematician John von Neumann, founder of the modern-day digital computer.

CLASH: *The world feels safer with the collapse of the Soviet Union, yes?*

TELLER: The world is much safer, but safer doesn't mean safe. America has to maintain its leadership position. We are now acting on a crazy basis that if we stop weapons research, advances will halt everywhere else. On that basis, actual dangers are going to arise—probably not in my lifetime, but almost certainly in yours.

CLASH: *How would you change the nuclear strategy?*

TELLER: I would certainly support military research. I would also support international cooperation. Today, international cooperation, to the extent it exists, says we should have agreements whereby this and that is not to be done. Our

181

agreements are negative. We should have positive agreements whereby we collaborate. Today people are afraid of whatever is new. This clearly is true about radioactivity. What do you think about cloning?

CLASH: *I have mixed views, as I'm sure most people do. In terms of pure science, of moving society forward, you have to pursue new knowledge. But I can also see where it presents ethical problems.*

TELLER: Look, cloning is a very old business—what is news is the cloning of a mammal. And that, of course, brings the possibility of cloning human beings much closer. In 1935 this discovery would have been welcomed. Now discussion has already resulted in cutting of funds. The fear upon us—the fear of what can be worse if it succeeds—is something we adopted in the past half century and is a great danger. Unless it is stopped, it will end the strength of the United States.

Here's a lady, her husband has died. She has a single child, one month old, and it's dying. Would you deny the possibility of reproducing the child painlessly and identically? Anything new can be applied well. And anything new can be applied wrongly. In other times, people would have said, "New, go ahead. If there's a problem, we'll deal with it." Today, it is, "New, better stop, we're going too fast." This is as un-American as can be.

CLASH: *Why has that happened?*

TELLER: Two reasons. One is that science sometimes makes discoveries—solid discoveries, undeniable facts—that are contrary to common sense. You and I are not sitting here at rest. We are moving through space at 10 miles per second with variable velocities, different in the morning and evening. Impossible! Denied by the Bible. It resulted in the trial of Galileo. Now such absurdities, which are real, occur in science, but not frequently. Some very important discoveries occurred around 1900. Will you kindly tell me what you know about relativity?

CLASH: *Relativity was Einstein's theory where he linked mass with energy and stated that, as you approach the speed of light, time slows down.*

TELLER: If you ask about understanding and absurdity: What does it mean that time slows down? Newton has written that time passes everywhere at the same rate. Was Newton wrong?

CLASH: *I don't know. Einstein seems to disagree.*

TELLER: Newton was wrong. If you read beautiful science fiction stories about an empire that extends over the galaxy—do you know how big our galaxy is?

CLASH: *Thousands of light-years.*

TELLER: It's 100,000 light-years. That means, of two events you think have occurred with a time difference of 50,000 years, you cannot say which happened earlier. It depends on the observer. An empire over the Milky Way is impossible because you don't know what has happened and you cannot influence what is going to happen, except in very small pieces of the Milky Way. This relativity of time, if you understand it, is simply contrary to common sense. But it's true.

Now let me come to the point. The two important basic discoveries of the century—relativity and quantum mechanics—have not been assimilated by people. Instead they ignore them and say, "Oh, that's science, and science cannot be trusted." They don't understand it, and therefore they don't like it. The second point is that the *un*-understandable—science—produces things like atomic explosions. The result is: "Stop, don't go so fast in science. Better not to know so much." Applied not only to radioactivity, but to cloning. After centuries of being pro-science, we are now in an antiscience era.

CLASH: *Do you use the Internet?*

TELLER: I am old and know less about it than I should. I think it's another way to communicate and use many facts on computers. It's the one real positive development of recent years. This development was started by a very good friend of mine. Do you know who I mean?

CLASH: *John von Neumann?*

TELLER: Right. He died in the early 1950s. Look, there had been primitive computers before Johnny von Neumann. But they were all hardwired. The program was built into the machine. Johnny's influence was programming a card to produce a flexible, digital computer you could tell what to do and vary it. One where the computer could essentially program itself and, to that extent, bring computers closer to human thinking.

[Teller had a long and strained relationship with J. Robert Oppenheimer, who had directed development of the atomic bomb at Los Alamos in the 1940s. A staunch anticommunist, Teller had reservations about Oppenheimer's motives and allegiance to the United States. He worked with Oppenheimer at Los Alamos, but quit just before the atom bomb was tested to pioneer the hydrogen bomb. Later, in the 1950s, Teller was a key witness against Oppenheimer at the McCarthy trials. Teller's controversial testimony ultimately led to Oppenheimer's security clearance being stripped.]

CLASH: *Let's talk about Robert Oppenheimer.*

TELLER: Oppenheimer was the only scientist I knew who was a scientist in order to promote his political views. During the war, my friend and fellow scientist Leo Szilard was in Chicago. I had been there, too, but went to Los Alamos. Sometime in June 1945, I got a letter from Szilard saying, "The Nazis have

184

surrendered. We are about to complete work on the atomic bomb. We should not use it on Japan, at least not without warning them first." He said there were a number of scientists who had signed a petition to that effect, and would I please get signatures of the scientists at Los Alamos? Well, at Los Alamos, I could not do that. Oppenheimer controlled everything. The only thing for me to do was go to Oppenheimer. It was the one occasion when I saw him get mad: "What does Szilard know? People in Washington know perfectly well what they're doing." So I wrote Szilard a letter saying that I am attracted to his idea and I'm also not sure that dropping the bomb is the right thing. But I told him that I could not circulate a petition. I did not mention my conversation with Oppenheimer because I knew that Oppenheimer would read my letter before it was sent. There was no privacy there.

What I did not know, and what Oppenheimer did not tell me, was that he was chairman of a very small group of prominent scientists who had been asked in higher secrecy what should be done. Oppenheimer wanted the bomb dropped right away. He convinced the others of the same. The recommendation went in to drop it. We then tested the bomb early on the morning of July 16 [1945] at Trinity. After the test, Oppenheimer talked to the press. Do you know his famous statement at the time? "I have become death, the destroyer of worlds." Now will you please tell me what kind of man is this who, when asked for scientific advice, made sure that the only advice to the president was "Drop it," then turns around to the press and implies the opposite?

CLASH: *You were at that historic test. What do you recall?*
TELLER: I was 20 miles away. The shot was canceled, then put back on. The countdown stopped at minus 30 seconds. An eternity passed—and I thought it was a failure, but it was just a

very long 30 seconds. I had on glasses that exclude light from welding. But, to be extra safe, I had put on an extra pair of dark glasses and suntan lotion. When I saw light—it was early in the morning before sunup—I tipped the welding glass and looked down at the sand beside me. It was as daylight.

CLASH: *Was it right to have used the atomic bomb on Japan?*

TELLER: I did not know what to do at the time. I am very sorry now that I did not make the recommendation that I should have. There was a way to act that would have been clearly better. I found out only later that we knew of Hirohito's attempts to make peace. I think we should have dropped the bomb near Tokyo Harbor in the evening—detonated it at an altitude between 10,000 and 20,000 feet—where we knew the Japanese, including the emperor, would have seen the firestorm. We could have told them what it was. But had we done the demonstration, no one would have been hurt. Perhaps if no one had been hurt, the whole thing wouldn't have been taken seriously. Perhaps it was best it happened as it did, because we had to kill quite a few thousand people in order to deter further warfare. I don't want this to be true, but maybe it is.

CLASH: *How did India and Pakistan get the atom bomb?*

TELLER: A half century ago I tried to write an atomic alphabet: *A* stands for atom, it's so small, no one has ever seen it at all. *B* stands for bombs—the bombs are much bigger, so let's not be so fast on the trigger. Do you know what *S* stands for?

CLASH: *Safety?*

TELLER: *S* stands for *secret*—you can keep it forever, provided there's no one else who is clever. India and Pakistan know that two and two makes four. You cannot keep scientific knowledge your own secret. We are the only ones clever enough to do it, right? If others have done it they must have copied us. Maybe, but I doubt it.

[Teller continued work on the more powerful hydrogen bomb after World War II, while many scientists and politicians were against it ethically. His reasoning: Even though the Soviets didn't have it, he believed it was just a matter of time before they did. To Teller, that was extremely dangerous. He didn't trust the Soviets, even back then, and felt if they developed an advantage over the United States in the nuclear arms race, they would exploit it. Russia ultimately did get the H-bomb, in 1953, just after the United States.]

CLASH: *You're known as the father of the hydrogen bomb. How did you feel when you finally realized your design would work?*
TELLER: Look, you work on something. If it succeeds, you like it. I have never had any doubts that knowledge is good. And I never had any tendency to be afraid of knowledge.

CLASH: *Is "father" an accurate label?*
TELLER: I worked on it more than anybody else. I made some essential contributions. But I have one distinction—I was for it when nobody else could or would be. And, quite possibly, if President Harry Truman had been faced with a unanimous scientific opinion against it, he might have acted differently. And now we would all be talking in Russian.

CLASH: *Had we delayed development, would Russia have gotten it first?*
TELLER: Quite possibly. They certainly got it independent of us. Look, the Soviets made their first atomic explosion in 1949. That set off debate on the hydrogen bomb, on which we had done little serious work for a long time. In October 1949, I think, a Democratic senator—Brien MacMahon—then

187

responsible for supervision of the Atomic Energy Commission (AEC), asked me to talk to him. I did not volunteer—I was asked.

I went to Washington. At the railway station, I was met by John Manley from Los Alamos, who was under Oppenheimer. He was important in getting a unanimous opinion to the president that the hydrogen bomb could *not* be done and should not be done. Manley said to me: "Now look, the president should be under the impression that scientists are unanimously against the H-bomb. Please don't talk to MacMahon." I would not agree to that and said, "I will let Senator MacMahon know I am not coming because you asked me not to." Then he gave in and said, "You had better go."

These people wanted to actively suppress any opinion that the H-bomb might be done. I gave my opinion to MacMahon, later to Lewis Strauss, who would later become the chairman of the AEC. These people had access to Truman and noted my opinion to him. I broke the anonymity of saying it could not be done.

CLASH: *Their efforts sound almost Communistic.*

TELLER: Look, Oppenheimer's mother was a Communist. His wife became a widow when her first husband—a Communist—was killed fighting in Spain. He was not a member of the Communist Party. And it's not my business to tell you why he did things. But it is my business to repeat to you essentially what I answered under oath at his trial: "I don't think he wanted to hurt the United States, but some of his actions are of the kind that I don't understand, and when the security of the United States depends on people, I want people who I understand more, and therefore trust more."

CLASH: *Where were you in 1952 when the first H-bomb was detonated in the Pacific?*

TELLER: I was busy at work in my laboratory. I was invited to go out; I didn't. But I knew the predictions. I went down to Berkeley to look at the seismograph and found that I could not see properly. My hand was shaking. Then came the appropriate time for the detonation. Nothing happened. I kept looking for travel of the sound wave through the ground. The shock arrived exactly when I had expected it. What I did then was a security violation at the time. Los Alamos did not know if the test was a success because the security people would not let them be notified. What I did was send an unclassified wire to the wife of the man who conducted the test saying, "It's a boy." This, of course, she immediately understood and circulated. It was the first Los Alamos had heard that the hydrogen bomb was a success. That is an accomplishment of which I am deservedly proud.

CLASH: *What are your thoughts on Stanislaw Ulam (Polish mathematician credited, with Teller, as coinventor of the staged, radiation-imploded H-bomb design)?*

TELLER: He was not a nobody. He did make many suggestions in what is called the Monte Carlo method in statistical mechanics. After I had known the solution to the H-bomb, and after the director of Los Alamos declined to listen to me, Ulam came to me with a part of the solution. I used that to get my paper published on a joint basis. He signed it. When it came later to defend it, he declined because he said he believed it would not work. I think his moral standards were a little higher—but not much—than Oppenheimer's. He was not working for the United States—he was working for fame; and he wanted to get credit. He got it, for very much more than what he did.

[In the 1980s, Teller was the major influence behind President Ronald Reagan's controversial Star Wars missile defense program. Many physicists said the concept was flawed and publicly questioned whether it could ever work. Teller's association with this project, to many, is the one scientific gaffe in an otherwise brilliant career.]

CLASH: *You worked with Ronald Reagan. What was he like?*

TELLER: Reagan was elected governor of California in 1966. Very shortly after—I hadn't met him yet—I invited him to visit us at the Lawrence Livermore Laboratories. I remember him listening to our arguments on why missile defense is necessary. He listened carefully. He asked a number of intelligent questions, but questions which showed that the whole topic was new to him. Then we had lunch together. He left without my knowing whether he was for or against it. Remember, that was in the 1960s.

He was elected president in 1980 and did nothing about missile defense. In March 1983, he made a famous statement fully supporting missile defense and making suggestions on how to do it. You know, he's accused of shooting from the hip. It took him more than a decade to draw, but he hit the target very accurately.

CLASH: *If enough money had been spent on Reagan's dream of an antimissile defense shield, would it have worked?*

TELLER: I don't know. I do know if you work only on things you know will work, you are not going to get anywhere. What I'm trying to propose is that you do not oppose people having missiles. But you require every big multiple-missile firing to be announced. And unannounced missiles should be brought down. Not just for the purpose of defending the United States, but for eliminating surprise attacks against anybody. That is the kind of positive action I think would make sense.

CLASH: *Do you keep in touch with the Reagan family?*

TELLER: When he was president, yes, and after that I visited him once. Already then, after he had retired, he seemed not to be completely there.

CLASH: *I'll name some others and you tell me what comes to mind. Albert Einstein?*

TELLER: Albert Einstein and I met twice, briefly, and he was already way over the hill. He did wonderful things until about 1920. After that, he did one or two things that were worthwhile—less and less as he became older, and practically nothing in his old age. He "wrote" a letter to President Franklin Roosevelt suggesting that nuclear energy be explored. The letter was actually written by my friend, Leo Szilard, who could do everything except drive a car. I was the historical personage who was Szilard's chauffeur that day. I drove him to the end of Long Island to show the letter to Einstein and to ask for his signature. From what I have seen of Einstein, I have no reason to respect him. But from what I know about Einstein—what he did before 1920—I have every reason to respect him.

CLASH: *President Harry Truman?*

TELLER: I didn't meet him while he was president. But after success of the H-bomb, *Time* magazine and other people got interested in me. I was giving a lecture in the Midwest, and a man came over and asked if I wanted to meet Harry Truman, who was celebrating his seventieth birthday in the same town. I said yes, met Truman, and we had a very nice conversation. He told me this story about himself, without any provocation on my part. "I wanted some money to publish my papers. I got an offer from the tobacco companies that if I might say something favorable about smoking, they

191

would give me the money. So I made a statement: 'When the Pilgrims came to America, we gave them tobacco and they brought us syphilis. I think it was a fair trade.' Guess what? I didn't get the money." Truman clearly was an honest person.

[For decades, there has been speculation that Werner Heisenberg, director of Germany's atomic bomb program in World War II and a former teacher of Teller's, deliberately stalled Germany's efforts to produce a bomb. Most recently, this drama was played out in the Tony-award-winning play *Copenhagen*. Heisenberg and Teller remained friends, even after Teller came to America.]

CLASH: *Werner Heisenberg taught you physics when you were young. What was he like?*

TELLER: Let me tell you. Heisenberg knew about the possibility of the atomic bomb. He went to his teacher, Niels Bohr, and proposed that there be an agreement between the Americans and Germans that neither side work on it. Bohr did not understand. He believed Heisenberg was secretly working on it. He spread that rumor to America and made life very unhappy for Heisenberg.

I will tell you the truth as I know it. Right after the war, a half-dozen really eminent German scientists were detained by the British for a few months in England. And, unknown to them, their conversations were recorded. In the mid-1990s, they were declassified. When we dropped the bomb on Japan, the Germans couldn't believe it. "We tried to do that thing. It cannot be done. What did the crazy Americans do, drop a reactor on the Japanese?" Now that, to my mind, proves as clearly as is ever possible that Heisenberg did not work seriously on the bomb.

CLASH: *It turns out the Germans were nowhere near as far along as the United States had thought, correct?*

TELLER: Their leader, Heisenberg, didn't want to do it and persuaded himself that it couldn't be done.

CLASH: *Do you think he didn't do it for moral reasons?*

TELLER: He certainly was not enthusiastic about doing it and was happy to find that it could not be done. Other Germans were not completely happy about the way he talked about it. Heisenberg was a proud German. A very nice man. He had a sense of humor above all that. But certainly, he was an anti-Nazi.

CLASH: *How would you like to be remembered?*

TELLER: I don't particularly care if I'm remembered. I never did anything for that purpose. When I go back to Hungary, now a member of NATO, people realize I did something and that makes me happy. I tell you, I would be a little happier if people would be less critical of my having found something dangerous and about my having hurt a sweet, innocent person like Oppenheimer.

CLASH: *For the most part, then, you feel good looking back at your life?*

TELLER: Let me tell you. I don't think I will go to hell. I think I will go to purgatory, but I don't think I will spend a lot of time there.

CLASH: *If you made a list of five great scientific minds of the twentieth century, who would be on it?*

TELLER: I feel I knew them all, and there were more than five. Despite my negative feelings about Einstein in his later life, without a doubt he'd be on it. Niels Bohr, with whom I disagree in connection with the Heisenberg business, would have to be on it. Heisenberg himself. Then, you know, my fellow Hungarians Leo Szilard, Johnny von Neumann, Eugene Wigner. . . .

CLASH: *Would you add your own name to that list?*
TELLER: I have to leave some job for you to do.

CLASH: *Do you believe in God?*
TELLER: I won't talk about things I don't understand.

CLASH: *Do you go to church?*
TELLER: No.

CLASH: *Are you disappointed that you never won a Nobel Prize?*
TELLER: I have a standard answer for that: I prefer when people ask me, "Why the devil did you *not* get the Nobel Prize," rather than, "Why the hell did you get it?"

CLASH: *Is there an element named after you?*
TELLER: No. I told you, with that respect, I'm am less ambitious than Oppenheimer. And even he does not have an element.

HAM RADIO: VICARIOUS TRAVELS

One March evening, amateur radio operator David Sumner carefully tuned his Kenwood transceiver across the 160-meter ham band. From the monotonous backdrop of static came a weak, echoey signal calling out, in slow bursts of Morse code, *CQ,* which is a ham's way of letting people know that he or she is in the market for a conversation.

Sumner, a Coventry, Connecticut, licensed ham for over four decades, responded quickly. He knew from the call sign—UA9CR—that the guy was in Ekaterinburg, Siberia. Such long distances on this low of a frequency (about the same as an AM radio) are exceptional. He tapped out his

194

response: UA9CR, followed by his own call sign, K1ZZ. Then he waited. A few seconds later Sumner heard his own call sign coming back in faint tones. Success: The guy had heard him! "It's the magic of radio," beams Sumner.

It may seem illogical in the age of the Internet and cheap cellular phones that anyone would find magic in picking up the faint sounds of Morse code. But there it is. Explains Sumner: "There's nothing to connect you—no telephone wires, no computer modems—just air, yet you're linked with someone on the other side of the world."

I know the feeling. Years ago, I got my novice-class ham license by studying radio theory and learning Morse code. On passing a Federal Communications Commission test, I was given a license and my own call—WN3JID—and was ready to communicate with any of the 750,000 hams licensed worldwide. I scrounged up $75 for a Heathkit HR-10 receiver by delivering Baltimore *Sun* newspapers before school. I remember many late nights working with my dad and a soldering iron to link exotic components—diodes, resistors, capacitors—within a maze of multicolored wires. For a transmitter, I purchased a used Hallicrafters HT-40 at a Hamfest for $25. My antenna: a home-built job consisting of two wires with insulators, strung to telephone poles across the front yard.

With only 40 watts of transmission power, I began working stateside hams in Florida, Kansas, California—even Hawaii. My best friend, Mike, also got his novice license, and the two of us competed for the most exotic contact. One night I reeled in Antarctica—KC4USN, right on the South Pole. Another night I conversed with VE8RCS, the Canadian research station in Alert, at the northern tip of Ellesmere Island, used by the thriller movie *Ice Station Zebra* as a model for its set. As my operating skills improved, I upgraded my license to general class (WA3JID), which allowed the use of more power (1,000 watts) and more of the ham band frequencies. By age 15, I had contacts with ham operators in more than 100 different countries, qualifying me for the prestigious DXCC Award—the ham's equivalent of the Academy Award.

Many of the contacts were from the former Soviet Union: Kazakhstan, Armenia, Uzbekistan. It was quite a thrill, considering it happened right in the midst of the Cold War. Most of the Russian operators were high-level Communist Party officials. Regular Joes in the Soviet Union were discouraged from using radios—for security reasons and because of the prohibitive cost. I even made a friend in Budapest—Dr. Lajos Horvath, a Hungarian doctor in his sixties, with whom I'd converse regularly at 10:00 A.M. on Saturday mornings.

But all that was long ago. My equipment, back home with my dad in Laurel, Maryland, is gathering dust now. Recently I became curious. Is ham radio still around? "I'd be surprised if there were any hams left," Bill Baldwin, the astute editor of *Forbes,* scoffed. "The Internet has probably siphoned them all off." It turns out Baldwin was wrong (or perhaps he was just goading me). The hobby is thriving. Over the past three decades the number of hams worldwide has quadrupled, to nearly 3 million, with about 700,000 of them in the United States. Since 1990, when the Internet started to become popular, ham ranks have jumped an average of 6 percent annually.

There's actress Priscilla Presley (N6YOS), former Tandem Computers chief executive James Treybig (W6JKV), and Walter Cronkite (KB2GSD). The late Senator Barry Goldwater (K7UGA) was a ham operator, as was Jordan's late King Hussein (JY1H). So are many of America's past and present astronauts. They get on the air once in a while from the space shuttle, thrilling earthbound hams who manage to contact them. Country singer Patty Loveless (KD4WUJ) likes the Morse code: She says the rhythms and pitch are downright musical. The magic is still there for a lot of people.

In the early 1980s, hams actually developed the first crude model of the Internet—packet radio. Information was typed into bulky computers that converted it to ASCII packets, then sent along using airwaves—rather than the phone lines used by the Internet today.

In the 1990s, amateur radio operators were among the first to adopt modern cybercommunications. The American Radio Relay League (www.arrl.org), amateur radio's largest organization, reports that three-quarters of its 170,000 hams are Internet users. But rather than replace ham radio, the Internet has become an ideal mate. A slew of web sites help hams reach one another. Say you're a ham interested in *DX*— the ham radio term for long-distance communications—like that guy Sumner contacted in Siberia. There's a web site in Finland that updates activity of rare hams in far-off lands. It's a luxurious improvement over shoot-in-the-dark methods I once employed to reach hams in Moldova, Australia, or India.

After they had exchanged radio signals that night, Sumner looked up Ekaterinburg's Alex Prikhodko (UA9CR) on the Buckmaster Ham web site. Sure enough, the fellow's cyberaddress in Siberia was listed. "I fired off an e-mail, and when I came home that night, there was a response," says Sumner. You might ask: Why not go the e-mail route to begin with if you want to reach someone in Siberia? "People who think like that just don't get it," Sumner laughs. "They've probably never run a marathon, climbed a mountain, or sailed a 14-foot boat across the Atlantic. They don't see the attraction of challenging themselves."

ROGER BANNISTER: FOUR MINUTES TO FAME

When *Sports Illustrated* ranked the top 100 athletic events of the twentieth century, the editors were divided on which should lead the list. On one hand, there was Edmund

Hillary's historic Mount Everest climb in 1953. On the other was Roger Bannister's sub-four-minute mile in 1954, a feat for centuries thought impossible. In the end, the editors gave the top spot to both men—in a tie.

Over the past half century, Everest has been scaled hundreds of times, and the four-minute mile is routinely broken at major track meets. But when Hillary and Bannister did it, they punctured their respective envelopes of dubious possibility, and for that each was knighted. It was an uncharacteristically rotten spring day at Oxford University when Bannister ran the mile in three minutes, 59.4 seconds—raining, windy, cold—not the kind of weather conducive to a world record, which makes his feat even more special.

Bannister, now in his mid-70s, disappeared from the track scene shortly after the record run. On graduating from medical school at Oxford, he devoted his life to medicine, initially in private practice as a neurologist, later as a researcher. In the 1960s he pioneered the idea of testing track athletes for drug use. A near-fatal car accident in 1975 kept Bannister from ever running again, but it didn't leave him bitter. He still lives with wife, Moyra, in Oxford—just a mile from where he ran his most famous race. He is happy to talk about his record and his research.

CLASH: *Your only Olympic appearance was in 1952, as a 23-year-old. How did you do?*
BANNISTER: I failed, came in fourth in the 1,500 meters. Very disappointed is an understatement. But if I had gotten a gold medal, I probably would have retired and never pursued the four-minute mile.

CLASH: *What was it about four minutes, anyway?*
BANNISTER: The world record then was four minutes, 1.4 seconds, held by Sweden's Gunder Hägg. It had been stuck there for

nine years, since 1945. It didn't seem logical to me, as a phys-
iologist/doctor, that if you could run a mile in four minutes,
one and a bit seconds, you couldn't break four minutes. But
it had become a psychological, as well as a physical, barrier.
In fact, the Australian John Landy, having done four minutes
and two seconds three times is reported to have commented,
"It's like a wall." I just couldn't see the psychological side.

CLASH: *Take us back to Oxford on May 6, 1954.*
BANNISTER: I went to do my rounds at the hospital in the morning.
I also sharpened my spikes and put graphite on them. There
are many things beyond your control, like weather. It was raining, with high winds, and that adds about four seconds to your
time. So you do the things you can. We were then running on
rough cinder tracks, made out of the disused ash from power
stations. Your spikes would accumulate bits of this grit and, at
the end of the race, were heavier than at the beginning. You're
talking maybe half a second. So why have a heavier shoe?

CLASH: *What's going through your mind on your first lap?*
BANNISTER: What I'm thinking, actually, is that pacer Chris
Brasher isn't going fast enough. I knew that if you didn't have
a fast first lap, you'd be in trouble later. I said, "Faster, faster."
I was just behind him. He took no notice. Well, he may have
taken a little bit of notice, because the first lap was 57.5 seconds, which is good!

CLASH: *As you crossed the finish line, what did you feel?*
BANNISTER: I felt exaltation. Whatever the result, it was over. It's
rather like a theatrical production. I felt like an exploded
flashbulb, without the will to live or die. Then you've got to
wait, and there was such a crowd. It was totally disorganized,
as university sport then was—1,100 people crowded into the
center of the track. I couldn't wind down. If you can't wind

down, your blood pressure suddenly drops. I did a momentary blackout. It was only a matter of seconds, but it was adequate proof I'd done the best I could. About the time I was coming around, the announcer said, "The results of event number 6 in the match between Oxford University and the Amateur Athletic Association: first, R. G. Bannister in a time which, subject to ratification, is a track record, English record, British native record, all-comers record, European record, world record. And the time is three minutes . . ." That was when everything exploded.

CLASH: *There are lessons in this for businesspeople as well as athletes. You were the entrepreneurial point man, but you had a lot of support.*

BANNISTER: I benefited from a coach, Franz Stampfl, who made me feel that I could do it and had to do it. He said, "I agree with you that it's a bad day. But I think you can do 3:56." That was the first bit of psychological preparation. I also had good friends who paced me. When Brasher tired on the second lap, Chris Chataway took over. There was the excitement from the crowd. Yes, we had all done it together, as it were— an English achievement.

CLASH: *Did you envision making money from your accomplishment?*

BANNISTER: It's never been part of my concern to have lots of money. When I wrote my book *The Four Minute Mile* [New York: Lyons & Burford, 1981], I gave away half the royalties to build the first track in the Wealdstone suburb of London, where I came from.

CLASH: *Are you at all appalled by the commercialism in sports today?*

BANNISTER: It's difficult to know how appalled to be about something about which we can do nothing. What I would say is that you can't control change. The real point is how many more young people now take part in sport. If, as a result of sponsorship, television, and continuing high prestige for the Olympics, there are 10 million Chinese athletes—where in the past nobody had ever heard of a Chinese athlete—that's good, and who am I to say that the few athletes at the top who get salaries of millions of dollars don't deserve them?

CLASH: *Is it true that your car accident in 1975 changed your life?*

BANNISTER: During recovery, I reviewed what I was doing and thought that the time spent seeing patients in private practice would be better spent if I did more research. Research is the engine that drives the whole of medicine. In a way, I was wasting some of my talents in private practice. And one thing I don't like in life is to feel I'm wasting time. The car accident said, "Well, if there's something you want to do, you might as well do it because after the next car accident, you might be dead."

CLASH: *How do you feel about drug use in sports?*

BANNISTER: I've always been against any chemical method of enhancing performance. In 1963, the problem of drugs was just emerging. Anabolic steroids had ceased to have an exclusively medical function. The story then was bodybuilding in California; American football's premium on size; and as we now know, East Germany's producing, at its height, perhaps 30,000 athletes on steroids and winning Olympic medals 600 times as often as Americans.

When I was made chairman of the Sports Council in 1970, I was given a budget for research. I found the best steroid biochemist at St. Thomas' Hospital. Our test was so good it could detect traces even if the athlete had stopped taking drugs two weeks before. I got the first real tests done in 1972, at the then Commonwealth Games in New Zealand. There were a number of positives—five or six. My real frustration was that the international bodies—the Olympic organizations and the International Amateur Athletic Federation—were slow to implement the tests. It wasn't until the Seoul Olympics in 1988 that the Canadian sprinter Ben Johnson was caught.

CLASH: *Is the drug testing working?*

BANNISTER: In the late 1960s through the early 1980s, the Communist bloc women held every record for middle-distance races. They broke the record for 800 meters at 1:53.3 in 1983; now they're doing only 1:58. This is evidence that drug testing is working—that nobody in certain events has been able to replicate performances at the height of the drug regime. I'd spoken to the East German minister of labor and sport. He denied any drug use but said, "We do give medical advice to heighten potential." I later realized that, of course, was a code for a secret operation. It was absolutely appalling.

CLASH: *What's the equivalent of the four-minute mile today?*

BANNISTER: I should think a two-hour marathon. They're doing two hours, five minutes now. The rate of improvement possible is greater the longer the distance, because it involves improving oxygen uptake, which just means more training. But whether people will look at two hours in the same light as the four-minute mile, I don't know. We'll have to wait and see. It's part of man's incessant search for some niche that will, for a while, ensure him a certain degree of permanence or fame.

TOMMY MOE: OLYMPIC GOLD

On February 13, 1994, Tommy Moe, fresh-faced and 23, streaked down the slopes at Lillehammer and into the record books with a time of 1:45.75 in the Olympic downhill. An American winning the downhill is akin to Germany's winning the basketball final; Moe is only the second ever to have done so (Bill Johnson, at Sarajevo in 1984, was first). Even more impressive was that Moe had never won a World Cup downhill ski competition until his Olympic race.

Moe now serves as ski ambassador to the Jackson Hole Mountain Resort (www.jacksonhole.com/ski), promoting it through endorsements and celebrity races. "If you want to ski one of the great mountains in the world, come to Jackson Hole," enthuses Moe. "I'll personally take you on one of the best runs of your life." In our interview, Moe remembers his most important race and what it was like to win the pinnacle of sport—an Olympic gold medal.

CLASH: *Take us back to 1994 and Lillehammer.*

MOE: I had a few thirds and several top-10 finishes that season. When I got to Norway, I asked myself, "When am I going to win? It's time." We were staying three-quarters of the way up the course, next to the downhill, while the rest of the teams were down in the Olympic Village, an hour's commute. It worked out perfectly because we were able to warm up and sleep a little more. In the last training run the day before the race, I got fourth. Andy Mill, a ski writer, said, "Tommy Moe, do you think you can win tomorrow?" I said, "We'll see. I'm feeling pretty confident." I believed I could get a medal.

CLASH: *But did you think it would be gold?*

MOE: I didn't really believe that, no. I was an underdog. Like I said, I hadn't won a big race. I remember sitting at the top of the downhill in a little warming station. I had my boots off with my feet up against the baseboard heater, and one of the other competitors, a German, said, "I feel crummy, I don't like this course." I said, "Well, you're not going to do very well today then." I just laughed, because he was already counting himself out. He knew that he didn't have a chance, and was trying to psyche me out.

CLASH: *There were 70-odd competitors. What race number did you draw?*

MOE: Eight. The favorite, the Norwegian Kjetil Andre Aamodt, drew seven. He uncorked a beautiful run: 1:47.79, the fastest all week. I tried to put it out of my mind. I just tried to remember my little mantra, "Outside ski, hands forward."

CLASH: *How important is the start of the downhill?*

MOE: It's huge, probably 20 percent of the run. If you are three-tenths slower in the first five seconds, you're already in fourth place. You need good upper body strength because you basically start from a flat spot, then hoist yourself out of the gate. It's like a bobsled start—rock back and forth, back and forth, then sprint until you're up to speed. As soon as I was out of the gate, everything clicked. I hit the top section the best I had all week, in some places topping 80 miles per hour. I was basically a missile. Where I won the race is at a jump about midway through—a flat spot over a hill where the contour of the course falls away. When I came to the lip, I picked up the tails of my skis and prejumped so as not to catch as much air. I remember my shoulder brushing the gate, and I landed 15 to 20 feet inside of everyone else's tracks. That's the shot on the cover of *Sports Illustrated.*

CLASH: *Did you know you had it won at the bottom of the course?*

MOE: I leaned back, got into the lowest tuck I could find and went through the finish line. The crowd was silent. Usually you can tell if you do well because there is cheering, but I had totally put a damper on the Norwegian domination. I just saw "1" on the board, jumped into the air and pumped my fist. It was a dream come true. All the stars were in alignment for me that week.

CLASH: *What went through your head up on the medal stand?*

MOE: I can tell you that it's 100 times happier than your happiest day. I couldn't even fathom what was going on. I remember looking out and seeing my dad, step-mom, and my girlfriend, Megan. They were smiling and clapping, and it was really emotional. A lot of people cry when they get up there, but I was too elated.

BAKER AND BRUCE: CREAM OF THE MUSICAL CROP

Shortly after the 1960s supergroup Cream was inducted into the Rock and Roll Hall of Fame in 1993, the band's aloof lead guitarist, Eric Clapton, became emotional. "I was moved," said the Grammy award–winning superstar. "I was in some other place. It's been so long since I've been around something from somebody else that's inspired me. For the past 20 years, it's been up to me to inspire me." The inspiration Clapton was talking about came from Cream-mates Jack Bruce and Ginger Baker. The trio had just run off a searing three-song set of their old material. It was the first time they had performed together since the band's breakup in 1968.

"There isn't a drummer on this earth that has the dexterity that Ginger has," Clapton went on to say. "And [Jack has] this powerful thing that happens when he starts to sing, and you're off on the side there." Clapton's remarks, which appeared in *Fresh Live Cream,* a video produced just after the Hall of Fame induction, offered hope to millions of Cream devotees that the short-lived group might finally come together again. But a decade later, much to the dismay of fans, promoters, and musicians, there's no hint of a reunion.

For the last few years, retread rock has been all the rage, so a Cream reunion would have been right in vogue. Kiss, for example, a marginal 1970s metal/show band, reunited in the late 1990s and grossed more than $100 million by the time the dust had settled. The band was even featured, of all places, on

205

the cover of *Forbes* magazine. Even bigger were reunion pay-checks for the Eagles and Pink Floyd. The Beatles also "reunited," using prerecorded tracks from the late John Lennon, and won Grammys for it. Even the Monkees—once derisively dubbed the "Pre–Fab Four"—recombined.

To get an idea of the importance of Cream in the annals of popular music, put the band into its historical context. In July 1966, Baker, Bruce, and Clapton haughtily named their new power trio Cream—blatantly proclaiming that they were the cream of the crop—and the music world didn't object. On the contrary, there was tremendous anticipation. Each band member—Clapton on lead guitar, Bruce on bass guitar, and Baker on drums—had already been proclaimed by music insiders as "the best ever" on their respective instruments. Overzealous fans, not to be outdone, used subway graffiti to dub Clapton "God."

Cream didn't disappoint: During its just-over-two-year life, it sold more than 35 million records. More important, though, Cream lived up to artistic expectations, producing a brand new form of "heavy" music that fused hard rock, blues, classical, and jazz. High-energy, improvisational concerts featuring songs like "White Room," "Sunshine of Your Love," "Crossroads," and "Toad" became the band's trademark. Its 1968 double album, *Wheels of Fire*—half of which was recorded in the studio, the rest live at San Francisco's Fillmore Auditorium and Los Angeles' Winterland—became the first-ever platinum album.

But the pressure of a seven-month, seven-night-a-week U.S. tour schedule took its toll. The band members had little time left for developing new material and, faced with a trinity of strong egos, couldn't survive their own fabulous celebrity. Nonetheless, Cream pushed the limits of modern-day music and paved the way for more commercial hard-rock acts that followed, like Led Zeppelin, and the modern-day heavy-metal knockoffs like Metallica and Poison.

Over the years, advances in digital recording–studio technology and slick live shows replete with sound stages, fireworks, and makeup have allowed lesser talents to garner more attention—and rake in much more money—than Cream ever did. So, you say, with retread rock hot, now's their chance. Why no reunion? A Cream devotee since my teen years, I decided to find out for myself and my fellow Cream lovers. First, I ventured to England to talk with Jack Bruce, the soul of Cream. In addition to singing lead vocals, Bruce played bass, harmonica, and piano, and, along with British poet Pete Brown, wrote the bulk of Cream's original material. Over oysters and drinks at London's famed meeting place, The Savoy Hotel, Bruce talked candidly.

"I'd like it to happen," said the Scotsman, more mellow and less contrary now than in his fiery Cream days. "Apart from the money—I have to be honest, I think it would generate a lot of income—that band tends to get overlooked these days. Led Zeppelin, for instance, has gotten a lot of recognition, and quite rightly so, but it seems to be forgotten that Cream and [Jimi] Hendrix really created that audience. A reunion would help clarify that."

He continued, "But I wouldn't be prepared to do it, really, unless it was a challenge. And the challenge would be to come up with new material somewhere close to as strong as the stuff from the old days." As for Kiss and retread rock—well, when I showed Bruce the *Forbes* magazine cover, his reaction was one of amusement, not bitterness. "Oh, I wish we could wear makeup like that," he joked. "At our age, we'd look a lot better. I think with Kiss, it's more about the show anyway."

Bruce now lives with his second wife and their children in Suffolk, just outside of London. He spends much of his time composing and performing, mostly his own creations. But don't think he's has abandoned rock 'n' roll. Occasionally, he will tour as bassist/vocalist with Ringo Starr and his All-Starr Band. And, for the record, Bruce will make himself available for a Cream reunion should the opportunity present itself.

Next, it was a visit with Ginger Baker. "A lot of people think I'm dead," laughs Baker, now in his early sixties. "But that's nothing new. In 1968, I was driving from Los Angeles to San Francisco in a Shelby Cobra with three gorgeous young birds. Suddenly, the radio program was interrupted to report that I'd just been found in my hotel room dead from an overdose." Baker's much-publicized heroin habit, which lasted for more than two decades, almost did kill him, but he insists he's been clean since 1981. Drummers Keith Moon (The Who) and John Bonham (Led Zeppelin) are deceased, he is quick to point out.

The man many consider the world's greatest rock drummer has bittersweet memories of Cream and told me over lunch at his modest ranch in Parker, Colorado—complete with five dogs, four cats, and nine horses—that he wouldn't rule out a reunion. But Baker is nowhere as enthusiastic as Bruce. "There was a point where I wanted to do it, when I totally went broke," Baker said. (He lost most of his money in a recording-studio venture in Nigeria in the 1970s.) "I went down to Eric and proposed it. He said he didn't want to do it just because I was broke. This really hurt at the time, but it was also absolutely true. That is not a reason to do something, you know." When shown the *Forbes* Kiss cover and told about their $100 million retread paycheck, Baker had a very different reaction than Bruce. "They credited us with the birth of that sort of heavy-metal thing," he scoffed. "Well, if that's the case, there should be an immediate abortion."

Though he looks more frail than in his younger days, when Baker takes the stage it's obvious that he hasn't lost a beat. At a performance at New York's Iridium Jazz Club, he launched into a series of innovative jazz solos that left no doubt that if there is a Cream reunion, he's the man to handle the sticks. Legendary drummer Max Roach, present in the audience, remarked, "I've never seen Ginger stronger. He's just fantastic." Replied Baker, an avid polo player, "It's because I live in Denver. We train at high altitude."

So, what about Eric Clapton? With his former band mates ready to rock, why isn't he ready to roll? Record industry insiders will tell you it's not Clapton, it's his handlers who are holding up a reunion. "If it ain't broke, don't fix it," says one record industry executive who wishes to remain anonymous. "His managers don't want to risk Clapton's commercial appeal. They've succeeded in making people think Clapton was Cream, when he was only a third of it. Reuniting the band now would just take the emphasis off Clapton." (Despite repeated efforts to reach him, Clapton would not comment on the feasibility of a Cream reunion.)

Ron Delsener, one of the biggest concert promoters in the United States, who has staged events for Pink Floyd and Led Zeppelin during his four-decade career, ranks Cream among the top five bands of all time. He thinks a Cream reunion could easily gross $100 million worldwide for a year's worth of work. But Delsener is another person who thinks it's Clapton's side that's holding things up. "Eric doesn't need the money," Delsener says simply. "It's Jack and Ginger who do." In a way, Delsener has a point; since Cream's breakup, Clapton has become a solo superstar while the other two have moved out of the spotlight. Baker moves in jazz circles in South Africa—Bruce more in classical and jazz in Europe—genres with lower profiles (and lower pay) than hard rock.

And Clapton keeps busy. He won three Grammys (one shared with fellow songwriter Wynonna) for the song "Change the World," featured in the 1996 John Travolta movie *Phenomenon,* and a fourth for a collaborative effort in tribute to the late blues guitarist Stevie Ray Vaughan. He's in demand. If you believe what Clapton said after the 1993 Rock and Roll Hall of Fame induction (and why not?), you must assume he'd like to do something with Cream, and not necessarily just for the money: "Immediately I went off afterwards and started thinking, 'What could we do? What could we do?' without it getting into the wrong hands, without it getting out of control. The first thing I thought was, 'Wouldn't it be nice to just go into the studio and play, and maybe do a bit of writing and see what happens then.' " Bruce's sentiments exactly.

If a promoter came up with enough up-front cash, Clapton's handlers might listen, says Margrit Seyffer, Bruce's manager and wife. Michael Cohl, the Canadian concert mogul who has bankrolled some Rolling Stones tours, reportedly guaranteed U2 a minimum of $100 million for its world tour, even if the group didn't sell a single seat. (They sold out.) If someone like Cohl approached Cream with a big up-front guarantee, says Seyffer, Clapton would be hard-pressed not to at least consider the deal. "It would only be fair to Jack and Ginger," she says. And to the millions of Cream fans worldwide.

According to Delsener, the gate money would be there. "If they did do something, I'd like to see a limited-edition tour, say 50 of the great cities of the world, at a million dollars a night to the band." That would mean the three members would split $50 million, plus maybe $10 million more of ancillary income from promotional stuff like T-shirts and hats. That's $20 million each. And it doesn't include recording royalties if there were to be a new album. The handlers would get a nice piece of all that—even at a conservative rate of 10 to 20 percent for a personal manager—perhaps as much as $3.5 million.

In the meantime, Polydor Records has reissued completely

remastered versions (from the original master tapes) of Cream's six albums, which has helped generate interest in a reunion. Plus this year will be the thirty-fifth anniversary of Cream's farewell concert (November 26, 1968) at London's Royal Albert Hall. A nice, round, promotable number. . . . Eric, are you listening? Jack, Ginger?

SURVIVOR: ESCAPE FROM THE WORLD TRADE CENTER

Sometimes an adventurer is an ordinary person thrown into extraordinary circumstances. The challenge, then, is making sense out of nonsense—and quickly. Just before 9:00 A.M. on September 11, 2001, Marilyn White, a senior vice president of institutional business development at New York's Fiduciary Trust International, was in her window office on the ninety-fifth floor of World Trade Center Tower 2, as an American Airlines 767 jet hit Tower 1. She and Michael Rohwetter, a coworker, managed to climb down 95 flights of stairs to safety, dodging, among other things, a fireball. Others were not as lucky; 88 Fiduciary employees ultimately perished, along with thousands more, in the Trade Center on that horrific day.

Why did White survive when so many others didn't? Part of it was pure luck. But not all of it. Because her family is in the fire-protection business (it owns and operates Reliable Automatic Sprinkler in Mount Vernon, New York), White knows a lot about fire. "This stuff was ingrained in me—checking closed doors for heat, avoiding elevators, dousing yourself with water," she says from her home in Scarsdale, New York. That knowledge and White's quick wits helped save her and her companion's life.

CLASH: *Where were you when the first plane hit?*
WHITE: I was working on my computer, and suddenly I heard a boom. It didn't startle me at first—it sounded like fireworks.

But when I heard screams and turned around to look, flames were outside my window. The blast from Tower 1 had sent fire and debris toward us, so you felt as if you were engulfed. The heat was so intense that my face was hot. Thank God the glass didn't break. I immediately got away from the window. We gathered in the lobby, and somebody looked to the elevator bank. Mike and I just yelled, "Stairs! Don't go there."

You never go near an elevator in a fire. You could get caught if the power goes off. We got down to the sixty-third floor in minutes, and an announcement came on. This is important, because people got different announcements on different floors. Some were told to return to their offices. Some were told to go to the roof. In our stairwell it was, "One World Trade Center has been hit by a plane. You can remain where you are or continue down." You got this false sense of security.

CLASH: *What happened when you got to the sixty-third floor?*
WHITE: We stopped at Morgan Stanley's offices to call our families. While talking to my husband, I looked out the window, and bodies were just cascading down. It was very surreal. You couldn't absorb the information. After I hung up, I looked at Mike and said, "What do we do? Do we want to go downstairs where all that mayhem is? Or would we be better staying here?" With that, there was a huge boom as the second plane hit, and we saw fire coming down the hall toward us. I screamed to Mike, "Duck into an office." We closed the door. Hopefully the fireball, if it was a back-draft fire, would go right past us.

CLASH: *What next?*
WHITE: We found a watercooler and started dousing ourselves. I took off my sweater, soaked it in water, and put it on the floor in the door crack. We waited for a couple of minutes. No

smoke came through, and the door wasn't hot, so Mike looked out; the fire had receded. That gave us an opportunity. We followed exit signs until we got to another stairwell and started scaling down steps like you wouldn't believe. People were helping each other. One fellow had a gash in the back of his head and was bleeding. People above yelled, "Wounded coming, step to the right." So you'd go close to the wall so this guy could pass.

Somewhere around the 30s I saw a fireman coming up by himself. I said to him, "It's so good to see you, but you don't want to go up there." And he said, "But I've got to go. That's why I'm here." He had a very stoic look. When we got to the bottom, we couldn't exit at Liberty Street. We had to go out underneath the plaza, that retail area, and come up by Borders Bookstore. Once outside, we just kept moving. At Broadway, we turned around for the first time and looked up. We saw the hole in Tower 2 and realized what we were just in.

CLASH: *What should we do when we find Osama bin Laden, the man widely believed to be responsible for the attack?*

WHITE: If we find him, bring him to justice in this country. But don't kill him. The terrorists are not scared of dying, they've shown that. Put them away in some obscure place for the rest of their lives. They will know that they're not martyrs, that nobody will hear from them again—that nobody cares. That will be their worst punishment because they will become an obscurity—not even a footnote in the history of humanity.

8

Space: The Final Frontier

When Neil Armstrong and Buzz Aldrin walked on the moon in 1969, the future for manned space flight looked, well, rather stellar. The landing inspired Wernher von Braun, the German-born rocket science genius behind the Apollo missions, to scribble into his notebook, "A Look at the Year 2000: Mars visited by man, small permanent station. Base on moon, manufacturing activities, radio astronomy station on the far side."

Today, von Braun, who died in 1977, would be sorely disappointed. The farthest NASA has sent anyone since the last moon mission in 1972 is a few hundred miles above the earth, in aging space shuttles.

The 1986 *Challenger* explosion, which killed a shuttle crew of seven, including a civilian schoolteacher, had a lot to do with the slowdown. The internationally televised launch and disaster seared into the minds of millions of viewers the dangers of space travel. NASA has never fully recovered. Other than shuttle flights, most of its efforts since then have focused on unmanned missions to Mars and other areas of the solar system.

The ultimate dream of the baby-boomer generation is, quite predictably, to do what John Glenn and Alan Shepard did: to go into space. Will it ever happen, other than for those rich enough (like Dennis Tito and Mark Shuttleworth) to pay the cost of a $20 million ticket? Weighing in are three experts: *Apollo 11*'s Buzz Aldrin, second man on the moon and an avid stumper for affordable space tourism; Wilshire Associates founder Dennis Tito, the first tourist in space; and Center of Science and Industry's chief executive Kathryn Sullivan, the first American woman to walk in space. In the meantime, if $20 million is too steep for you, there's always Space Adventures' MiG-25 flight to 84,000 feet, as far into space as most civilians can go now. That one costs a mere $12,000.

Regardless of how far into the final frontier you may want to travel, this chapter reveals the reasons for, and benefits of, exploration. In any context, whether scientific, business-related, or personal, the healthy curiosity that drives exploration is the fire that sparks innovation.

THE RIGHT STUFF: TOURISTS IN SPACE

Picture this: You're aboard a rocket, strapped in tight as the countdown ticks off in your headset. At T minus two seconds comes ignition, then the powerful rumble of engines at full throttle. The takeoff pins you to your seat. You accelerate to the speed of sound, then twice that . . . three times. In a few minutes your vessel reaches a height of 62 miles and touches the outer edge of the atmosphere. You can see the arc of the world below, a delicate curvature enveloped by a thin, translucent blue halo. Above is cold blackness. Suddenly, you are weightless. You're in space.

Believe it or not, such flights soon could be available to anyone with the physical stamina and financial resources to buy a ticket. More than a dozen small companies are currently building spaceships and, through booking agents, selling advance tickets to well-heeled customers. In five years there's a good chance that anyone with a spare $100,000 will be able to buy a ticket on a rocket ship.

Until recently, private space travel has been dogged more by insufficient capital than by lack of technology. Now the money is starting to trickle in, enough to help lift a half-dozen space tourism companies off the ground. Encouraged by demand from wealthy individuals like Dennis Tito and Mark Shuttleworth, private investors are beginning to make sizable bets on space tourism. Richard Garriott, son of Skylab astronaut Owen Garriott and a software developer who made $30 million building Origin Systems, has put down a five-figure deposit with the booking agent Space Adventures in Arlington, Virginia, to secure a good place in line. "I've been to the South Pole and the bottom of the ocean," he declares. "The only direction left is up."

Space Adventures' main business now is taking thrill seekers to the edge of space in Cold War–era MiG fighter jets. But Eric Anderson, who runs the company, says he has collected more than 100 refundable deposits of $6,000 each toward the $98,000 price of a space trip. At least 10 prospective astronauts have paid in full up front. Anderson's brochure advertises that regular liftoffs will start as early as 2005. That may prove optimistic, but customers include Taco Bell, Pizza Hut, Dole Food, and First USA, all of which hope to use space trips as contest prizes. Another booker, Incredible Adventures of Sarasota, Florida, is also taking deposits, of $5,000; it, too, is aiming for 2005.

Who's going to carry the space tourists? Not NASA, which is still shell-shocked over the 1986 *Challenger* explosion. Not Boeing or Lockheed Martin—they're more interested in their joint partnership with NASA, called United Space Alliance, to develop a cheaper, next-generation shuttle. (The shuttle, now two decades old, was supposed to reduce the cost of space travel by reusing the spacecraft. But through a series of compromises, it is only partially reusable, and NASA's cost per pound to put a payload into space has increased from $8,400 during Apollo to over $22,000 now.) Other governments with proven space technology, including France and China, are too busy launching military and commercial satellites. And Russia, while it has taken Tito and Shuttleworth to the International Space Station in Soyuz rockets, doesn't have plans for regular tourist missions in the near future.

A 1997 joint NASA/Space Transport Association study predicts that there will be a private space-tourism industry, $10 billion to $20 billion a year, by 2010. Before then, there is the X Prize (www.xprize.org), created in 1996 by Dr. Peter Diamandis, an aerospace entrepreneur and founder of the International Space University in Strasbourg, France. Echoing the $25,000 Orteig Prize that spurred Charles Lindbergh to fly across the Atlantic in 1927, the X Prize promises $10 million to the first privately funded group to take a pilot plus the weight equivalent of two passengers to a suborbital height of 100 kilometers (62 miles), bring them back safely, and repeat the feat, using the same vehicle, within two weeks.

So far, 20 teams from six countries (the United States, England, Russia, Canada, Argentina, and Romania) have entered the competition. Diamandis, who lives in St. Louis, Missouri, has raised over half of the $10 million from individuals, including Tom Clancy, and business leaders in St. Louis, including Andy Taylor, CEO of Enterprise Rent-A-Car, and John McDonnell, chairman of the McDonnell Douglas Foundation. In addition, money has been raised by First USA, which has issued a series of X Prize Visa cards.

The X Prize recognizes that in space tourism's early stages, you're not likely to see golfers teeing off on the moon, as Alan Shepard did on his second space trip in 1971. Instead, the first tourists are likely to do something similar to what Shepard did on his first trip in 1961—fly a 15-minute suborbital parabola. This would offer a great view, a few minutes of weightlessness, and invaluable bragging rights—assuming that the passenger makes it back. What about full orbital flight? This requires rockets that can fly at 17,500 miles per hour, fast enough to enter orbit. Combined with the fiery business of reentry into the atmosphere, this means orbital space tourism, other than the occasional Tito or Shuttleworth, is still 7 to 10 years away.

Burt Rutan, founder of Scaled Composites, in Mojave, California and an entrant in the X Prize competition, already has a working aircraft, called Proteus, capable of carrying 3,000 pounds—a small capsule, perhaps—up to 12 miles. Rutan won't tip his hand about whether he's building that capsule, but insiders believe he is. Rutan also plans to build a space-pilot school in Mojave and charge $10,000 for a weeklong course that includes a 1-in-10 chance at a flight into space. Rutan compares space tourism today to the fledgling aircraft industry in the early 1900s. After Wilbur and Orville Wright began selling rides to the public later that decade, interest in flying increased exponentially. By 1911 there were 40,000 pilots in 31 countries.

How safe will early tourist spaceships be? Rutan guesses that a few dozen people will die this decade, as space tourism begins. But put that in context: In 1911 alone, he reminds us, there were 139 aircraft fatalities, as aviation took off. "In the entrepreneurial world, we make daily decisions to take risks," says Rutan. "If it breaks or makes a smoking hole, by God, we know more than we knew yesterday."

BUZZ ALDRIN: THE VIEW FROM NUMBER 2

On July 20, 1969, Buzz Aldrin became the second man to step onto the lunar surface, 19 minutes behind *Apollo 11* mission commander Neil Armstrong. Since then, Armstrong has retired to his farm in Ohio, ducking press interviews.* But Aldrin, who wrote a science fiction novel, *Encounter with Tiber,* in 1996, still reaches for the stars through his ShareSpace Foundation, a proposed lottery that would allow ordinary citizens a chance to go into space.

Aldrin is sorely disappointed with the rate of progress of manned space exploration in the past three decades. Whom and what does he blame? An increasingly cautious approach to manned space travel, for one. The end of the Cold War, for another. At the height of the Apollo program, NASA's $6 billion budget accounted for just over 4 percent of the federal budget; today, at about twice that, it is less than 1 percent.

CLASH: *Why haven't we done much in the way of space tourism?*

ALDRIN: One impediment is the fear of catastrophe. And I'm not sure how you deal with that. Does it mean we don't fly civilians in space? Do we only do it from our couches? Is the destiny of the human species to sit back and play with our mouse and computer and imagine, fantasize? We are scared out of our wits. We are a risk-averse society now.

CLASH: *Did the 1986* Challenger *explosion traumatize us?*

ALDRIN: Yes, the TV coverage did. Now, you don't want to deny freedom of the press. And the value of human life is very

---

*I have tried on many occasions to interview Neil Armstrong, always without success. Finally, I met him in person at the 2001 Explorers Club Annual Dinner, where he was the honored guest speaker. After waiting in a long line in the VIP room, I shook his hand and asked why he doesn't do interviews. The perfectionist that he is, Armstrong candidly told me that he doesn't like first drafts, and an interview is a first draft. A fourth or fifth draft is preferable, he said. Trying to be playful, I asked him if his famous phrase, "One small step for man, one giant leap for mankind," was a first draft. He smiled coyly and said, "Well, I had some time to think about that one."

high. We need to keep a balance. But the explorer, the climber of mountains, all those who want to go out and do these things ought to be able to without having the risks exaggerated.

CLASH: *Should NASA start sending civilians into space again?*

ALDRIN: There's essentially an understanding that only government employees will go. Yes, it should revert back to where the operator of the shuttle is able to take ordinary people. It's time that the billions of dollars in contributions from taxpayers result in taxpayers being able to go into space. You don't have to be superhuman. If a 77-year-old like [former astronaut and retired senator] John Glenn, no matter how good a condition he's in, can go into space, so can a robust 25-year-old.

CLASH: *How would the ShareSpace concept fit in?*

ALDRIN: Even the rosiest of forecasts predicts it will be a long time before the average price for a ticket into space is affordable to ordinary citizens. Is space tourism, despite its potential promise of space travel for all, destined to replace a well-trained NASA elite with a well-heeled economic elite? Not necessarily. There's a classic mechanism for ensuring that a high-priced asset is distributed in an egalitarian manner— the lottery. I'm proposing that for a nominal price of, say, $10, ordinary citizens gain access to a space lottery. Prizes in the near future could include suborbital and orbital flights. There is no reason why later prizes could not include trips around the moon and Mars.

CLASH: *If you could return to outer space, as John Glenn did, would you?*

ALDRIN: I think that those of us fortunate enough to participate in Apollo and fly to the moon had our share of rewards for the time we put in. To try to edge into another space flight on board the shuttle is kind of incongruous. The shuttle is an aerospace transport; it carries people and cargo. It's not an exploration command module or a lunar lander. It's not a pioneering vehicle.

CLASH: *Are you disappointed that we haven't sent a man to Mars yet?*

ALDRIN: I've kept abreast of the space program and realized that sending humans to Mars is not going to happen until the cost of rocket launches comes down. The best way for that to happen is spacecraft reusability. And that requires a high flight rate with valuable payloads. People fit into that category. If you put people into space, you need at least to bring down the container that took them up, and if it's a two-stage rocket, we need to recover the larger booster and reuse it, too. An inspired political leader with the backing of Congress and corporations could get us behind a commitment that would take people to Mars within 20 years. Every five years we could accomplish something of significance. We could improve the shuttle in five years. In 10 years, we could begin to replace the shuttle.

CLASH: *Has celebrity status helped you promote space tourism?*

ALDRIN: There is no doubt that the public focuses on achievements of significance, and certainly I was fortunate to be part of *Apollo 11*, a very significant achievement. It lends credibility and a desire to at least listen to what that participant has to say. But you don't want to misuse that just because you achieved something in the past. It doesn't mean you necessarily know much about the future or the present.

CLASH: *Were you ever afraid, in space or as a Korean War fighter pilot?*

ALDRIN: There's always an interest in safety and dealing with something that goes wrong. But for the high-visibility performer, the pilot, his reactions are so important. Not making a mistake is more important than a fear of physical danger. A mind concerned about danger is a clouded mind. It's paralyzing.

CLASH: *What do you remember about your lunar landing in 1969?*

ALDRIN: Obviously, when we touched down, we were very relieved. Neil and I acknowledged that with a wink, a nod, and a pat on the shoulder. The immediate surface was very powdery, as best we could see looking down from 15 feet. Off in the distance was a very clear horizon, maybe with a boulder. And, of course, the brightness of the sunlit surface was almost like looking out at sunlit snow. Your pupils close down, just as in orbit when the sun is on the spacecraft. The sky is black as can be, but there's no way you can see stars. They're there, of course, but you can't make them out, because they're too faint with all the ambient light in your eyes. Knowing that we were going to call ourselves Tranquility Base—but we had never rehearsed it because we didn't want people to know— we hadn't inserted that historic announcement into our procedures checklist. So when Neil said, "Tranquility Base here, the Eagle has landed," it struck me as, "Gee, we're in the middle of something, Neil, don't do that."

CLASH: *Did you two say anything as Neil prepared to exit the lunar module?*

ALDRIN: I don't think it occurred to either of us to say something private. It's just not the way we related. The discussion had to do with procedure not, "Have a good time out there, I'll see you in 20 minutes."

CLASH: *When Neil stepped onto the moon, what did you feel?*

ALDRIN: I could probably manufacture all sorts of wondrous things. But in retrospect, I felt like we were proceeding with things on the checklist, such as carrying the camera down. There are lots of little things, more than meets the eye.

CLASH: *How about when you stepped on the moon yourself?*

ALDRIN: Can you give me some multiple choices I can pick from to describe my emotions? I don't go through life verbalizing what I feel. After the fact, it's really kind of difficult. I guess if you're used to a lot of describing, those things come easily. We were not really picked to do that. That's why, I guess, the greatest inadequacy I've experienced in my life is when someone asks, "What did it feel like?" I have a very hard time trying to tell someone.

CLASH: *What were your first words on the moon?*

ALDRIN: I don't know that they had any significance. I don't know what the first ones were. The ones I felt were most descriptive were very spontaneous: "magnificent desolation."

CLASH: *Any disappointment that Neil was first?*

ALDRIN: No, not at all. I recognized when we, as a crew, were picked to be the first landing mission, there would be a great loss of privacy, a great burden of public speaking, which never appealed to me. If I were given a choice, there was something inside that said, "You might be better off, Buzz, on the second or third lunar landing, because you won't have as much of this. You will also get to do more things when you're on the moon. Maybe the burden of being on the first landing is something you'd just as soon not have to put up with." But the competitive nature of everybody was such that you weren't about to turn down something offered to you. You may never get another chance.

CLASH: *Do you believe there is life in the universe other than on earth?*

ALDRIN: I'm pretty careful with what I say I believe in. If you say you believe in something, you are beholden to defend it. Somebody has to be at the top. We're not bad, we're pretty advanced for a species. But somebody has to be leading the pack in this universe. And chances are, somebody else is.

CLASH: *When you look up at the moon now, can you believe you were there? Does it seem real to you?*
ALDRIN: Well, it was very real, but it's a categorized realness. It fits into a niche. The moon I see now is the same moon I saw before. Except that before, when I looked at it, it was in anticipation of what it would be like when I got there. That's behind me now.

CLASH: *Anything you want to say to NASA?*
ALDRIN: We've got government careers now that are based on the latest polls. This is the epitome of short-term thinking. You're asking somebody to vote on something he has no responsibility for later. What's necessary is to look beyond the problems of the moment, to project where we'd like to be in 20 to 30 years. Mars should be within our grasp by then. A number of us feel that it's inevitable there will be a permanent base there. And that within 500 years, we will journey to the stars. It's inbred within us to do that. It's human curiosity. If we don't, we'll fall by the wayside.

DENNIS TITO: EXECUTIVE IN SPACE

In 2001, businessman Dennis Tito became the first paying tourist in space, living the dream of countless American baby boomers who grew up in the early 1960s when astronauts were our heroes. Strangely, it was the Russians—America's Cold War space foes—that took him into orbit for eight days for a reported $20 million (Tito insists that he paid less, but won't elaborate). Tito has since quietly settled back into his job as a founding partner at Wilshire Associates, the well-known stock index firm based in Los Angeles that made him rich enough to take the flight. In our interview, he talks about NASA's resistance, the future of space tourism, and the flight itself.

CLASH: *Describe your takeoff from Kazakhstan.*

TITO: You feel a slight vibration but don't hear the sound of the rocket engines. Gradually, acceleration builds as the fuel burns off. There are three separate stages; at the end of each you have maximum acceleration, because at that point the fuel is almost gone. I had a card in my right hand listing the time from liftoff to when each stage would jettison. I kept a stopwatch on my left arm, so I knew to the second when each event was occurring. They all happened exactly as scheduled, so nothing was frightening to me. The entire launch sequence, from liftoff to orbit, was just 8 minutes, 50 seconds.

CLASH: *How did you know when you were in orbit?*

TITO: When the third stage burns out, pencils hanging by strings in the cabin start to float. You, too, are weightless but don't feel it because you're so tightly strapped in. I don't recall looking out at Earth on the way up; I was concentrating on the instrument panel and on my sequence of events. Once we achieved orbit, though, I turned to my right and glanced out and could see the black blackness of space and the curvature of the earth. It was a euphoric feeling because I knew that at that moment I was in orbit. I said to myself, "I've done it. I'm in space."

CLASH: *Did you like the experience?*

TITO: I could have stayed up there for months. I took close to a thousand photographs and four 40-minute videotapes. I floated while listening to opera. And unlike most people who have been in space, I didn't have a list of tasks to perform, so I was really able to enjoy it.

CLASH: *Sounds like heaven.*

TITO: In fact, that's how I've described it. Religious art depicts angels with little wings that could never lift their weight. I see that as the weightlessness. Then the earth is below, because in heaven you're above the earth.

CLASH: *Were you ever scared during the flight?*

TITO: When I got back, I asked the Russians what my heart rate was during ascent. They said it never got beyond 72 beats a minute. It gets higher than that looking at the stock market indexes. But reentry was more exciting. It turns out that we had a much steeper entry into the atmosphere than normal—a maximum G load, as I understand it, of seven—almost three times what a shuttle astronaut experiences. It was hard to breathe because of the weight on your chest. You just take short breaths and know it's not going to last long—five minutes or so. The more Gs, the faster the vehicle is slowing. There's only so much speed you can take out.

CLASH: *Compare your space flight, which cost a reported $20 million, to your MiG-25 ride to the edge of space, which cost just $12,000.*

TITO: The MiG, which takes you 85,000 feet up, gives a feel for what it might look like from space because the sky is dark and you can see a slight curvature of the earth. The actual flight into orbit is much more fascinating, in part because you are weightless. The International Space Station is 240 miles up. Viewing the earth from there allows you to look out in each direction to a distance of 2,000 miles on the horizon, so the earth's curvature is very distinct. Your speed in orbit—about five miles a second—is 10 times faster than the MiG.

CLASH: *Do you get a feeling of speed so high up without reference points like clouds?*

TITO: Yes, because you go over areas of earth you're geographically familiar with, and they pass in no time. You're over the Great Lakes, then within a few minutes, Boston. To photograph Southern California, I had to position myself when I was over Hawaii.

CLASH: *How did you feel when you returned?*

TITO: I was amazed that so much attention had been drawn to my flight. People would be walking along Fifth Avenue in New York and see me and say, "Oh, that's Dennis Tito." Usually you don't become a celebrity at my age—you're a lot younger. It was also satisfying to see how much my flight inspired people. There was so much bad news that year. Aside from the attack of September 11, we had a sliding stock market for a year and a quarter before my flight. School kids were killing one another. This was one of the few stories people could feel good about.

CLASH: *Do your coworkers at Wilshire treat you differently now?*

TITO: Some of the younger people at Wilshire stare at me when I'm in the elevator because, well, here's the boss who actually went out and did it—flew in space. But my senior partners and I are mainly same-old same-old. I have four who have been with me for 20 years or more. It was their cooperation that allowed me to do this.

CLASH: *But there must be a time each day you talk about space?*

TITO: Are you kidding? I love it. I get invited to luncheons as the keynote speaker. I tell people I'll give a speech—as long as it isn't about the stock market.

CLASH: *Do you want to go back up?*

TITO: I do not. I have the experience, the pictures, the video. I'm still enjoying my space flight. It's part of me, and no one can take that away. I only wish that I were younger so I could enjoy it for a longer part of my life. The best thing I can do, and which gives me great satisfaction, is communicate my experience to others. It would be a little greedy if space tourist number 3 were Dennis Tito. I want to do something different. Who knows what? Maybe there will be an opportunity to help cure a disease.

CLASH: *Do you think your orbital experience will dampen enthusiasm for suborbital rides planned by the small rocket companies?*

TITO: I don't think that a suborbital vehicle that pops up to 62 miles and gives you five minutes of weightlessness would be much of an experience, other than to give you bragging rights to having been in space—if 62 miles up is considered space. I also think that a suborbital flight will cost more than the $100,000 they're projecting—it will be more like $300,000. If you've flown on the MiG for $12,000, you'll get 80 percent of the thrill, less the bragging rights. And it will have been less dangerous. Those suborbital vehicles haven't been built yet, let alone tested.

CLASH: *Why was NASA so against your flight?*

TITO: The real issue was: Who really manages the International Space Station? Could one partner unilaterally fly someone other than the choice of NASA? The Russians had a good point when they said, "Look, it's our taxi spacecraft. We can choose whom we want, as long as they're trained and qualified." The argument NASA used was that I wasn't qualified. The Russians have been training cosmonauts for 40 years. It was an insult to suggest that they would slip in somebody who was untrained. Yes, they need funds, but that doesn't mean that they're willing to compromise their space program. For me, writing the check was a small part of it. For eight months, I trained in the cosmonaut center outside of Moscow on a Soviet-style military base; I lived in a two-room flat, made my own bed and cooked my meals.

CLASH: *When you testified before Congress, what did you say?*

TITO: First, we really ought not discourage the Russians from having paying passengers on future taxi missions. To the extent that you can create more demand there, private capital will come out of the woodwork. Two, the United States should reinstate the Citizen in Space program it terminated with *Challenger.* The marginal cost to make available that seventh shuttle seat is practically zero. People from all walks of life should get to go. Our culture will then reflect the more heavenly—and less technical—aspects of space. Let's get over *Challenger.* If consenting adults—as long as they have full risk disclosure—don't come back, they don't come back. It doesn't have to be a tragedy. I heard Dan Goldin [the former NASA administrator] once say, "But we killed that schoolteacher." If you're so worried about dying, we can ban drinking, motorcycles, and skydiving. We can have a repressive society that confines us to rocking chairs. Of course, then we'd all probably die of heart disease.

KATHRYN SULLIVAN: SPACEWALKER TURNED CEO

Kathryn Sullivan was the first American woman to walk in space, spending three and a half hours outside the shuttle *Challenger* in 1984. Just over a year later, that spacecraft exploded 73 seconds into flight, killing its crew of seven, including Sullivan's friends Francis Scobee, Ellison Onizuka, Judith Resnik, and Ronald McNair. Undaunted, Sullivan flew again, not once but twice—in 1990 on *Discovery* and in 1992 on *Atlantis.* "I had to," she says without hesitation. "We were all there because we believed this was important work for the country. If it was sufficiently unimportant that one painful moment was grounds to give it up, then we had made the wrong estimation."

Sullivan has retired from NASA and now oversees more than $100 million in public and private funding as the chief executive of the Center of Science and Industry (COSI) in Columbus, Ohio. The structure features interactive displays ranging from lifting a car with your own strength by means of levers to manipulating laser beams through a series of mirrors. Sullivan says that centers such as COSI are important not only for children but for adults, too. "The average American adult comprehension level of science is something around the sixth-grade level," she says—the knowledge of a 12-year-old. I asked Sullivan to reflect on her achievements both as an astronaut and as a businesswoman.

CLASH: *Why did you become an astronaut?*

SULLIVAN: As early as I can remember, I had a broad geographic curiosity. What are places like? What are people like who live there? We were not a family that went on European vacations and attended boarding schools in Switzerland. It was dreaming and reading—those were the avenues of exploration long before it was practical to do it with my own two feet. In graduate school at Dalhousie University [Nova Scotia, Canada] in 1978, I studied oceanography. I was looking for an education that would give me a life that centered around traveling the planet. Along came NASA looking for astronauts. There hadn't been a selection in over a decade. It was a pretty easy leap—seeing myself mainly as an explorer interested in the world more than being absolutely wedded to a discipline such as oceanography.

CLASH: *What do you remember about your first space walk in 1984?*

SULLIVAN: A lot, and not very much. Those are pretty intense experiences, and you're focused. If you ever want to do a second one, it's probably a good idea to get this one right. There are safety reasons as well. There's nobody there but you and the equipment—the only thing between hard vacuum—so you tend to pay close attention. The walk is really like swimming, reminiscent of the pool in which we had trained. But the view's a whole bunch better. At one point I looked down, and there was Venezuela sliding by beneath my boots.

CLASH: *What's it like up there?*
SULLIVAN: It's almost schizophrenic. If you just told me this was magic, it would make some sense. But it's not. You feel outrageously normal, given the outrageously not-normal place you are. In fact, it's so normal that you're wearing gym shorts and sipping hot cocoa and listening to a rock band on your Walkman. The main thing you're thinking about is, will I miss some steps on the checklist, and will things go okay so I can get home for dinner on Thursday? And yet you look through the window and what's outside doesn't fit normal at all.

CLASH: *Describe what's outside.*
SULLIVAN: Just when you think you've picked the one most beautiful sight, there is another. Like realizing that when you see a continent-size mass of thunderstorms from above, there is never a moment there isn't an electrical discharge in that mass. It's the illusion of being at one place on the ground that makes you think lightning is intermittent. Meanwhile, on the day side, going over parts of the earth that you know is exciting. You can see a lot of detail with the bare eye. I don't know where the myth came from that you can only see the Great Wall of China. You can see airports, dams, baseball stadiums—even the spot we had launched from.

232

CLASH: *What do you remember about the 1986* Challenger *disaster?*

SULLIVAN: I was in California testing components of the Hubble Space Telescope. We'd been working all night, so I was actually on an airplane en route to a connection in Dallas. I called the office to check in and got the news. And, of course, went right to the space center, because who can go home at that point? You're stunned. Words don't come. And then you think, what could have done it? What happened? There are long phases of just being numb, and then you fall into the necessary activity patterns of looking after families and showing proper courtesies. And finally the world begins to move again a little bit, and you get into trying to figure out what really happened and what we are going to do about it.

CLASH: *Did you ever think, "I'm not going to go back up if I get another chance."*

SULLIVAN: No. My father was in aerospace, and my brother's an aerospace nut. I grew up with families that know what airplane crashes and explosions are. This business consists of riding bombs. And if you do absolutely everything right, you can marshal the energy to do something astonishing, like put yourself into orbit. If you do even a few things wrong, it's going to act like a bomb.

CLASH: *What did you learn as an astronaut that applies to your job as the chief executive of COSI?*

SULLIVAN: The systems way of thinking. Astronauts have a central, although not genuinely authoritative role. You sit at the focal point of everything, you have a hugely integrated perspective on how a flight needs to come together, you certainly have responsibility for final results. But you don't have direct classical authority over anybody except yourself. So you do get a perspective on how to integrate many different complex strands—technical, engineering, cultural, political. With

COSI, it's similar but more like: Who's your food service operator going to be? What kind of ticketing system and software are you looking for? Does it need to connect to something? How about point-of-sales systems? With all of these, as with space flight, you do not really have the luxury of time or excess funds to just try something and then go rip it out and try again.

There is no way you can do it all yourself. You've got to surround yourself with good people; you've got to hold up your end of the bargain, but also find ways to draw them in and give them the chance to really own part of it. So it seems a lot better to me to keep an open, peer-group approach, where my job is to say, "Look, we're going this direction as opposed to that direction." But within that playing field there are a thousand decisions a week we need to be clever about. I really want to know what they think.

CLASH: *Why are interactive science centers like COSI important?*
SULLIVAN: Research shows that retention is higher if there's active engagement on the part of the learner. For some, that can happen just listening to a lecture. But often you have to be actively engaged on more levels. And there are differing modes by which people learn. With some, it's visual. Others have to be able to turn it over in their hands. In the kinds of highly interactive environments we design, we create a mélange of all of those channels that have a capture point for any learning mode.

CLASH: *As the first American woman to walk in space, are you a role model for other women?*
SULLIVAN: I have a twin view. That would have been my first space walk if 10,000 people had done it before me. So, from the point of view of the experience itself and its meaning to me, that little historical fact doesn't play any role. But when it's

234

parents, teachers, or young high school folks figuring their way through the world—if I'm identifiable as having something worth saying to help someone figure out the road ahead—I think that's an extraordinary opportunity. So I enjoy that and whenever possible try to do what I can.

CLASH: *There are small companies building rockets to take tourists into space. And then there's Russia and NASA. What do you think about space exploration today?*

SULLIVAN: We're not where I wish we were. I mean, I wish we had kept more of an active exploration vein. I wish we had more knowledge about Mars and maybe had sent at least one scouting party there. But again, if you look at the history of exploration—whether it's jungle or polar—there are always cycles. I think it would be great if we get results from the small rocket companies. That would make space a more commonly shared experience. Furthermore, if you democratized it that way, you would find, as with other forms of travel, the price would be driven down as the engineering becomes more clever. The best analogy is the Wilbur Wright and Ford Trimotor days. In the early years, no one could have imagined airplanes as mass transit. But it happened, because you got safety and reliability up and costs down. Transformations like that might someday happen in space.

MACH 2.6 IN A MiG: 'SCUSE ME WHILE I KISS THE SKY

"If I say: 'Jim, eject, eject, eject'—this is not command for discussing, only for fulfilling." In broken English, Russian pilot Alexander Garnaev is prepping me on emergency evacuation procedures for the MiG-25 fighter jet while his ground crew straps me into the restrictive cockpit. I am listening carefully. Garnaev is about to take me to the edge of space at upward of two and a half times the speed of sound—a mile every two seconds. "But don't pull this handle," he adds, gesturing at the ejection mechanism near my seat. "You could eject me."

When I signed up for this adventure, I knew it wasn't going to be a first-class excursion in a Learjet, but accidental ejection of the pilot—well, that was something I hadn't really considered. No matter, here I am in Russia, donning a pressurized flight suit, helmet, and oxygen mask. My heart is racing. Is this how Alan Shepard, the first American into space, felt before his historic flight in 1961? Shepard's Mercury Redstone topped out at just over 100 miles above the earth's surface. My ride is only supposed to go to 16 miles. But since that's above 99 percent of the earth's atmosphere, much of what one sees—the blackness of space, the curvature of the earth—is similar to a space flight.

We've gathered at the Gromov Flight Research Institute, Zhukovsky Air Base, about 20 miles southeast of Moscow. During the Cold War the place was so secret it didn't appear on maps. Now tourists—many of them Americans—test their intestinal fortitude from here. A few hundred souls have braved the MiG-25 before me. On the supply side, times are tough for the Russian military. Soldiers are receiving reduced pay, if any at all, while their equipment sits idle. Outside entrepreneurs such as Space Adventures pump needed money into the Soviet economy and give tourists the thrill of a lifetime. You can't do this sort of thing in the United States; commercial aircraft cannot legally break the sound barrier over land. That's why the Concorde doesn't fly across America or Europe.

At my preflight briefing in the morning, I learned that the MiG is quite an aircraft. Designed in the 1960s to intercept America's SR-71 Blackbirds, the MiG-25 holds the world record (23 miles) for altitude by a jet. After the big buildup, I'm not quite ready for what awaits me on the runway. The plane looks ancient—like something out of *Dr. Strangelove*—and unkempt. Frayed seat harnesses. Chipping paint. Nothing digital in the cockpit. No sleek, futuristic lines. To make matters worse, I'm to fly in a separate cockpit on the nose of the jet. Garnaev, about 10 feet behind in another cockpit, will communicate via radio; I must push a button every time I talk.

After a jolting takeoff powered by full afterburners, we quickly rise to 35,000 feet—the height at which passenger jets cruise—but we do it subsonically. Supersonic speed can only be achieved up high, Garnaev explains on the radio, because a sonic boom near the ground would break too many windows down below. As we approach the speed of sound—some 750 miles per hour—Garnaev asks me to watch the instrument gauges. The needles—and the plane—should jerk when we break through it. Sure enough, just as the gauge flashes Mach 1, there's a shudder, then the ride becomes incredibly smooth. For the first time in my life, I am traveling faster than thunder.

We continue to accelerate to Mach 2. There is no jolt this time, and the sensation of speed is hard to judge because any frame of reference is absent; we are way above the clouds. Then, at Mach 2.3, we circle back toward the air base, already 180 miles away, and start a steep climb. I really begin to feel the G-forces. The small camera in my right hand (we are turning left) suddenly feels like it weighs 10 pounds.

At 12 miles up we reach Mach 2.5 and are still climbing. The sky has turned a very deep blue and the earth below is distinctly curved. At 16 miles, the sky is cold black and a translucent blue hue hangs over the curvature. By God, that is the entirety of the atmosphere, I think. I'm astonished by its thinness. We now slow appreciably. There isn't enough air for the jets to push against to maintain our speed, explains Garnaev. It feels as if we are hanging in the sky. There's a distinct sense of peacefulness here at the edge of space. I take some photos of the haunting vista.

Suddenly, with no warning we are in a steep, screaming dive. I am alarmed (no, I didn't pull the ejection handle) until

Garnaev radios that we had just reached our apogee. In his judgment, to continue to climb—and therefore to slow—would have risked the plane's losing its aerodynamics; we could have fallen out of the sky like a lead pipe.

Once we stabilize at 30,000 feet and slow to subsonic speed, descending is fun. The ground is up, the sky down as Garnaev does a 360-degree roll to the left. I feel slightly nauseated. He asks me to conduct the same maneuver. (Since we are in a trainer, I have a throttle stick, too.) The stick handles heavily, like a car without power steering, but I manage to muscle it around. When Garnaev radios again—this time suggesting a roll to the right—I beg off. I know if we try it once more, I'll get sick. And with the pressure suit and oxygen mask, that would be a disaster.

Just before landing, Garnaev asks me to touch the cockpit glass. It is hot, even though the air temperature outside was −77°F a few moments ago. As thin as the air is up that high, Garnaev explains, our speed was so great that friction was able to overcome the cold and heat the aircraft skin. That's why rockets—which travel much faster—can burn up during re-entry, even in a thin atmosphere.

Safely back on the ground, Garnaev and I shake hands. He tells me we've just burned over 5,000 gallons of jet fuel, rocketed upward by 85,000 feet, and reached Mach 2.6—all in about 35 minutes. I'm a bit wobbly, but happy—no accidental ejections, no incidents. A few weeks later in New York, I showed one of my air photos to Buzz Aldrin. Is this what space looks like, I wanted to know? Aldrin scrutinized the photo. Then, smiling, and with a glint in his eyes, he replied: "It's pretty darn close." I can live with that.

TRAVELER'S NOTEBOOK: MiG-25 trips run year-round for about $12,000. That includes everything but round-trip airfare to Moscow. You must be in reasonably good health (Russian doctors give you the once-over the morning of your flight) and willing to sign countless release forms (my last one was in Russian, on the runway, as I boarded). Want to try weightlessness? Group flights in an Ilyushin-76, a modified cargo jet capable of parabolic flight, are also offered at Zhukovsky Air Base. You get bursts of 30 seconds of weightlessness at a time. One trip will set you back $5,000. Finally, to test your G-force limits with top gun–style acrobatics, flights in other MiGs (the -29, -23 and -21) range from $5,000 to $10,000. (Warning: All will test the limits of your stomach.) Contact: Space Adventures (www.spaceadventures.com) or Incredible Adventures (www.incredible-adventures.com).

Author's Note: As we were going to press, the space shuttle *Columbia* and its crew of seven were lost during reentry over Texas. When I heard the news, I immediately thought of former astronaut Kathryn Sullivan's poignant words regarding her own shuttle experiences (page 233): "This business consists of riding bombs. And if you do everything right, you can marshal the energy to do something astonishing. . . . If you do even a few things wrong, it's going to act like a bomb." On the morning of February 1, 2003, after 27 successful flights dating back to 1981, unfortunately *Columbia* did just that.

But I also remember Sullivan's inspiring words about whether she gave pause to going back into space after *Challenger*'s 1986 ill-fated flight. "I had to [fly again]," she said without hesitation. "We were all there because we believed this is important work for the country. If it were sufficiently unimportant that one painful moment was grounds to give it up, then we had made the wrong estimation." Perfectly phrased. Space exploration will go forward. But not without sadness and some valuable learning from what went wrong on *Columbia*'s last flight. Our prayers go out to the families of the seven astronauts—some of the first true heroes of the twenty-first century.

Acknowledgments

Thanks to Julie Androshick, Wendy Bahlav, Bill Baldwin, Donna Barfield, Lee and Todd Brayton, Robbie Buhl, Susan Casper, Duncan Christy, Jeff Cianci, Andrew, Ben, Liz, Michael, Nancy, David, and Thomas Clash, George Clissold, Kathy Coleman, Emily Conway, Beau and William Croxton, Mark Decker, Deborah DeBlasi, Laurie Dhue, Dylan Fitch, Miguel Forbes, Tim Forbes, Christine Furry, Mary Beth Grover, Michele Hadlow, Scott Harrington, Ray Healey, Tucker Hewes, Nigel Holloway, Amy Jedlicka, Dale Kokoski, Jon Krakauer, Glenn Kramon, Ginger Kreil, Larry Light, Heather and Robert Lutz, Doug MacKay, Chris and Rick Mears, Steve McNeely, Sue Miller, Gretchen Morgenson, Eleonora Negrin, Norbu Tenzing Norgay, Jamling Tenzing Norgay, Jessie Noyes, Michael Oakes, Renee Obester, Mark Patterson, John Pew, Bill Pinsky, Kitty Pilgrim, Kris Ann and Steve Quinlan, Al Read, Tim Reis, Andrea Rigo, Bob Rodriguez, Tim Rue, Holly Saunders, Sam Schmidt, Rita and Wolfgang Schutt, Will Schwalbe, Jeffrey Slonim, Suzanne Siguenza, Patricia and Shelby Shupert, Sophie, Barbara Strauch, Airié Stuart, Andrew Torres, Ed Tryon, Laurie Weisman, De De Weiss, Paul Wiltz, Pat Wright, and Jody Yen. (Thanks, too, to a handful of people who tried to discourage my pursuit of adventure. I'm reminded of the words of Friedrich Nietzsche: "What does not kill me makes me stronger.")

Index

Aamodt, Kjetil Andre, 203
Abercrombie & Kent, 3,
    96–100
  cost of trips offered by, 99
Ackerman, Peter, 36
Aconcagua, 12–23, 91, 160
Acute mountain sickness (AMS).
    See Altitude sickness
Adventure:
  as a business, 95–109
  cost of, 2
  cultural attitudes about, 162
  motivators for, xiv–xvi, 1,
    3–4
  preparing for, 5–6
  revenues from, 3
  risks of, xvii, 4–6
  See also Mountain climbing
Adventure Network Interna-
    tional, 2, 125

Advertising, effects of adventure
    travel on, 4
Africa, adventure travel in,
    96–100. *See also* Mount Kili-
    manjaro
Alaskan Arctic Adventures, 130
Aldrin, Buzz, 215, 216, 220–226,
    239
  interview with, 221–226
Altitude:
  effects of, 58
  sickness, 17–19
American Alpine Institute, 32
American Radio Relay League,
    196–197
Amundsen, Roald, 112
Anderson, Eric, 217
Anderson, Robert, 45
  interview with, 81–94
Andretti, Mario, 161

Andretti, Michael, 104, 144
Andrew, Prince of England, 161
Anker, Conrad, 44, 123, 125
    interview with, 62–65
Antarctica, xiv, 122–126
    cost of traveling to, 2, 57, 123
    travel tips, 125–126
Armstrong, Neil, 215, 220, 224
Askin, David, 175
Askin Capital Management, 175
Athans, Pete, 92
Atom bomb, 178–180, 185–186
    attitudes toward, 179–180
    development by India and
        Pakistan, 186
    use on Japan, 184–186
Audi VW Group, 163
Aviation industry, 220, 236

Babcock, Susan, 124, 125
Baker, Ginger, 205–209
Baldwin, Bill, 196
Ballard, Robert, 130–131
Balmat, Jacques, 29
Bannister, Sir Roger, xviii,
        197–202
    car accident of, 198, 201
    interview with, 198–202
Barents, Willem, 114
Bass, Richard, 2–3, 5–6, 44, 123
    interview with, 56–61
Bauce, William, 170
Bearzi, Mike, 93
The Beatles, 205
Bergholm-Lindgard, Beate,
        116
Bertil Roos Racing, 104, 145
Big Daddy, 97–98

Bingham, Deborah, 179
Bjerrang, Mathias, 115
Blaton, Jean, 168
Blessed, Brian, 5
Blevins, Lisa, 179
Boeing, 217
Bohr, Niels, 192
Bonham, John, 208
Bonington, Chris, 57
Boyarsky, Victor, 127
Branson, Richard, 105
Brasher, Chris, 199, 200
Brayton, Lee, 152
Brayton, Scott, 152
Brayton, Todd, 152
Brayton Racing, 152, 156
Breashears, David, 58, 60, 66, 74,
        108
Brokaw, Tom, 10
Brown, Pete, 207
Bruce, Jack, 205–207, 209–210
Buck Baker Racing, 151
Buffett, Warren, 96
Buhl, Robbie, 156, 157, 161
Buigues, Bernard, 118–120
Burkle, Ronald, 167, 169, 170
Butler, George, 112

Cage, Nicolas, 170
Canaletta, 22
CARE, 33
CART, 102
Carstensz Pyramid, 42
Carter, Jimmy, 96
Castroneves, Helio, 158
Cayambe, 19
Center of Science and Industry
        (COSI), 231, 234–235

244

Challenger explosion, 215, 221, 230–231, 233
Chamonix, 29
Chandler, Otis, 168–170
Chapman, Max C., 10, 28
Charles, Prince of Wales, 98–99
Chase, Bernard, 168, 170, 171
Chase, Marc, 168, 170
Chataway, Chris, 200
Cheno Island, 106
Churchill, Winston, xiv
Citizen in Space program, 230
Clancy, Tom, 218
Clapton, Eric, xviii, 205–206, 208–210
Clinton Group, 171
Cloning, 182
Cohl, Michael, 210
Columbus, Christopher, xiv
Concorde, flight paths of, 237
Cook, Frederick, 112
Cooke, Brian, 126
Cope, Derrike, 104
Corr, Jerome, 124
Cotopaxi, 19
Cousine, 105, 107
Coys International Historic Festival, 167
Crampons, 14
Cream, xviii, 205–210
Cronkite, Walter, 196
Crysdale, Kris Ann, 21
Curtis, Tony, 105

Dead Sea, 135–137
    cost of traveling to, 135
    evaporation of, 137
    salinity of, 136

Deep Ocean Expeditions, 2, 131
Delsener, Ron, 209, 210
Destivalle, Catherine, 71
de Vries, John, 152–153
Diamandis, Peter, 218
Diamox, 19
Dolganes, 119
Douglas, Lord Francis, xv
Drake Passage, 123–124
Driving 101, 101–103, 151–152
    cost of, 103
d'Urville Monument, 125

The Eagles, 205
Earnhardt, Dale, 149
Ecclestone, Bernard, 168
The Eighth Summit, 61
Einstein, Albert, 191
Encounter with Tiber, 220
Endurance, 112
Ershler, Phil, 19, 57
Everest, 73–74, 107–108
Extraterrestrial life, 225
Extreme travel, 111–112
Exum Mountain Guides, 8, 11

Faul, Skip, 161
Ferrari:
    Enzo, 163
    250 GT Sperimentale, 167
Fiduciary Trust International, 1, 76
Firestone, Adam, 103
Fischer, Scott, 32, 34–35, 43, 58, 73
Fischer, Timothy, 42
Fisher, Sarah, 161
Fontana, Sergio, 163

Forbes, Timothy, 10, 27
Four-minute mile, 198–199
  modern equivalent of, 202
The Four Minute Mile, 200
Foyt, A. J., 140
Franz Josef Land, 128
Fregate Island, 107
Fresh Live Cream, 205

Garnaev, Alexander, 236–239
Garriott, Owen, 217
Garriott, Richard, 217
Gates, Bill, 96
Genova Products, 1–2, 131
George, Tony, 161
Getty, Gordon, 99
Glenn, John, 222
Glieberman, Bernard, 170
Godovanik, Victor, 117–118
Goldin, Dan, 231
Goldwater, Barry, 196
Gordon, Robby, 103
Gossage, Eddie, 157
Grand Couloir, 29
Grand Teton, 8–11
  cost of climbing, 8, 9
  tips on climbing, 11
Greco, Giuseppe, 162, 163, 165
Gromov Flight Research Insti-
  tute, 237

Hägg, Gunder, 198
Hall, George, interview with,
  171–176
Hall, Rob, 58
Ham radio operators, xix,
  194–197
  celebrities as, 196

and the Internet, 196–197
  in Svalbard, 115–116
Happel, Otto, 107
Harrington, Scott, 153, 159
Hedge funds, 171–172, 173,
  175–176
Heisenberg, Werner, 192–193
Hemingway, Ernest, xvii, 39
Hendrix, Jimi, 207
Higgins, Paul, 36
High-altitude cerebral edema
  (HACE), 18
High-altitude pulmonary edema
  (HAPE), 18
Hillary, Peter, 46, 93
Hillary, Sir Edmund, xiii, 5,
  69–71, 197
  interview with, 45–56
  relationship with Tenzing Nor-
    gay, 67–68
  work among Sherpas, 44, 46,
    52–53
Hindery, Leo, 102
Hoey, Marty, 60–61
Hongbao, Wang, 62
Hornish, Sam Jr., 158
Horvath, Lajos, 196
Hunt, John, 67
Huntington, Lawrence, 1, 45
  interview with, 76–81
Huntley, Peter, 107
Hussein, King of Jordan, 196
Hydrogen bomb, 181, 187
  first detonation of, 188–189

Icebergs, 127
Ilyushin-76, 239
IMAX, 107–109

Incredible Adventures, 217, 239
Indy Racing League (IRL),
    152–153, 157–158
International Space Station,
    228
International School of Moun-
    taineering, 28
Internet, 184
  ham radio and, 196–197
Into Thin Air, 5, 59, 74
Irvine, Andrew, 62, 64
Islands, selling/renting, 103–107
Isola Galli, 107

Jackson Hole Mountain Guides,
    11, 21
Jackson Hole Mountain Resort,
    202–203
Jagged Globe, 87
Jefferson, Thomas, xiv
Johnson, Ben, 201
Johnson, Bill, 202

Kadoorie, Sir Michael, 170
Kangshung Face, 81
Karges, Louis, 168
Keiko, 131–132
Kennedy, Michael, 124
Kent, Geoffrey, 3, 96–100, 129
Kent, Jorie, 99–100
Kent, Joss, 100
Khatanga, 118
Kiss, 205, 208
Kokoski, Dale, 152
Krakauer, Jon, 43
Kreil, Ginger, 161
K2, 72–73
Kursk, 129–130

Lamborghini, 162–166
Land Rover, 135
Landy, John, 198
Langhorne, Will, 158
Laternser, Martin, 27
Leaf Cay 2, 106
Led Zeppelin, 206, 207
Lembrik, Alexander, 127
Lennon, John, 205
Lewis and Clark expedition, man-
    date of, xiv
Lindbergh, Charles, 218
Lindenberg, Cathy, 38, 39, 40
Lindenberg, Marc, 38, 39
The Living Sea, 108
Lockheed Martin, 217
Long-Term Capital Management
    (LTCM), 172, 175
The Lost Explorer, 62
Loveless, Patty, 196
Lutz, Glenn, 101
Lutz, Robert, 100–103, 158

Macchio, Dennis, 104, 145
MacGillivray, Greg, 107–109
MacMahon, Brien, 187–188
The Magic of Flight, 108
Mallory, George, 44, 50, 62–64
Mandles, Martinn, 126–127
Manley, John, 188
Marianas Trench, 131
Mars, exploration of, 222–223
Martin, John, 158, 161
Matterhorn, xv, 23–28
  fatalities on, 24
  versus Grand Teton, 8
  tips on climbing, 28
McCaw, Bruce, 166, 168, 170

McCaw, John, 167, 170
McDonnell, John, 218
McGehee, Robby, 152
McLaren, Alfred, 127
McNair, Ronald, 231
McNeely, Steve, 156, 158, 161
Mears, Rick, 146, 147, 155–156
  interview with, 140–145
Meriwether, John, 172
Messner, Reinhold, 45, 57, 71, 72, 75
Metallica, 206
MiG-25 flights, 216, 228, 236–239
  cost of, 2, 239
  travels tips for, 239
Mill, Andy, 203
Mille Miglia, 167
Minard, Lawrence, 15
Moe, Tommy, 202–204
  interview with, 203–204
Molchanov, 123–124
The Monkees, 205
Mont Blanc, 28–32
  fatalities on, 28
  tips on climbing, 32
Mont Blanc du Tacul, 30
Monterey vintage car race, 167
Mont Maudit, 30–31
Moon, exploration of, xiv, 223–225
Moon, Keith, 208
Moores, John, 170
Mosher, Howard, 135, 136
Mountain climbing, 7
  for charity, 33
  client/guide ratios, 58–59
  cultural attitudes about, 68
dangers of descent, 23
earnings from, 71–72
equipment used in, 49, 63–65, 79
fatalities in, 92–93
guiding, 86–92
reasons for popularity of, xvi, 7, 57, 83
risks of, 4–5
training for, 9, 13, 58–59
traits for success in, 51, 75, 78–79, 83–86
types of, 12–13
value of experience in, 17, 19
without oxygen, 72–73, 75–76
See also specific mountains
Mountain Madness, 34
Mountains over 8,000 meters, 76
  challenges of climbing, 88–90
Mount DeMaria, 125
Mount Elbrus, 25, 28
Mount Everest, xiii, xiv, 1, 43–94
  commercialization of, 47
  cost of climbing, 2, 4
  fatalities on, 4–5, 35, 46–49, 57–59, 68, 79–80, 90
  50th anniversary expedition, 93–94
  IMAX film about, 73–74, 107–108
  pollution of, 49–50
Mount Kilimanjaro, 32–40
  cost of climbing, 4
Mount Kosciusko, 40–42
Mount McKinley, 33
Mount Rainier, 13–15
Mount Townsend, 42

Mount Washington, 8
Murcielago, 162–165
    cost of, 163
Murphy, Kathy, 24
Myshkina, Marina, 122

Nardo Prototipo, 162–163
NASA:
    future of, 221–222, 226, 235
    partnership with Boeing and
        Lockheed Martin, 217
    post–moon shot programs,
        215–216, 221
NASCAR, 139, 148–149
Neiman, Bradley, 124
Newton, Isaac, 183
Norgay, Jamling, 45, 93
    interview with, 65–71
Norgay, Tenzing, 48, 55, 65–67,
    69–70
    relationship with Sir Edmund
        Hillary, 67–78
North Face, 62
North Island, 107
North Pole, 117–122, 126–130
    cost of traveling to, 2, 118, 119,
        126
    open water at, 128
    travel tips, 122, 130
Northwest Passage, 130
Novaya Zemlya, 127–128
Nuclear weapons:
    attitudes toward, 181–182
    development by Nazi Germany,
        192–193
    development by Soviets, 187
    See also Atom bomb; Hydrogen
        bomb

Obrist, Albert, 169
Oceans, pressure below, 133
Olsen, Dave, 38
One Sport, 38
Onizuka, Ellison, 231
Oppenheimer, Robert, 184–185,
    188
Orizaba, 16, 17
O'Rourke, P. J., 165
Orteig Prize, 218

Paccard, Michel-Gabriel, 29
Packet radio, 196
Pahlavi family, 105
Patterson, Mark, 149
Peary, Robert, 112
The Performers, 108
Peterson, Bart, 161
Petty, Richard, 101–102
Phenomenon, 209
Phurba, Ang, 58
Piccard, Bertram, 131
Piccard, Jacques, 131
Pink Floyd, 205
Pinsky, William, 156
Pittman, Sandy Hill, 5, 59
Plimpton, George, 95
Poison, 206
Popocatepetl, 16
Presley, Priscilla, 196
Prikhodko, Alex, 197
Proteus, 220

Quark Expeditions, 2, 126
Quinlan, Steve, 21

Race car driving schools,
    100–104, 145–166

Racing, 139–176
  average speed of, 139
  in boats, 171–176
  popularity of, 139
  strategies of, 149–150
  traits for success in, 140–141,
    143
  types of tracks, 145, 147
  with vintage cars, 166–171
Racing for Kids (RFK),
    156–161
Rainier Mountaineering, Inc.
    (RMI), 13
Ray, Greg, 158
Read, Al, 10
Reagan, Ronald, 190
Relativity, 183
Resnik, Judith, 231
Rheinberger, Michael, 76–77,
    79–80
Richard Petty Driving Experi-
    ence, 102
Ridgeway, Rick, 57
Rimes, LeAnn, 103
Rita, Ang, 52, 53
Roach, Max, 208
Rock group reunions, 205,
    207
Rockport Capital, 36
Rohwetter, Michael, 211, 212
Ross, Diana, 105
Ruester, Peter, 107
Russia:
  ham radio operators in,
    195–196
  space tourism in, 2, 218, 219,
    230–231, 237, 239
Rutan, Burt, 219–220

Sam Schmidt Paralysis Founda-
    tion, 157
Sand dune climbing, 97–98
Sanna, Giorgio, 163, 164, 165
Schmidt, Sam, 157
Schumacher, Michael, 165
  earnings of, 139
Schutt, Rita, 127
Science, attitudes toward,
    183–184
Scobee, Francis, 231
Scott, Robert, 112
Self-arrest, 14
Setton, Jacques, 168
Seven Summits, 2, 44, 56
Seyffer, Margrit, 210
Shackleton, Ernest, xiv, 112
Shapovalov, Vladimir,
    179–180
ShareSpace Foundation, 221,
    222
Sheen, Charlie, 170
Shelley, Percy Bysshe, 29
Shepard, Alan, 218–219, 236
The Shining, 108
Shipton, Eric, 51–52
Shuttleworth, Mark, 216, 217
Simonson, Eric, 15
Skip Barber Racing School,
    147–148
  cost of, 148
  fatalities at, 149
Ski racing, 202–204
Sky Riders, 108
Sneva, Tom, 151, 161
Snowbird Ski & Summer Resort,
    61
Sonic booms, 237

250

South Pole. *See* Antarctica
Space Adventures, 217, 219, 237, 239
Space shuttle, 215, 217–218
Space tourism, 2, 215–239
   cost of, 216, 217, 226, 230
   future of, 218–219, 220
   impediments to, 221
   in Russia, 2, 218, 219, 230–231, 237, 239
Spigot Peak, 125
Spitzbergen, 113
Sports:
   commercialism in, 200
   drug testing in, 201–202
Squire, Billy, 5
Stampfl, Franz, 200
Starr, Ringo, 207
Star Wars missile defense program, 189–190
Stewart, Jackie, 161
Strauss, Lewis, 188
Strzelecki, Paul, 41
Sullivan, Kathryn, 216, 231–236
   interview with, 232–236
Sumner, David, 194, 197
SUVs, naming of, 4
Svalbard, 112–117
   coal mining in, 114, 116, 117
   travel tips, 117
Symbolic Motor Car Company, 168, 170
Szilard, Leo, 184–185, 191

Tackle, Jack, xvi
Taylor, Andy, 218

Teare, Paul, 82
Teller, Edward, 180–194
   interview with, 181–194
   relationship with Robert Oppenheimer, 184–185
Titanic, 2, 130–135
   cost of traveling to, 2, 131
   plumbing of, 134
Tito, Dennis, 2, 216, 217
   interview with, 226–231
To Fly, 108
Torres, Ricardo, 16
Touching My Father's Soul, 65
Towering Inferno, 109
Treybig, James, 196
Trieste, 131
Trinitite, 178, 179
Trinity fund, 171
Truman, Harry, 187, 191

Ulam, Stanislaw, 189
United Space Alliance, 217
Unser, Al Sr., 140
U2, 210

Vail, Lawrence, 103
van Wyk, Menno, 38
Vaughan, Stevie Ray, 209
Venables, Stephen, 82
Viesturs, Ed, 45
   interview with, 71–76
Vintage cars, 166–171
   cost of, 168–170
   events involving, 167
Vladi, Farhad, 103–107
Vladi Private Islands, 105
von Braun, Wernher, 215
von Neumann, John, 184

Waitt, Ted, 170
Walker, Catherine, 36
Walsh, Don, 131
Walton, S. Robson, 166–168,
    170
Wealdstone, England, 200
Webster, Ed, 82
Weisman, Laurie, 10–11
Wells, Frank, 2–3, 56
Wheels of Fire, 206
White, Marilyn, 211–213
White, Vanna, 170
White Sands Missile Range,
    178–180
  radioactivity levels at, 179
  tips for traveling to, 180
Whittaker, Jim, 13

Whittaker, Lou, 13
Whymper, Edward, xv, xvi
Wickwire, Jim, 57
Williams, Robert, 1–2, 130–135
Wilshire Associates, 2, 226
Woods, Tiger, earnings of,
    139
World Trade Center attacks,
    211–213
Wright, Patrick, 158, 161
Wynonna, 209

X Prize, 218

Yamal, 126

Zhukovsky Air Base, 237

About the Author

James M. Clash, a mountaineer and Fellow at The Explorers Club, writes "The Adventurer" column for *Forbes Global* (www.forbes.com/adventurer). He also covers mutual funds for *Forbes* and is a commentator on *Forbes on Fox,* the magazine's weekly business show on the Fox News Channel. Clash has been at Forbes for more than a decade, initially as a reporter, then as a staff writer. In 1998, he wrote a pivotal story on hedge funds, warning investors of the risks and high expenses. When Long-Term Capital Management collapsed six months later, *Forbes* ran a national advertising campaign ("Business Reporting as Tough as Business Itself") themed around Clash's story, and he was promoted to associate editor.

An avid adventurer, Clash's experiences while at Forbes include a climb of the Matterhorn; a MiG ride at two and a half times the speed of sound to the edge of space; driving Indy cars in excess of 200 miles per hour; climbing virgin mountains in Antarctica; and two visits to the North Pole.

Before coming to Forbes, Clash worked at the New York

advertising agencies Grey, Ally & Gargano, FCB-Leber Katz, and Fred/Alan. He has an MBA in marketing and finance from Columbia University and a BA in English from the University of Maryland. Clash, who grew up in Laurel, Maryland, resides in Manhattan.